HOW SHAKESPEARE SPENT THE DAY

HOW SHAKESPEARE
SPENT THE DAY

IVOR BROWN

HILL AND WANG

NEW YORK

CONTENTS

I. The Missing Man, 7

II. The Daily Round, 25

III. The Sharers, 38

IV. The Fellowship, 53

V. Preparing, 71

VI. Getting the Play On, 87

VII. Quality of Player 106

VIII. Training and Touring, 119

IX. At the Desk, 135

X. In the Study, 152

XI. Money Matters, 171

XII. Medical Report, 186

XIII. The Last Years of Work, 198

XIV. Work Ended, 217

Note on Books, 231

Index, 233

CHAPTER I

The Missing Man

BOOKS ABOUT Shakespeare continue to appear in multitudes. The annual list recorded every year in the *Shakespeare Survey* published by the Cambridge University Press must strike panic into the hearts of librarians, whose shelves are already loaded with Shakespeariana, and appal the student who wants to keep afloat on the flood. Here is yet another for which apology is due and excuses must be made. My attempted justification is a feeling that something is still absent, the man at his job or rather his variety of jobs.

In the spate of articles and volumes, conjectures, theories and interpretations, all surely has been said unless new factual discoveries are made—and there is still Dr. Hotson at hand with his genius for discovery. Argument can and will go on concerning biographical detail, Shakespeare's education and his reading, the architecture and stage-arrangements of the theatres for which he wrote, the origins and validity of the texts that we possess, and the sources of his plays. There is no end to examination of his thinking, his personal philosophy, and his affairs of the heart. Some submit his psyche to analysis. One cannot read all, but I do read as much as I can, and am constantly impressed by the amount and quality of research, reflection, and scholarship which they contain. Yet, at the end of my reading, I feel baffled. I feel myself no closer to one side, and a very important side of Shakespeare, the man who worked to the clock, to the need of his colleagues, and to the hard facts of theatre finance. Since I am as much interested by the staging and performance of a play as by the writing of it, I find no satisfaction for my curiosity about this Shakespeare, actor, manager and investor, as well as author, Shakespeare the man going down to rehearsal and back to his desk, working with a team, counting his money, and fitting all into the hurrying day. Pursued in treatise after treatise and in endless elaboration of theories, this Shakespeare of

7

the daily round and nightly diligence or diversion escapes the hunting pack. He is the missing man.

We know something but not enough of a career so devoted and so versatile. Robert Greene's sneering phrase about the young, emerging, immensely energetic actor-author, 'an absolute Johannes Factotum', remained honourably applicable throughout Shakespeare's life. With youth behind him he did not cease to be a jack of all playhouse trades. He was a theatre man to the full while, as our lord of language and our first of poets, he was so much more than a theatre man. He read enough for his purposes, he used what he heard in conversation, and he kept his eyes open to the lively spectacle of the boisterous human comedy and of the social and political crises and disasters with their sharp turns of tragedy so amply provided by Elizabethan and Jacobean England. He could also make and watch shrewdly his investments in land and houses. He could not be charged with avarice, but we know quite enough about his purchases of property to see that he did not disdain financial calculation and had a normal share of the acquisitive impulse. While as a poet he had his head in the delicate air of fancy, as a citizen and as the earner of an income he had both feet upon the ground of workaday fact.

We might agree on 1588 as the starting-date of his life's work in London, when he was twenty-four. Since almost everything about Shakespeare is disputed, even the authorship of the plays that bear his name, that date is not always accepted; but it has fairly general support. If we agree on 1613 as a closing date for his major operations, a point on which there is less dispute, we have a working-life of twenty-five years. During this time he wrote all or most of thirty-seven full-length plays and contributed to others, probably to a piece of composite authorship on the life of Sir Thomas More, and almost certainly to *The Two Noble Kinsmen*, in which he assisted John Fletcher. He may well have had a hand in other pieces owned by his company, the Chamberlain's and later the King's Men. The vanished *Cardenio* might be one of these. He wrote, just before he was thirty, two long narrative poems, *Venus and Adonis* and *The Rape of Lucrece*. He also wrote sundry other poems and the *Sonnets*, perhaps more than the one hundred and fifty-four that we possess since some may have been lost or suppressed. Many of the poets of his period were rapid and profuse writers: not all, for John

Webster confessed his slowness. But with all allowances for general speediness this would be a reasonable output for twenty-five years if the author was a writer only and stayed with his books, his thoughts, and his papers. Shakespeare often packed more into a speech or even a line or two than others could manage at full length. Capable of rapidity, as some of the lesser work indicates, he can hardly have written the best of his immensely pregnant plays without some pauses for rest and reflection.

But Shakespeare was not an author only: he began as an actor and an actor he remained at least until 1603, an actor in repertory with all the demands which that entails. That is certain, since we know from the list of players appearing in that year in Ben Jonson's tragedy *Sejanus* that Shakespeare was one of the cast: as he is named second after the star Burbage he may have taken a part of length and importance. Jonson stated that in the first version of this play, which was not the one printed, 'a good share' of the work was by 'a second pen', whose owner he described as 'a happy genius'. Some have thought this to be a reference to Shakespeare: if that is so, here is a further addition to his labours at a time of his own most active and remarkable composition. Here was Shakespeare, the multifarious man, member of a team with which he worked nearly all his life, and ready for all the jobs that needed to be done. His readiness to co-operate was constant. After the greatest of his writing he would lend a hand to the novice Fletcher or rescue *Pericles* from its disastrous opening acts.

So we must visualise him in 1603, memorising, rehearsing, and acting in a piece not his own. Thus to study and rehearse a fair-sized role is a whole-time and fatiguing task during the period of preparation: to keep up later performance after production would certainly interfere with full-time attention to his own affairs. *Sejanus*, it is true, did not greatly please and presumably was not often given; but it was an interruption of Shakespeare's own work. There is no evidence that he continued to be an actor after this, but he was undoubtedly involved as 'a Sharer' twice over, as a Property-Sharer concerned with the ownership and upkeep of two theatres, the Globe and Blackfriars, and as an Actor-Sharer responsible for the finding of plays and players and getting those plays on to the stage. Margaret Chute, authoress of *Shakespeare of London*, thinks that he was constantly engaged as a player himself and continued to take important parts. Fripp in his *Shakespeare, Man and Artist* even assumed that he came up from the country for the Court season of 1613–14 and acted some of his old roles. There is no documentary support for this view; but, if it is correct, it is a further indication that he was still a theatre man to the full almost to the end of his life and was not only a retired poet musing among the flower-beds and water-meadows of his country home two and a quarter years before his death.

From some of the academic speculations on Shakespeare's mind, faith, and philosophy one gets the impression of a sequestered sage, who had pondered at length the problems of English dynastic history and carefully brooded over the first and last things of human duty and destiny. That picture leaves out the man I want to find. Obviously his mind ranged widely, but he was not a consistent and committed man with a clear-cut philosophy. Amid a life of such various activities, his thinking was quick, impulsive, and intermittent. He was obviously no tenant of an ivory tower: we know that he lived beside his work in the busiest parts of the town, at one time amid the close-packed squalor of the Southwark Bankside with its stews and bear-garden as well as its theatres. Later, perhaps more comfortably, he lodged north of the river with the Mountjoys in the Cripplegate ward of the city.

There is no evidence of his having acquired a town house of quality or any sizeable establishment of his own. He would have his hired room and work in that, but a lodger is not in a position to build up a considerable library and he cannot command peace when others are noisy. Presumably his fellow-writers were accustomed to scribble away at any time in any place; they were not study-dramatists or solitaries who had to retire to a mountain-top or a beauty-spot to find their inspiration and let the music flow. Shakespeare belonged to a bustling urban society. As the pamphleteers so angrily complained, London was a noisy town of narrow, crowded streets and raucous street-cries. No doubt he treasured the tranquillity of Stratford when he returned there, but during most of his life he could do quite well without it.

In his early London years Shakespeare had the patronage of the Earl of Southampton: the warmth of his second dedication to the Earl, that of the *Lucrece* narrative poem, suggests more closeness of friendship than was usual between a nobleman and a worker in the theatre. Leaving out altogether the much-vexed and seemingly insoluble problem of the male recipient of the *Sonnets*, we can reasonably surmise that Shakespeare had, for a time, access to what the auctioneers call 'A Gentleman's Library' in the Earl's house in Holborn and possibly also at the country house at Titchfield in Hampshire. In the Southampton circle he would certainly meet John Florio, the Anglo-Italian scholar from Oxford who was tutor to the Earl and subsequently, with his renown for scholarship and probably for tact as well, tutor also to King James's elder son, Prince Henry. It is beyond dispute that Shakespeare had read and drew upon Florio's translation of Montaigne's *Essays*.

So in that quarter there was a contact with the fashionable world and its culture and an opportunity for reading and writing when the theatres were not claiming his full attention. But the Southampton friendship was not, apparently, maintained and the Earl's foolish adherence to the rebellious Earl of Essex, followed by a spell in the Tower, would have made a member of the Lord Chamberlain's own company of players prudently shy of that social connection. The terrible and all too frequent outbursts of plague, a curse as well as a peril to the players whose theatres were closed by order, could bring a chance to the actor who was also an author. The epidemic of 1592–4 and the consequent shutting of the London theatres were both loss and gain for Shakespeare. Johannes Factotum, not busily studying parts, could busily write them and was very much at his workshop bench. His first great tragedy, *Romeo and Juliet*, and his comedies and histories began to pour out in a stream: if some had been written during the plague-break, all had later on to be brought to the stage and seen through rehearsal with the added possibility that the poet was also a player in many of them and supervised the preparations. It is hard to believe that a dramatist who could act and expressed his views about acting in a forthright way handed a script to the company and left them to it.

This bustling life continued. There were at least two plays a year to be written in the next ten years; one or two years may have included three. (In our own time our principal poet-dramatists T. S. Eliot and Christopher Fry produce plays at the rate of one in four years or so—and they not actors or engaged in theatrical management.) In addition to its routine work in the public theatres Shakespeare's company had to give command performances at

Court and in noblemen's houses; there were also the labours of a tour. Some of these journeys Shakespeare may have been spared in order to enable him to get on with his much-needed writing, but there is a strong tradition, for which documentary evidence apparently existed but has unfortunately been lost, that he was with the King's Men when they played *As You Like It* for the Earl and Countess of Pembroke at Wilton House in Wiltshire in December, 1603.

The transport of players and their properties on wide-ranging tours was of a jog-trot kind with exposure to all weathers. The roads were rough and made dangerous by armed thieves. The improvisation of stages and the direction of production in the differing conditions provided by the halls at the universities, country mansions, and country-town guildhalls or inn-yards imposed a further drain on the players' time and energy. Thus it must have been impossible for Shakespeare to do much writing on tour unless he was wholly proof against fatigue and had an uncanny genius for scribbling the immortal passage in an odd half-hour or amid a tavern hubbub of local chatter and of players 'talking shop'. Mainly in London, amid a whirl of productive activity, or if whirl be deemed too strong a word, under constant pressure, the writing went on, uneven but mostly of a kind that has been the wonder of the world. It might be easy for a practised hand to knock off in a fortnight *The Merry Wives of Windsor*, with its faded Falstaff and its facile repetition of the same comic situation. It was, says tradition, royally requested at short notice and even a hint from the throne would be a command to the Lord Chamberlain's Men.

There were advantages not possessed by the dramatist of today. The writers of Shakespeare's time had no need to worry about nagging and fussy criticism. The approach of the Tudor public to its entertainment was very different from ours. In our mainly realistic theatre we are concerned with likelihood. So we at once ask whether this or that person in the play which we have just seen would have behaved as he is made to do. Was that piece of behaviour in character? Did the motives and actions make sense and hold together? We demand probability, but Shakespeare's audience cannot have bothered for a moment about probabilities in the plot and about consistency in the characters. Likelihood was no schoolmaster to them. With a good appetite richly served they would, like mackerel, swallow anything that glittered. This eased the strain for one who could make words shine as well as sing and gorge the public with what it wanted most.

It was an accepted convention of Shakespeare's stage that men who have fallen in brawl or battle or on their own suicidal swords, instead of retching blood or groaning in scarcely articulate agony, will produce the finest poetry in perfection of phrase. It was also understood that, if a character put on a disguise, not even his closest friend would recognise him. A well-known ruler in a hooded cloak could pass unnoticed among his subjects. When a girl was dressed as a boy, she would be so readily accepted as a man that even her lover would be completely taken in. These failures to see through an obvious pretence are nonsensical to us who are the slaves of probability. But if the 'penny knaves' on the ground-floor or the gentry in the galleries had cried 'Rubbish' when such make-believe was made the essence of Shakespeare's story, then he would have stopped using plots of that kind. Bad receptions there could be. But a tall story was not the cause of that. If it had been, Shakespeare would have had failure after failure.

If such major defiance of likelihood was accepted, there would be no boggling over a conflict of minor detail. So Shakespeare, with this uncalculating public and free from our fetters of realistic consistency, could drive into *Hamlet* without deciding his hero's age. Readers, for whom he was not writing, may first discover that Hamlet was still a student-prince 'with intent to going back to school in Wittenberg' (Act I, Scene 2) and this at a time when the entrance to Oxford and Cambridge Universities was made at fourteen or even earlier. Yet the Prince seems to be a man of thirty in the graveyard scene at the opening of Act V. (I have never understood why King Claudius found Hamlet's return to Wittenberg 'most retrograde to our desire'. Would not the King have been safer with Hamlet out of the way?) Wherever the reader turns in *Hamlet*, and in many other of Shakespeare's plays too, there are the 'difficulties' which evoke the endless arguments of the scholars but which the firmly gripped audiences of the past have not noticed and the playgoers of today, despite all their notions of likelihood, accept quite readily. Those who scrutinise the text are much concerned about the time-scheme in *Othello*. I have never heard members of a modern audience expressing bewilderment on that score.

So the hard-driven author with the players urgent for a new and profitable piece and a script to handle immediately was under no obligation to be careful in his shaping of a play or logical in his handling of characters and events. He could let it rip. Theatrical conditions have radically altered. Now there are floods of plays on paper and sixty authors in search of a good manager instead of less than six companies in search of a good author. One reason for that is the long run which awaits any London success and so bars a theatre to new entrants for years at a time. But there were no long runs for Shakespeare and his rivals: a play that was liked would go into the company's repertory and stay there if it continued to fill the house. The failures, of which even Shakespeare had some, fell out at once and had to be rapidly replaced.

More, more, more, was the cry, and there were the wretchedly underpaid quill-pushers, often working in partnerships of two, three or four, to grind the stuff out and meet demand. To comprehend the conditions of authorship it is well to remember the life and hard labour of Thomas Heywood. It is true that this paragon of industry lived nearly twenty years longer than Shakespeare and so had larger opportunities for the consumption of paper and the service of stages. He was a busy actor, yet in his seventy years he claimed to have had 'an entire hand or at least a main finger' in no less than two hundred and twenty plays. So Heywood, if we allow Shakespeare a main or minor finger in a few plays outside those normally accepted as his, still achieved six times the output of the latter. In his preface to *The English Traveller* (1633) Heywood added to this prodigious claim of authorship an illuminating statement about a dramatist's work in his time:

'... true it is that my plays are not exposed to the world in volumes, to bear the title of works (as others): one reason is, that many of them by shifting and change of companies have been negligently lost. Others of them are still retained in the hands of some actors, who think it against their peculiar profit to have them come to print, and a third that it never was any great ambition in me to be in this kind voluminously read. . . .'

Such was the flux and chaos of theatrical writing and theatrical life amid which Shakespeare worked.

Once established and with the profits of management coming in he had no need to emulate the desperate speed of the hungry and thirsty hacks driven to sell a whole play for five or six pounds. Fortunately his company were less negligent in the handling of texts than those which Heywood served, but he too had no ambition 'to be in this kind voluminously read'. *Hamlet* was never meant for the bookish, and its author might be horrified to find it made a compulsory educational item and a theme for a world-wide flow of lectures which the years cannot quench and constantly enlarge. Like Heywood, Shakespeare had no wish to be the author of complete and formidable Works with a capital 'W'. For that kind of reputation he had no concern.

The dramatist's existence then, when compared with that of a playwright now, made less demands on nervous fears about his work's reception but was inevitably fevered from time to time with a high emotional temperature. The people attracted to and succeeding on the stage include all types, even the phlegmatic; but there is naturally a fair proportion of those with a volatile temperament and a leaning to exhibitionism, types easily excited and easily depressed. No harm in that: the player is there, as Shakespeare himself said, 'to strut' and to be seen to the author's and the company's advantage as well as his own. Without some practice of showmanship he or she would be less the attraction which the public seeks and relishes. But the possessors and exploiters of panache and of a vivid personality are not likely to be easy colleagues.

The displays of egotism and the jealousies and tantrums of those who cannot help and may actually enjoy being 'difficult' are stimulated nowadays by the blaze of publicity which beats upon the stage. The big lights and big headlines can be valuable at the box-office. But the focusing of so much attention on the leading figures must add to the tensions inevitable in public appearances and amid the anxieties of a 'first night'. There are the apprehensions of a failure which will become a headline matter and the dreaded sting of bad 'notices' which may be more remembered than the acclaim of a success. There can be unhealthy ranklings of resentment after censure: there can be no less unhealthy glorifications of success. A newly arrived player who has been highly praised is now showered with offers from the other and more rewarding media of film and television: even the playwright, though less likely to be a vessel of glamour, can be lifted by a winning venture, especially if it be a first play, to the level of television interviews and a sovereign position in the gossip columns. It is difficult for those receiving this sudden and immense promotion to keep their heads and to maintain a steady stance and a sense of proportion.

Shakespeare and his fellows were not thus harassed. Their agonies as well as their exultations were on a smaller scale. They had their verbal critics in the audience and some of these could be rude and boisterous when displeased; but the talk of the town or a part of the town was all that authors and players had to expect. They were not in the limelight. The boy-players who scored in tremendous parts might, by the standards of today, have been the heroes of the hour; but we hear almost nothing of their identities and achievements. Players had only recently worked their way up from the status of vagabonds and still had numerous and powerful enemies. They were 'known to their own', not widely glorified.

The surviving comments on the plays and players of the time are mostly of a generous kind, the tribute of play-loving men. The drama too, was not subject to that continual analysis and discussion which go on nowadays; our air buzzes with broadcast arguments about trends and problems in the arts which usually give the impression of more error and failure than achievement. There is also in print as well as vocally a flow of nattering about 'What's Wrong with the Theatre?', an institution which seems never to have anything right with it. Christopher Fry, who courageously addressed a meeting of the London critics and spoke from the playwright's angle, observed that as soon as an acorn sprouted in the field of authorship it was expected to become an oak and censured for not doing so. But there is the other side of this, the over-praise of somebody who has made a lucky hit and is immediately beset by photographers and interviewers wanting to know his opinions on everything under the sun.

The emerging Shakespeare did not have to spend his time in that bewildering and hysterical atmosphere. He did not pick up a newspaper and see in large letters 'Is Shakespeare Slipping?'. The poets and players could get on with their job as contributors to the new mixture of art and industry which they were creating; they were technicians in this rewarding craft of exciting and amusing, full-time professionals who had become increasingly skilful. So there was less cause for the nervous to be kept on edge and less cause also for the exhibitionist to enlarge his vanity.

Now there is excessive attention paid to a 'flop'; failures in the theatre are inevitable and should be quickly forgotten. Presumably in Shakespeare's theatre they were forgotten: one cannot imagine a flow of continuous and vexatious chatter over the cold reception of, say, *The Two Gentlemen of Verona* and of *All's Well that Ends Well*. There was no lavish investment of capital in a single play and things moved rapidly. Off with the old and on with the new. The players went bustling into a new addition to their repertory. 'Sweet Mr. Shakespeare' of the honeyed pen was not repeatedly rebuked in a score of criticisms if he failed to please when turning to a bitter and a biting temper. Playwrights and players had no Press-cutting books.

The demand for new plays and the scramble to get them ready for a play-hungry public meant hasty work, and for many life was chancy and precarious. But for a man established with one company it was assured work. He did not have to look round and wait over long periods to obtain a production. This may be the fate even of playwrights of repute, with many successes behind them, in the theatrical conditions of today. They have not only to write their plays: after that they and their agents have to market them and to do that they must not only suggest the right casting, which may be easy, but to collect the suggested players, which is not. If the latter are in demand they have ample and tempting invitations to work and to work for very high fees in the other forms of entertainment. Then large financial backing must be found to meet continually soaring costs of production and a suitable London theatre obtained. At the end of months or even years of negotiation the whole design may collapse and the author may be left with the play on his hands.

As J. B. Priestley, writing from long experience as a dramatist, has put it: 'It is as if an author of books had to find not only the right publisher but also the right paper-maker, the right compositors and machinists, the right binders, the right salesmen.' Mr. Priestley has further described, and according to my knowledge of what happens in Shaftesbury Avenue and Broadway, has

17

accurately described, the Monte Carlo and almost mad-house conditions in which the dramatist finds himself.

'In the English-speaking Theatre, you are compelled to exist in an over-heated atmosphere of dazzling successes and shameful flops, you are a wonder man in October, a pretentious clown in March, you are in, you are out. Hardly anybody can be found in theatrical London or New York who takes you for what you really are—neither a genius nor a fraud but simply a man trying to do a difficult job as best he can, a writer who does not deserve to make a fortune out of one lucky hit and equally does not deserve to have his work unrewarded and derided. No competent English or American playwright is as good or as bad as managers, theatrical press and public, say he is: they are playing roulette with him. It is this gaming-house atmosphere that makes serious work in the theatre so difficult.'

But, when all allowance has been made for the absence of casino finance and of the lunatic nonsense of modern publicity, Shakespeare's travel to prosperity was not made through entirely calm waters. The excitements of the player's life must have drawn to it the quick-tempered and explosive types and have created at least some of the tensions which now exhaust and exacerbate. The Elizabethans were people of spleen as well as of spirit. From what we know of their social behaviour they were quicker to show their choler than to contain their anger and to exhibit a stiff upper lip. They quarrelled easily and drew a sword in sudden rage. So we cannot envisage their actors' world as a placid mill-pond of equable tempers. The winds of rivalry blew keenly and storms arose. There was a battle of wits in their 'War of the Theatres' and there were other more lethal battlings too. Such a fiery particle as Marlowe, who was once in prison for his part in a duel and died of a dagger thrust, may not have been typical. But one minor dramatist slew another in 1599 when John Day killed Henry Porter; and Ben Jonson fought and killed his man, Gabriel Spencer, a fellow-player.

The adjective 'gentle' was applied to Shakespeare by several others as well as by Jonson in the lines which accompanied the Droeshout engraving in the First Folio. 'Gentle' probably signified a well-mannered man, affable, and a good mixer rather than meek.

Shakespeare was evidently not of the hand-on-hilt and 'Draw-cansir' type. But he could not keep altogether clear of serious trouble. He was involved in a somewhat mysterious and nearly violent episode when Francis Langley, owner of the Swan Theatre, was in dispute with the Surrey magistrate, William Gardiner, a fraudulent and tyrannical rogue who appears to have used and cheated his step-son, William Wayte. He was associated with this weakling in seeking from the Sheriff of Surrey 'sureties of the peace' against William Shakespeare, Francis Langley, and two unknown women, Mrs. Dorothy Soer and Anne Lee, 'for fear of death and so forth'. Langley sought a similar surety 'for fear of death and so forth' against Gardiner and Waite. Fortunately there appears to have been no death and the curious menace implicit in the words 'so forth' may not have been followed up by either side. But the affair sharply reminds us that Shakespeare, however gentle himself, was working amid the tumult and high tempers of Tudor London and its 'roaring boys' and not in any niche of bookish serenity and isolation.

There is a wide separation between the problems and pressure of playhouse life and the themes of the modern lecture-room when the philosophy of the tragedies is under discussion. What curious discoveries are made by the probing and learned academic mind! For example, in *The Question of Hamlet*, Professor Harry Levin of Harvard, who has carefully read his way through the deterrent jungle of Hamlet literature and can tell us in brief what the scholars have told us at length down the centuries, decides at one point that 'Hamlet is re-enacting the classical Eiron, the Socratic ironist who practises wisdom by disclaiming it. More immediately, Shakespeare was dramatising the humanistic critique of the intellect as it had been generally propounded by Erasmus.' Of the 'to be or not to be' soliloquy Professor Levin writes: 'Such is the doubter's mode of dialectic which leads him back—through complementary semi-circles—to his binary point of departure. This is the question, *esse aut non esse*, which metaphysicians from Plato to Sartre have pondered.... The ontological question becomes an existential question and the argument lifts from metaphysics to ethics.' One can imagine that Shakespeare, confronted with a commentary of that kind, would have torn in bewilderment what hairs may then have been left on that exalted head when he was reaching middle age.

Desiderius Erasmus (1466–1536) was a Dutch scholar of European renown who recommended the study of plays, and his treatise on speech, *Copia Rerum et Verborum*, had been introduced to the curriculum of English education. Shakespeare may have had to cope with that work, whether he liked it or not, in the Grammar School at Stratford. We can credit him with a memory above the ordinary, and much of his early reading may have stayed in his mind, if only in the confused and fragmentary form that is the normal long-term residue of much of our education. But that he was in full recollection and comprehension of the Erasmian 'humanistic critique of the intellect' when he was writing and rehearsing *Hamlet* with his colleagues to their great advantage in finance and in repute seems to me as improbable as anything can be.

Those who believe that Shakespeare was written by Bacon can gladly accept such discoveries of a profound academic scholarship in the plays. In that case, the Socratic Eiron as well as the Erasmian critique of the intellect may have been stored fruitfully away in the brain that was to give us Hamlet's taste for bawdy, his theatrical gossip, and his dramatic criticism, as well as his brilliance in a loftier form of reflection and of argument. But if, with the vast majority, we accept the authorship of Shakespeare, the playhouse man able and ready to tell the actors a thing or two, we can picture a very different background to the composition of this turbid and tremendous piece of theatre.

This Shakespeare of the lecture-room, with his intellectualism and his ethical message, did not exist for the Elizabethans and their immediate successors. The references to him made in his lifetime and for some time after give no sign that he was regarded as a sage and a seer. Study of the valuable *Shakespeare Allusion Book* makes it plain that the part most remembered was, with good reason, that of Falstaff, with Hamlet in second place. On the evidence of quotations in other men's work, as well as of direct references, the plays which most lingered in men's minds were *Romeo and Juliet*, *Hamlet*, and (to our astonishment) *Pericles*. But most enduring, not only in memory but in present enjoyment, was the narrative poem *Venus and Adonis*, with *Lucrece* slightly behind it in the reader's favour. In *The Return from Parnassus*, performed at the Cambridge about 1600, the character Gullio says: 'Let this duncified world esteem of

Spencer and Chaucer, I'll worship sweet Mr. Shakespeare and to
honour him will lay his *Venus and Adonis* under my pillow.'
    So it went on. As late as 1640 a character in *The Noble Stranger* by
Lewis Sharpe cries, 'Oh, for the book of *Venus and Adonis* to court
my mistress by', and in 1646 Samuel Sheppard, in *The Times
Displayed in Six Sestyads*, said that 'never as well as Shakespeare'
could even the Greek Aristophanes display such 'fancy'.

> *Witness the Prince of Tyre, his Pericles;*
> *His sweet and his to be admired lay*
> *He wrote of lustful Tarquin's rape shows he*
> *Did understand the depth of poesie.*

Sheppard's phrasing is awkward, but the valuations are plain. In
our later opinion Shakespeare's 'poesie' had gone rather deeper
than that, but his Caroline readers and playgoers stressed, as a rule,
his 'comic vein', his 'natural' art, his 'smooth and easy strains' and
'his muse's sugared dainties'. There was frequent contrast of
Jonson's weighty efforts with Shakespeare's lighter touch. Sir John
Suckling wrote of

> *The sweat of learned Jonson's brain*
> *And gentle Shakespeare's easier strain.*

The author of what we call the 'bitter comedies' and of the doom-
burdened and sometimes misanthropic tragedies was much less in
mind than was the wielder of the enchanting quill. To Milton,
Jonson was learned and Shakespeare a warbler of native woodnotes
wild. But *King Lear* and *Timon of Athens* are hardly to be described
as warblings.
    Not only *Venus and Adonis* but the collected plays were regarded
as agreeable stimulants and manuals of the tender passion. John
Johnson in *The Academy of Love* (1641) noted that 'Shakespeare, as
Cupid informed me, creeps into the women's closets about bed-
time and, if it were not for some of the old out-of-date Grandames,
who are set over the rest as their tutoresses, the young sparkish
girls would read in Shakespeare day and night'. We are losing touch
with Socrates and Erasmus. Reference to Shakespeare as a scholarly
sage was indeed made in the inscription under the bust in Stratford
Church which pompously and absurdly likened his intellectual

attainments to those of Nestor and Socrates and his art to that of Virgil. This kind of tribute was exceptional and solitary and, as Dr. Johnson observed, the writers of epitaphs are not on oath.

It was not forgotten in the mentions and tributes that Shakespeare was an actor as well as author and therefore a doubly occupied man, trebly occupied if we include the managerial cares on which the greater part of his income depended. Twenty years after his death an anonymous elegy was written on that 'famous writer and actor'. Once more there was praise of the 'smooth rhymes' but unfortunately no description in detail of his prowess on the stage or naming of the parts which he played. In 1643 Sir Richard Baker, writing on *The Reign of Queen Elizabeth*, was contemptuous of stage-players when matched with the high company of statesmen, writers, and divines; but 'seeing excellency in the meanest things deserves remembering', and noting that the Roman Roscius had been commended in history, he stooped to pay compliments to Burbage and Alleyn, and the clown Tarleton for their unmatchable qualities. 'For writers of plays and such who had been players themselves' he selected as most eminent Shakespeare and Ben Jonson. Baker added a note, 'William Shakespeare, an excellent writer of comedies'. He was either ignorant of the great tragedies or, like many of his period, he regarded them as scarcely worthy of mention.

Much of our modern Shakespearian interpretation is concerned with the import of his tragedies, the purpose of their symbolism, and their underlying ideas: there is ample consideration of his moral testament, especially his praise of mercy in an age of savage punishments and persecutions. *The Tempest* seems to be written in a valedictory mood and Prospero can be viewed as a self-projection of the matured poet who has in mind to leave the theatre, a purpose fortunately not wholly fulfilled. Consequently his closing speeches with their forgiveness of his wrongdoers are taken as declarations of the author's faith and his moral code. The moving Epilogue spoken by Prospero in eight-syllable lines is more remembered for its mention of prayer

> *Which pierces so that it assaults*
> *Mercy itself and frees all faults*

than for its earlier statement of the author's wordly hope and purpose,

*Gentle breath of yours my sails
Must fill, or else my project fails,
Which was to please.*

In other words, he craved applause and support for this and presumably all his work, whose principal aim was conveyed in the simple words 'to please'. To please the public has been the honest, unaffected ambition of the stage through the centuries and Shakespeare here declares himself to be the professional, not the professor. It is worth noting that the word project at that time had a particular commercial meaning. Merchant adventurers and capitalists developing industrial undertakings were commonly called projectors. Shakespeare and his colleagues were theatrical projectors.

The habit of adapting the deity or idol to one's own tastes is a frequent occurrence in the history of religions. It is conspicuous in the Shakespeare-reverence which Shaw called Bardolatry. So we have had a procession of Shakespeares, all imagined according to personal proclivities and creeds. He has been paraded as Catholic and Protestant, a patriotic monarchist and a hater of the Court and all things courtly, a profound thinker and moralist and a tortured sensualist. I do not find these views completely contradictory: a great man will always appear as all things to all men. After education had taken over Shakespeare the bulk of academic criticism came from those who regarded the plays as fruits of the intellect with especial appeal to the intellectuals. The actor, director, and sharer in management was overlooked. It is fair to say that some of the most esteemed Shakespearian expositors would have been far happier to join the conversation in a senior common-room than in a player's dressing-room: what a clumsy organiser of rehearsals, a piece of bad casting, or a careless stage-manager could have done to ruin the theatrical life of a play is not in their reckoning. Nor, one may conjecture, have they often discussed with practising dramatists of the modern theatre what they were trying to do, what they suffered, what defeated them, and what surprised them, either for disgust or delight, when the written word became the acted and the spoken thing. I surmise that if Shakespeare had an opportunity to revisit London today he would be far happier with entertainment at the Garrick or the Green Room Clubs than at the Athenaeum.

How, having written, did Shakespeare get his plays off the paper and on to the stage? This process must have been speedier and less taxing than it is now. We need not imagine anything comparable with the discussions and delays which precede an important theatrical production in London or New York today. As all modern dramatists know to their cost, plays, even by writers of repute and with some success behind them, are kept months in script while the arguments about financial backing, rewriting, casting, and the choice of producer drag on. Plays now often reach their presentation some years after they were written. To write on a contemporary topic is hazardous since the topicality will have vanished when the play at last is seen. Shakespeare was free of the palaver and postponements suffered by the modern playwright. Since the theatrical turnover was so rapid decisions had to be made rapidly. Shakespeare was in the thick of it as actor and sharer so that the greatest of all English writers can almost be called a spare-time author. I can visualise him spending far more hours 'messing about in theatres' than he did at his desk.

Here is the Shakespeare of the continuous grind whom I find missing amid the just and eloquent tributes to his genius. If we turn to the index of many of the valued books about the master-dramatist and look for the words production and rehearsal they have no mention. Yet these activities were at the heart of his life-work. It is true that the documented facts are scanty, but there are side-lights and stray pieces of information. Conjecture there must be, but we have a fair amount of matter on which to base it. I can only hope that the picture here presented will interest, even if it does not convince, those who have felt a frustration similar to my own, and that the attempt to count the Shakespearian hours as they ran will do something to fill the gap in our vision of William Factotum.

CHAPTER II

The Daily Round

❧

TO BE in the thick of it as player, playwright, and shareholder was a gruelling life. There is good reason for supposing that the actors in Shakespeare's time had to be early at work. Nowadays professional actors generally rehearse in the morning and afternoon with a short break for a light lunch. But in Shakespeare's day the performances in the open theatres were given in the afternoon. Thus the time for preparing the next production was awkwardly curtailed or broken up. The prevailing system was a repertory with plays coming in and dropping out rapidly according to their degree of popularity. Even those most liked did not have 'a run', as we call it. They were, of course, given more often, but ten or twenty scattered performances would be taken as evidence of a considerable hit. The more the failures, the more replacements were needed. So there can have been few days in which rehearsals of some kind were not going on, not only in the preparation of new plays but also in the brushing-up of productions brought out of stock.

It has been estimated that Shakespeare's own company staged fifteen or more new plays in a year, provided that the year's work was not interrupted by an outbreak of plague, the closing of the London theatres, or a departure on a tour round the country towns. (In a way these epidemics may have come as a relief, since old plays could be used afresh and there would be less rehearsal needed and less drudgery in the learning of new parts.) Assuming the estimate of fifteen new productions a year to be correct, Shakespeare and his fellow-players, if they stayed in London and worked continuously, had just over three weeks in which to launch each new venture.

To a company engaged in contemporary British repertory that may seem ample time, since its members may be called on to be ready with a new production every fortnight and in many cases every week. But these companies are usually handling plays that have been presented previously in London and are available in print together with the stage-directions made by the original director. In that case the director of the repertory company has had a good deal of his work done for him in advance. The repertories do offer new pieces from time to time, but their novelty is not likely to be a *King Lear* or to involve fencing-matches or scenes of battle with scurrying armies. That was the kind of task that Shakespeare's team had to tackle in the stride of their tragical-historical-comical repertory. Furthermore the leading players in that company, in addition to learning and rehearsing new and long parts, were administrators and no doubt were glad to be their own masters even though it meant more worry. Their day's work included commissioning new plays, considering plays submitted, front-of-the-house management, coping with the balance of costs and takings, discovering talent, and training 'the young entry'. That again was a matter of great importance. There were, as far as we know, no academies of dramatic art, pouring out apprentices with a two years' course of instruction behind them. The companies were their own drama schools in which the boys learned as they went and by watching rehearsal and performance; but there must have been some teaching too and portions of valuable time must have been allotted to that.

The working-pace of the Chamberlain's Men, if the assumption of fifteen plays a year be at all accurate, was less than that of similar output elsewhere. The papers of Philip Henslowe have fortunately been preserved and give us precise information, with most imprecise spelling, about the amount of work in hand. Henslowe was not an actor himself, but a business man who had been a dyer, a pawnbroker, and a dealer in landed property before he entered Show Business: that term is fairly applied to this man who was as ready to make money from the bloody arena of the popular Bear Garden as from the works of the poets and players. He took no part in acting and authorship himself, being what now would be called a capitalist employer, in which function he was a keen maker of contracts and bargains. He kept his accounts, as his later rivals, the Chamberlain's Men, must have kept theirs. If the latter had been preserved in addition to Henslowe's we should have fascinating news of the receipts earned by Shakespeare's plays and would know which pleased and which did not. But there was no such lucky survival of the figures in this case.

Before the formation of the Chamberlain's Men in 1594, Henslowe employed Lord Strange's Men, who contained the nucleus of the future Chamberlain's company, and he had the use of one of the plays included in the First Folio of Shakespeare's plays. This was *Harey the VI*, almost certainly the piece known to us as *Henry VI, Part I*. It was one of Henslowe's great successes. Nashe in his satire *Pierce Pennilesse*, published in August, 1592, wrote of 'the brave Talbot' triumphing again on the stage after two hundred years in his tomb and having his bones 'new embalmed with the tears of ten thousand spectators at least (at several times) who in the Tragedian that represents his person, imagine they behold him first bleeding'.

Henslowe was less fortunate with many of his other plays, but Marlowe was a stand-by among his authors and Edward Alleyn a magnetic star among his actors. The striking feature in his records is the information that he offered his public fifty-five new or newly revised plays within a period of one hundred and twenty-six weeks. There was an amazing quantity of output; as to the quality we can only guess. It is not unfair to imagine an occasional 'shambles'.

This programme allowed little more than a fortnight for the preparation of each new or newly revised piece. Some of the new ventures were likely to be particular or total failures: consistent success is very rare in the history of the theatre. But the value of old 'hits' was then experienced since they could be brought in to take the places of those that were quickly taken off. The takings varied considerably: Henslowe's list of plays and the receipts at the Rose Theatre in February, 1592, are evidence of that. There must have been some chilly afternoons at that season of the year and the amount which each play took may have been conditioned by the state of the weather. One can see Henslowe and his men looking anxiously at the midday sky. But during this week there were no abandonments: a shower did not kill a performance. Tudor players and playgoers must have been tougher than the cricketers of today, who, in matches of the first-class, run for cover if a few drops fall. Here is the statement of work done and payment received during that week.

Feb 19	Fryer Bacune	17s 3d
21	Mulomurco	29s
22	Orlando	16s 6d
23	Spanes comodye, Donne Oracoe	13s 6d
24	Syr John Mandevell	12s 6d
25	Harey of Cornwell	32s
26	the Jewe of Malltuse	50s

It can be seen that Marlowe's *Jew of Malta* drew almost three times the audience attracted by Greene's *Friar Bacon*. Just after that, on March 3, *Harey the VI* had a record attendance: 'the house' was worth a hundred and fifty-three shillings and sixpence. The piece was repeated thirteen times and this shows the small number of performances which even a particular favourite would receive.

The machine had to keep grinding on: the pressure on the pens of the writers and the memories of the actors was continuous. If Henslowe's men and boys appeared in all or nearly all of the plays in hand their life must have been a scramble from rehearsal to performance and back again. Henslowe was not one to let his workers off lightly and we hear of no defensive trade unionism to insist on reasonable wage-rates, overtime payments, or 'days off'. Shakespeare and his colleagues, when they had their own company, may have worked in more tolerable conditions; they were then their own masters, but everywhere the pace was hot.

Sunday playing was forbidden, but there seem to have been some evasions of that rule by Shakespeare's company and, if they were so arduous in seeking a profitable audience, the notoriously greedy Henslowe would not have been missing his chances. A Privy Council order in the year 1600 commanded two companies, the Chamberlain's and the Admiral's, to 'refraine to play on the Sabbath daie', which suggests that the offence was being committed. Officially Lent was a forbidden season for the theatres: if that ordinance were observed there would be six welcome weeks in which to prepare the plays to come. But it was not observed. We know that in 1592 Lord Strange's Men, working for Henslowe, were busy nearly every day between the middle of February and the middle of June. Later the Admiral's Men were not in trouble although they had public performances three days a week during Lent. In 1615 several companies, including Shakespeare's, were summoned to the Privy Council and accused of Lent-breaking. But evidently there could be a blindness of the official eye if money eased the way, for in 1616, a month before Shakespeare's death, the King's Men and other companies could obtain a Lenten Dispensation for a payment of forty-four shillings. So the break was certainly not a complete one. It was a very commercial theatre in which Shakespeare spent his working life.

How, amid this hurly-burly, were the various jobs fitted into the divisions of the day? The usual daily performance was at two in the afternoon or a little later. By that time there was a sufficiency of leisured and wealthy or of poorer men with a free afternoon to create an audience. One of the epigrams of Sir John Davies, a poet and play-fancier of the period, gives a picture of an unquenchable addict of the theatre.

> *He's like a horse, which, turning round a mill,*
> *Doth always in the self-same circle tread:*
> *First, he doth rise at ten; and at eleuen*
> *He goes to Gyls, where he doth eate till one;*
> *Then sees a Play till sixe, and sups at sovon;*
> *And after supper, straight to bed is gone;*
> *And there till ten next day he doth remaine,*
> *And then he dines, and sees a Comedy*
> *And then he suppes, and goes to bed aguine:*
> *Thus round he runs without variety.*

It is interesting to learn that some of the plays lasted till six: if the start was at the usual time 'the two hours' traffic of our stage' mentioned in the Prologue of *Romeo and Juliet* was not a practice always observed. The subject of the epigram was obviously a good sleeper, with or without company.

Nor were the penniless less eager than the men of means to get a place at the play. There was a complaint made in 1603 by Crosse, the author of *Vertue's Common-Wealth*, that 'pinched, needy crea-tures, that live of almes, with scarce clothes for their backs or food for their bellies, make hard shift that they will see a play, let wife and children begge and languish in penury'. Exaggeration perhaps, but some evidence of the appetite for more than bread and meat.

A general picture is given by Thomas Nashe. In the course of his defence of the drama against 'shallow-brained censurers' he pictured the players' patrons thus: 'For whereas the afternoon being the idlest time of the day, wherein men who are their own masters (as Gentlemen of the Court, the Inns of Court, and the number of Captains and Soldiers about London) do wholly bestow themselves upon pleasure and that pleasure they divide (how virtuously it skills not) either into gaming, following of harlots, drinking, or seeing a play, is it not better (since of four extremes all the world cannot keep them but they will choose one) they should betake them to the least, which is plays? Nay, what if I prove Plays to be no extreme, but a rare exercise of virtue?'

Nashe omitted to mention the women who came with them, at least to the galleries, but he has given us a general picture of the masculine crowd assembling for their after-dinner 'exercise of virtue'. The nobility or prosperous middle class could take an afternoon off from their social round or financial concerns and would be eager to do so if news of something good to be seen had gone round the town. The Inns of Court students had attended their morning lectures and done their morning's reading, if they faced any part of either task; many of them were noblemen or sons of rich parents unlikely to be bothered by close study for a legal career. The standing-room close to and around the stage was occupied by the groundlings or 'penny knaves', the fighting men on furlough and artisans, unemployed perhaps but with a penny to spend, or enjoying a trade or public holiday—and public holidays were numerous. In the winter the performances in an open theatre must have provided some damp or icy sessions, but the performances went on though the results at the pay-doors could be disappointing. John Webster attributed the lack of attendance at his powerful tragedy *The White Devil*, produced in 1612, to its appearance 'in so dull a time of winter and in so open and black a theatre'. In midwinter matinées would have to be over before the early darkness and a two o'clock start would be essential. Thomas Platter, of Basel, who visited England in 1599, went to see 'the tragedy of the first Emperor Julius Caesar' on September 21, and stated that to do so 'about two o'clock I and my party crossed the water to a house with a thatched roof.' If his journey was made at that hour, the performance on a day of summer or early autumn might have begun at two-thirty.

The usual dinner-hour was from eleven o'clock onwards. There must have been morning rehearsals of the new play in hand, unless the actors were to be up half the night, and there was then daylight by which to work. But they had surely to break off by noon: they may not have taken a large midday meal, but they had to stop for some rest and refreshment before beginning the major business of the day. They would have to be in the tiring-room well before the trumpet sounded for a start. So we can assume that rehearsals were abandoned about noon. Actors of today do not relish matinée performances. They expect a smaller audience than they look for at night and it is a drowsy time when yawning comes easily and the quickening response of a full and alert house is unlikely. But for the Tudor actors, and audiences too, this was the time to be at their liveliest and best. Heavy feeding would be a handicap.

If all were over by half-past four they may, after a drink or two, have rehearsed again, in summer-time on their own open stage or in winter by candlelight in the tiring-room or some other covered premises. Since daylight was necessary in the open theatres the six-o'clock ending mentioned by Sir John Davies was not a general occurrence. By the late afternoon, whether they had been playing for three and a half hours to the public or playing for two hours or so and then rehearsing, they would be needing a good supper: after that there would be a natural readiness to linger in a tavern, drink, gossip, and talk 'shop'. But there were the new parts to be studied, a formidable piece of homework for the night hours.

Furthermore at night, possibly following an afternoon performance for the public, they might be called to serve a special and exalted audience at Court or at a nobleman's house. There was, for example, a presentation of *Love's Labour's Lost* at Lord Cranborne's or the Earl of Southampton's house in January, 1605. Perhaps the severity of the weather at that time of the year limited their work on the open-air stage of the Globe, so that such extra engagements, which were a compliment and well rewarded, would be welcome; and there might be a free and generous supper to follow. But when such additional labours were ordered much hurried work in shifting the costumes and properties and adapting the presentation to a different kind of stage was necessary. The players were frequently engaged in what we call 'fit-up' productions as well as in their ordinary routine on their familiar stage. They would be used to such improvisation because it was inevitable when they travelled the country, but anybody who has worked in our own time on 'fit-up' tours knows the endurances that have to be faced. And we have cars and motor-lorries and are not dependent on horse-power or walking or the service of a barge which had to be loaded and unloaded on a journey to Greenwich or Richmond. Travelling 'on the hoof', as Nashe called it, was a familiar exercise.

Nocturnal rehearsals were obligatory when plays were 'pre-ferred' for performance before Queen Elizabeth or King James at Whitehall or wherever they desired. There was a regular series of such commanded performances after Christmas and the arrange-ments were passed on by the Lord Chamberlain to the Master of the Revels, who was responsible for the political seemliness of all plays. Absence of comment on matters of State was necessary to pass this censorship, whose vigilance was keenly directed to political and religious references. We are apt to link the ideas of censorship and sex, but the presence of the 'broad' jest and 'blue' line was not what worried authority in Tudor and Jacobean times. The quality of entertainment and of spectacle, as well as political propriety, was a matter for the application of strict standards. Their revelling Majesties were to have the best of showmanship and there were funds for procuring it.

Throughout most of Shakespeare's life the Master of the Revels was Sir Edmund Tilney. He was established at the old Priory of St. John's in Clerkenwell which had been turned to secular uses after the Reformation. His winter task was to ensure excellence in the plays which were, according to Heywood, 'often perused and necessarily corrected' by Tilney and his subordinates. Their respon-sibility was artistic as well as political and they scrutinised the preparations as well as the texts, looking for the highest professional capacity. The rehearsals were held at night in the Great Chamber at Clerkenwell in a room well warmed with a great fire and by the light of torches and candles. The Revels Accounts which have been preserved contain much valuable detail concerning these preludes to a command performance.

In the weeks before Christmas there was immense activity at Clerkenwell and this involved the cartage (and from Southwark perhaps the ferrying) of the players' dresses and gear, which could be supplemented at Clerkenwell. Since Queen Elizabeth was at Greenwich for the Christmas of 1594, where the keeper of the

Palace hired eight extra men to assist the preparations for entertainment, this meant much use of water transport. This was safer
and quicker than a journey on the wretched and sometimes
robber-infested roads but could be far from comfortable on rough
nights amid the wind and the rain.

Money was expended by the players on their costumes with
astonishing liberality and so extreme care had to be taken of them.
A cloak of splendour was not to be roughly packed or exposed to
risk of theft: a great price might have been paid for it. The star
would insist on a conspicuously stellar glory in his robes if he were
playing a kingly part, as he often was. As Mr. Bridges-Adams puts
it in *The Irresistible Theatre*, 'In a time when to be splendidly turned
out was almost a mania, the players, largely dependent on the more
fashionable public, could not afford to lag behind. Accordingly
even the careful Henslowe has to note some hair-raising items.
Twenty pounds or so for a cloak is two hundred and more in the
money of today. The lavish Irving did not use cloth of gold, finding
that under the gaslight much cheaper stuff looked better: in the
more searching light of day Henslowe did and it cost him the
equivalent of five pounds a yard.' A playwright, then paid five or
six pounds for a whole tragedy, may well have taken a poor man's
view of twenty pounds for a cloak. The snarls of the writers about
the peacock-players are the more understandable.

For Court performances especially the best would be worn and
all things must be in trim, with weapons gleaming, wigs newly
combed, and properties repaired and repainted. If Shakespeare
was himself acting and if one of his plays was 'preferred', as it often
was, he would be in the thick of all this. He has given us a glimpse
of the last-minute urgencies in *A Midsummer Night's Dream*.
Bottom, charging his hempen homespuns of the Athenian crafts
to be spick-and-span, speaks for amateur performance, but the
professionals must have had a similar bustle to face, with apparel to
be made perfect and memories refreshed.

'. . . All that I will tell you is, that the duke hath dined. Get your
apparel together, good strings to your beards, new ribbons to your
pumps; meet presently at the palace; every men look o'er his part;
for the short and the long is, our play is preferr'd. In any case, let
Thisbe have clean linen; and let not him that plays the lion pare his

nails, for they shall hang out for the lion's claws. And, most dear actors, eat no onions nor garlic, for we are to utter sweet breath; and I do not doubt but to hear them say it is a sweet comedy. No more words: away! go; away!'

Commanded performances of plays at the Royal palaces or great houses took place at a late hour, at ten o'clock or even after. A letter from Sir Gerrard Herbert to Sir Dudley Carlton describes a very late sitting in honour of French visitors at Court in 1619. 'In the King's great Chamber they went to see the play of *Pericles, Prince of Tyre*, which lasted till two o'clock. After two acts, the players ceased till the French all refreshed them with sweetmeats brought on China voiders and wine all in bottles; after, the players began anew.' (Voiders were not only receptacles for removing scraps and dirty plates; they were also trays for carrying round cakes and such like.) In this case the players would not be home until three or four in the morning, since one may assume some further refreshment when the play was ended.

This revel was in the month of May when the open-air Globe would be in full use. How soon were the actors up and about again? Did they rehearse their next piece for some hours before noon and then give their usual afternoon performance? Shakespeare, three years dead, was not troubled by that call to Court; but he had plenty of similar exhausting experience: before such an audience nerves would be on edge too. But none would wish to miss a Court appearance, especially as the payment to be shared, ten pounds for the company, was reckoned to be most attractive, apart from the honour of the command.

To be a constantly committed playwright in the midst of such a scurry of activities was nothing rare. The prolific Heywood was esteemed so good an actor that Henslowe bound him by contract in 1598 'not to play anywhere public about London, not while these two years be expired, but in my house'. Henslowe was not one to leave any of his Hired Men, especially one whom he so much wished to tie down, without an assignment when casting was being done. Yet Heywood must have knocked off some of his two hundred and twenty plays during those years. Shakespeare could and did fit it all in to the extent of thirty-six plays and 'extras'. But he did not stay a long life's course like Heywood, who managed to pass the age of seventy. Richard Burbage died, like Shakespeare, at fifty-two. But Burbage had no retirements to a garden in Stratford and the toughest of Shakespeare's life was over when he was forty-five. But he had been carrying a treble load; Burbage, actor and sharer, did not have to write plays too. Both had good reason to be tired out in what we call middle age.

To get through a reasonable amount of rehearsal before the twelve o'clock break the players must have been early at breakfast. That was not the practice of the rich, if we are to believe Dekker's picture of his Gull, who was advised to follow the practice of 'the fairest liers in the world, the simpering merchants' wives' who made eleven their common hour of rising. There is no mention of the Gull's breakfast or of any early refreshment. Unless he is faced with the cold and biting weather of winter, he must first yawn, stretch, and gape, thus sending out 'his lively spirits, like vaunt-couriers, to fortify and make good the uttermost borders of his body'. Then he is to take a little walking exercise in his chamber, either in a thin shirt or stark naked. (Some praise of nudity follows.) Next, having inquired of an inn with 'an ordinary of the largest reckoning, whither most of your courtly gallants do resort', he is to go there at half-past eleven, when 'most of your fashion-mongers are planted in the room, waiting for meat'. That was an easy way of life for the wealthier members of the matinée audience. The players in their humbler quarters may have yawned, stretched, and gaped to start the day and even taken a little exercise, shirted or in the nude, as recommended for the would-be gallant, but that would have been at a much earlier hour. Also they would need to make a good breakfast with a hard morning's and afternoon's labour ahead and no time for a solid meal in the middle of the day.

It is difficult for us to imagine a life without tea or coffee to ease the approach to the day's work and soothe its intervals. For children there was water or milk: for men, and doubtless some women too, beer. In the Induction of *The Taming of the Shrew* Christopher Sly, waking after his heavy drinking, cried, 'For God's sake, a pot of small ale.' The nobleman's servants offer him a cup of sack and conserves. A thick type of sherry as an eye-opener sounds almost nauseous to us and so it did to Sly. He knew nothing of sack and did not care for it. If conserves there must be, then let them be conserves of beef to go with his draught of light beer.

Whether or no Shakespeare faced a cup of sack and the kind of breakfast before rehearsal that Mr. Jorrocks liked before hunting, he had no comfort from our morning stimulants. If rehearsals were proceeding there had to be an immediate journey to work. For a while, soon after his rise to some position in the theatre, he was living in Bishopsgate Street which lay south of Shoreditch and led to the direct route through the City to London Bridge. We know that in 1596 he was living in the Parish of St. Helen's, Bishopsgate, where he was assessed for local taxation as the owner of goods to the value of five pounds. There were two demands, for five shillings in 1596 and thirteen shillings and fourpence in 1598. By report gentle and amenable among his friends and colleagues, he evidently had less regard for tax-collectors and evaded, or at least neglected, payment. (The response of Tudor London to taxation of incomes as we know it would have been, one may fancy, open rebellion.) Shakespeare was not alone in this lack of concern when orders to pay were delivered. A fifth of his fellow-parishioners were also defaulters.

By 1599 he had gone across the river to live in Southwark, close to his work at the Globe. He was then living 'in the liberty of the Clink' which was under the jurisdiction of the Bishop of Winchester. The Bishop's officers seem to have caught up with him there and no more is heard of his failures to pay. The South Bank was a busy and tumultous district, and, if Shakespeare chose to stay there, he was evidently not seeking the peace and quiet deemed appropriate to a sequestered literary man. But a Bankside lodging saved travel.

Mr. M. M. Reese, in his careful and valuable book *Shakespeare*, suggests that Shakespeare may have had 'a substantial house' in Bishopsgate and that his wife had brought the children up to live with him there before the purchase of New Place in Stratford in 1597. This surmise is based on the size of his assessment in the parish of St. Helen's, but five pounds does not seem to be a great sum and there was one valuation of three hundred pounds in that area. Shakespeare can hardly be regarded as living in affluence because of that rating. But New Place does come into the matter, since he must have been considering and saving up for the purchase of what was indeed 'a substantial house' at the end of 1596. So he must have been counting his money carefully when he was being a dilatory, and even evasive, ratepayer.

After the stay in Southwark he moved north again. By 1604 he was lodging with the Huguenot tire-maker Christopher Mountjoy at the corner of Silver and Monkwell Streets in the Cripplegate ward. The suburb north of the City was a theatrical area. Here James Burbage, father of Richard, had built the Theatre in 1576–7, and here too was the Curtain Theatre. The Chamberlain's Men, founded under the protection of Lord Hunsdon, and taking over the functions and assets, if there were any, of Lord Strange's and Lord Derby's Men, were probably at the Curtain during some years. Thus those dwelling in Shoreditch and thereabouts would be close to their place of work until the move across the river to a tenancy of the Swan and occupation of the Globe. Richard Burbage continued to live there all his life, even when Southwark would have been more convenient. Another member of the company, Richard Cowley, was a Shoreditch resident. Marlowe had also been a lodger in this area.

When Shakespeare lived in Bishopsgate and later with the Mountjoys and was working at the Globe, he had a moderate journey to make: he may have kept a horse and ridden over London Bridge or he could walk to the river and either walk over the Bridge or be ferried across the water. Mr. Reese pictures him going by Cheapside and St. Paul's, but that was out of his way and time was short if there were morning rehearsals. He was closer to his work in both his North London lodgings than was Burbage, whose journey from Shoreditch to Southwark was of the same distance as a walk from Kensington to Knightsbridge. With a long day of rehearsing and playing exacting parts ahead of him, Burbage would probably spare his legs by riding. But for Shakespeare a leisurely walk to work may have been helpful: the talk and traffic of the streets were part of his raw material and, if he walked alone, he had his thoughts for company and fresh air for inspiration in both senses of the word. A. E. Housman has told us that a pint of beer and a walk on the open heights of Highgate and Hampstead were a frequent source of his poetry. So may some of Shakespeare's lyrical fancies have come to his mind and lips as he went across the water to the Bankside through a riverside breeze.

CHAPTER III
The Sharers

BEFORE CONSIDERING the actual rehearsals and the methods of directing them employed in Shakespeare's time there are the earlier labours to remember. A play has to be chosen or contracted for before the allotting and memorising of parts can begin. There can be abundant worry in that and it must have been a constant anxiety either to an independent manager like Henslowe or to a self-governing fellowship like the Chamberlain's Men. The 'Hired Men' and boys would have little or no say in this. The responsibility lay with the leading actors who held the shares in the venture.

The sharers were of two kinds. There were the House-keepers who held the lease, if they had not the freehold, of their building. When Cuthbert and Richard Burbage moved from North to South London and built the Globe on the Bankside there were seven House-keeper Sharers with ten shares to be divided. The Burbages held five of these and five of the players, Shakespeare, Heminge, Phillips, Pope, and Kempe, held one each. When in 1608 the company, now the King's Men, took over the lease of the Black-friars Theatre Phillips had died and Pope had disappeared, either through death or retirement. (He was not mentioned in the list of the King's Men on the accession of James I in 1603.) Their places were taken by Condell and Sly. Kempe had left the company soon after the opening of the Globe and had been replaced as the leading player of Clown parts by Robert Armin, who is not listed as a House-keeper. So the sharers of this kind were one less at the Blackfriars than at the Globe, and Shakespeare's chances of a good profit were now the greater since there was one fewer to claim a dividend and the takings at the roofed and more comfortable Blackfriars are known to have been considerably larger than at the Globe.

In 1635 there was frequently trouble about shares held by actors passing into other hands, a process which would mean divided control and consequent disputes. The matter was carried to a high level when the King's Men petitioned the Lord Chamberlain, then the Earl of Pembroke, for an order that would grant them the right of compulsory repurchase of the shares, three in the Globe and two in the Blackfriars, which had been quietly sold outside the company by Heminge's son William after his father's death for five hundred and six pounds. So the value of a House-keeper's Share was then about a hundred pounds, considerable money at the time. To own one House-keeper's Share in the Blackfriars was to have a capital sum as large as the income earned, at least among the lesser men, by writing as many as fifteen full-length plays.

Fortunately we have the text of Cuthbert Burbage's statement to the Lord Chamberlain. (Their claim, incidentally, was successful and the players won their case for the retention of theatre shares.) In it he is stressing, for obvious reasons, the hardships of the House-keepers and he describes the expense of building the Globe 'with more sums of money taken up at interest which lay heavy on us many years'. He adds that in this undertaking 'to our selves were joined those deserving men Shakespeare, Heminge, Condell, and Phillips and other partners in the profits that they call the House'. Pope's name, it will be seen, has dropped out, and 'other partners' are mentioned without identification. So Armin may have taken up Kempe's share if he had the money to do so when he came in.

The statement further explained that at the Blackfriars the boy players, Underwood, Field and Ostler, 'growing-up to be men', were taken in 'to strengthen the king's service'. Underwood and Ostler became House-keeper Sharers in both the Globe and the Blackfriars, and their shares were part of their estate after death. From this it is plain that the players, if they did well, could be men of some property and would naturally be eager to watch the finances as well as to be highly spoken of for their acting.

The House-keepers had to find the interest on money borrowed and pay local taxes and ground-rent. When the Globe was built there was a thirty-one years' lease of the site for which the rent, payable to the landlord, Nicholas Brend, was fourteen pounds and ten shillings a year. Local taxes had also to be met and the building kept in repair. Standards of amenity in the seating of the audience were not high and many patrons were packed into a space which we would consider intolerably uncomfortable. But, whatever the standards, their observance was the House-keepers' business. Presumably they drew profits from the refreshments available which certainly included beer, since we know that at the burning of the Globe in 1613 one man whose breeches were on fire 'had the benefit of a provident wit' who put out these flames 'with bottle ale'. The eating of fruit in the theatre of the time was common and nut-cracking was as much a nuisance as the fidgeting with chocolates is today. There were no matinée tea-trays to clink and clatter, but the service of the 'bottle ale' may have been no less noisy and probably quite as profitable. In his theatres Henslowe would see to that and Shakespeare's men would not let the opportunity slip. 'The bars' are usually a valuable asset in the modern theatre and probably were so then.

The shareholders were a small, close set and not, like shareholders in most joint-stock companies of today, a large number of outside investors who get information about the year's business in reports and are entitled to attend an annual meeting but hardly can, or will, ever do so. In theory they control, but actually they do not; they leave directions to the directors and only occasionally, in the case of serious losses or some alleged scandal, do they come to the meeting in large numbers and seek to make themselves felt. But the Theatre-Sharers of Shakespeare's time were the directors, a small group exercising total control, and in daily touch with the problems and profitability of their enterprise. The fact that they were nominally the Sovereign's or Lord X's Men gave them status and security from persecution, not endowment. The noblemen did not come to the rescue of their 'Men' financially: Lord Southampton's legendary gift of a thousand pounds to Shakespeare, a story with no contemporary support and generally regarded as incredible because of its size and his lordship's financial troubles, would have been, if ever made, a present to a favourite poet. James I did indeed compensate the King's Men in the plague-stricken period of 1608–9 for being 'restrained from public playing within the city of London in the time of the infection'. Otherwise the Theatre-Sharers had to look to themselves and live on their earnings. If we regard the King's Men as containing the essence of a National Theatre they had no regular subsidy on which to count, and the modern idea of a non-profit-making company would have horrified them.

Shakespeare's holdings of House-keeper Shares are known: how far he was committed to House-keeper duties is uncertain. It may be thought that with his parts to learn as well as his plays to write and perhaps to direct in rehearsal, he would have refused to be bothered with the accountancy of buildings and their maintenance and with 'front-of-house' administrative detail. But it is obvious from what we know of his life that he was property-minded and that the use of money interested him keenly. So we cannot be certain that he took his functions as a House-keeper lightly and was an absentee from the meetings and discussions which the House-keeping involved.

It is plain, however, that much of the business management was taken over by Heminge. He was the Treasurer to whom payments for command performances were made. There were numerous tasks for him to face in what office premises he may have had, including supervision of the money-takers at the doors and partition of the receipts between the House-keepers and the Actor-Sharers. These two bodies were largely identical in the case of Shakespeare's company, but not wholly so. Cuthbert Burbage remained a House-keeper only; he was never an actor.

Presumably Heminge had assistance in his office, especially from Cuthbert. During the first years, more than fifteen, of his association with the company he was desperately busy, since he was one of the leading players as well as the Treasurer and the most important member of the House-keepers. He gave up acting soon after 1611, but in 1619 and 1621 he headed the list of 'our well-beloved servants' in the Royal Licence 'to use and exercise the art and faculty of playing'. His name disappeared from the cast-lists of the King's Men after the production of Ben Jonson's *Catiline* in 1611. Burbage, Condell, and Lowin continued to play the leads. Heminge did not appear in Webster's *The Duchess of Malfi* (1613). So it seems that in 1611, with nineteen years of working life before him, and later on with the joint-editorship of the First Folio to combine with his business management, Heminge sat at a desk and was a general and valuable counsellor. The more he concentrated on administration the less would be the worries of the other House-keepers.

Throughout nearly all Shakespeare's working life Heminge had been not only Treasurer but a leading actor and much appreciated. The eighteenth-century Irish scholar and Shakespearian editor Malone stated that he created the part of Falstaff. We have no evidence for that, but, according to the cast-lists in Ben Jonson's Folio, he had appeared in *Every Man in his Humour* (1598) and *Every Man out of his Humour* (1599), in *Sejanus* (1603), and *The Alchemist* (1610). Heminge made one great error in his life. He omitted to put the cast-lists of Shakespeare's plays in the First Folio, which he might easily have done from what records there were as well as from his own memory. In that volume's 'Names of the Principal Actors in all these Playes' he put himself third after Shakespeare and Burbage. Shakespeare headed the list since it was his volume and not from any idea of his primacy as a performer. Burbage undoubtedly ranked first.

How much time Shakespeare gave to the House-keepers' affairs it is impossible to say. Certainly he remained a sharer of that kind until the burning of the Globe in 1613; but by then the number of the House-keepers had doubled or he had sold half his holding, for then he had only a fourteenth of the stock. The second Globe, made ready in less than a year with a new elegance and a tiled roof to replace the inflammable thatch which had spread the fire, cost fourteen hundred pounds. So Shakespeare could have been called on for a new investment of a hundred. We do not know his response. He may have preferred to drop out; if he were then living mainly at Stratford, as is generally supposed, he might have wanted no more part in the discussions and responsibilities of management. But it was a likely venture which would appeal to a man with the investing habit. If he did take up his share he had sold it, as well as his interest in the Blackfriars, before his death; there is no mention of theatrical property in his will.

The case of the Actor-Sharers is less documented. It is therefore more difficult to be precise about their number, functions, and profits. Our information comes from the Henslowe papers, and the arrangements made in Shakespeare's company may well have been different. There is a general tendency among scholars of the Elizabethan and Jacobean theatre to suppose that there was one general pattern both in the architecture of the playhouse and the organisation of the players. But here was a rapidly developing industry of entertainment carried on by inventive, as well as industrious, men. They were experimenters, not traditionalists. They were also rivals, competing to catch public attention. In all their professional concerns they were likely to go their own way to what they considered their best advantage. So we cannot assume that Henslowe's methods of organisation and rates of pay were always followed by others.

There was, however, a fairly general system of ranking the actors in three tiers. At the top were the leading men and chief players of supporting roles, mostly Sharers. Then came the Hired Men: then the boys. Boys whose voices had broken and were no longer suitable for women's parts presumably went on to be Hired Men, unless they were considered to be inadequate performers and were relegated to other jobs, in or out of theatrical life. The brilliant ones, like the famous Dicky Robinson, could rise quickly to the first tier and become Actor-Sharers.

We know enough of the young Robinson's progress to visualise the rapid moves possible in the rise of a talented player. He appeared in women's parts for the King's Men in some cast-lists of 1611. Eight years later he was named in the Royal Licence granted to the company. This implies his possession of an Actor-Sharer's status during his early twenties. He had passed quickly from the ranks of the Hired Men and it is possible that the boys who had done exceptionally well could become Actor-Sharers without any interval in the middle grade. Perhaps the term middle grade is questionable since the boys, playing women's parts, had some roles of the first importance, far beyond anything likely to be left to the Hired Men. Robinson was still with the King's Men in 1647 when there can have been little for the Sharers to share owing to the disturbance of the Civil War and the defeat of their Royal patron by the enemies not only of King Charles but of all persons and things theatrical. Incidentally, it is alleged that Robinson married Richard Burbage's widow, but as Burbage was nearly forty when Robinson was born and Mrs. Burbage had borne her husband eight children, it was hardly a case of 'boy meets girl' and it seems an unlikely story. There were other Robinsons about.

Could Shakespeare have entered the profession as a boy? Yes, if there is any truth in the supposition that he was the 'William Shakeshafte now dwellynge with me' commended by Alexander Houghton of Lea in his will of 1581 to Sir William Hesketh of Houghton in Lancashire, a supporter of a team of players. It was a period with no strict ideas about the spelling or even the form of names. Shakeshafte had been used by Shakespeare's family and it is conceivable that William went north, using this name, after leaving school. The case for it has been argued strongly by Alan Keen and Roger Lubbock in *The Annotator*, a book of which more will be said later.

If that was so, he must have come back to Stratford with money in his purse or another job in hand in time to marry Anne Hathaway in 1582. But there is no general support for this suggestion, and it is more likely that Shakespeare left Stratford some time after the birth of his twins in 1585 and joined a touring company which was visiting the town. With them, at his age, he would begin as a Hired Man.

There has been much conjecture about the company or companies which he served before the Chamberlain's Men got together and began their long, unbroken, and happy association. The problem is fully investigated in all the major books on Shakespeare's life and need not be further probed here. What is important for a survey of the Sharers and Shakespeare's part in their activities and responsibilities is the fact that in the winter of 1594 Shakespeare, then thirty, had reached the top rank of the actors' professional grading. In December of that year, with Kempe and Burbage, he was officially named as one of three payees for two Court Performances. Like Bottom and his team Shakespeare and his two colleagues could say, 'We are preferred', and he himself was one of a trio representing his own fellowship. That he became a House-keeper Sharer before his certain participation as such at the Globe in 1599 is likely. That he was an Actor-Sharer in 1594 is made certain by the statement in the list of Court payments. A Hired Man would not have been mentioned in that way. Heminge is not mentioned and so cannot yet have become the Treasurer, in which office he was to serve so long and so well.

We know the number of House-keepers at various stages in Shakespeare's life. It was small and the Actor-Sharers may have been more numerous. The list of 'The Principall Actors in all these

Playes' given in the First Folio in 1623 mentions twenty-six and it is assumed that all these were Actor-Sharers at one time or another. The names (in the Folio spelling) are:

William Shakespeare	*Samuel Gilburne*
Richard Burbadge	*Robert Armin*
John Heminge	*William Ostler*
Augustine Phillips	*Nathan Field*
William Kempt	*John Underwood*
Thomas Poope	*Nicholas Tooley*
George Bryan	*William Ecclestone*
Henry Condell	*Joseph Taylor*
William Slye	*Robert Benfield*
Richard Cowly	*Robert Goughe*
John Lowine	*Richard Robinson*
Samuel Crosse	*John Shancke*
Alexander Cooke	*John Rice*

Of course these were not all Sharers at the same time and we have enough knowledge of the players and their fortunes to trace the pattern of the comings and goings. Shakespeare, Burbage, Phillips, Kempe, Ostler and Cowley had died before the Folio was published. Taylor was a late arrival who came in, a matured player with a reputation already made elsewhere, to take Burbage's roles after the latter's death in 1619. John Downes, who was a prompter for forty years in the Restoration theatres and wrote in 1708 *Roscius Anglicanus or an Historical Review of the Stage* said that Betterton, the great Hamlet of his period, was 'instructed in every particle' of the role by D'Avenant, who had seen Taylor's Hamlet. Downes added that Taylor was instructed by Shakespeare himself; this could only have happened if Taylor had understudied or deputised for Burbage before he formally joined the King's Men three years after Shakespeare's death. Shank, described as a comedian, was another late-comer who may have played the chief Clowns and Fools after Armin's death in 1615. Benfield could have replaced Ostler, who died in 1614.

Of the boys recruited Gilburne was described by Phillips as his 'late apprentice' in 1605. Underwood came from the Chapel Children's company and was an adult actor with the King's Men in 1610. Robinson's career has already been noted. Rice was apprenticed as boy to Heminge in 1607 and was still with the company in 1625.

So we can assume that of the twenty-six men named by Heminge and Condell in 1623 there were usually a dozen or so Actor-Sharers at one time. We know that the number of Royal Grooms in 1604 was not less than nine. The chief players in the Royal service were appointed Grooms: for this, however, they received no extra pay, but had their place in ceremonial occasions and for that purpose were granted two uniforms every second winter, a heavy one for winter and a lighter one for summer. The Grooms who were each given four and a half yards of red cloth by the Master of the Great Wardrobe 'against his Majesty's royal proceeding through the City of London', i.e. for the Coronation of King James, were Shakespeare, Phillips, Fletcher, Heminge, Burbage, Sly, Armin, Condell and Cowley. (Fletcher had been 'comedian to his Majesty' in Scotland and so, when brought to London, could claim to take Groom's rank.) He died in 1608 and since he was not mentioned among the twenty-six principals in the First Folio he may never have been a Sharer with the King's Men. Not all Sharers were Grooms, nor all Grooms Sharers. So we need not decide that because nine Grooms are mentioned as due for special Coronation costumes the Actor-Sharers were only nine at the time. Shortly after the Coronation the number of Grooms was increased to twelve. This would bring in Lowin, who is in the *Sejanus* cast of 1603 and was to be an extremely important member of the company and a House-keeper in the Globe and Blackfriars.

To become a Sharer in either class meant a precious financial gain, and that was important, for the pay of the Hired Men was meagre in the extreme, though we cannot take it that Shakespeare's company paid as badly as Henslowe did. This exacting employer bound the Hired Men as servants under covenant to himself personally for terms of two years, and he demanded bonds of forty pounds for their service during the period. Since the Hired Men's weekly wage ranged from six to seven or at the most ten shillings it is hard to imagine how they managed to put up bonds of forty pounds unless they had rich and kindly friends. The title of Hired Men covered not only the minor actors but the Book-keeper, who was the prompter, the Tire-man, who was the wardrobe master, the musicians, and stage-hands. The number of minor players and supers was not great. F. E. Halliday in *The Shakespeare Companion* writes, 'It looks as though Shakespeare would have been able to count on six or seven regular hired actors and ten or twelve supers, as well as the twelve Actor-Sharers (nine before 1604) of the company.' In the Prologue to *Henry V* Shakespeare apologised for the five or six 'most vile and ragged foils' who had to do the work of an army. Here is a plain statement of the small numbers engaged.

Six shillings a week was reckoned to provide a living of sorts in Elizabeth's London. Professor Alfred Harbage in *Shakespeare's Audience* decided, after close examination of the figures available, that the average weekly wage for artisans in England was about five shillings and threepence-halfpenny. London workers, presumably because of higher rents and prices, got slightly more, say fourteen or sixteen pence a day compared with the national average of a shilling. The writer concluded that 'we shall err by very little and probably on the side of generosity, if we place the average weekly wage of London workmen at seven shillings in the year of *Hamlet*'. So a Hired Man acting in the theatre was on the same economic level as the building-worker who provided him with his workshop and his home.

We have then an organisation in which Shakespeare was one of seven or eight House-keepers and one of a dozen or so Actor-Sharers. The work to be done by both classes was far from light. The House-keepers could, as was suggested, leave some of the business detail to their Treasurer and a non-playing member of the body such as Cuthbert Burbage. The Actor-Sharers may have been glad to assign important decisions to three or four of their group, but this must be only a surmise. If there was an executive sub-committee composed of the most important Sharers Shakespeare, as the principal dramatist of the time and the only actor-dramatist in his fellowship, must have been one of this smaller group. (Ben Jonson was a free-lance contributor to their stock of plays and a most useful one. But he was never a Sharer of either kind with the Chamberlain's or the King's Men.) Shakespeare's plays were their principal asset and he would naturally insist on a governing voice in the casting and mounting of them.

The matters to be settled, either in full session of the Actor-Sharers or in sub-committee, were numerous as well as vitally

47

important. While the House-keepers were watching their side of the budget, the players were the owners of the valuable costumes and had to agree on additions and renewals. They had to decide on the new plays to be given and the old ones to be kept in the repertory. They had to apportion the parts and Shakespeare knew his men and could suit them. Unconscious that he was writing for all time he was well aware that he was writing for Burbage and the others.

Further problems to be settled were those of recruiting and maintaining an efficient staff. This included the acceptance of new Hired Men looking for work and the parting with those found to be unsatisfactory. Moreover, when there was enlisted in this class a recruit who had not been through the mill of a boyhood apprenticeship, he would need training, and only the senior actors could provide that. The audiences came from a world in which music was widely made and keenly appreciated. So the choice of musicians for the theatre was extremely important and their preparation for each production would be carefully supervised. Shakespeare himself had his knowledge of music and devotion to it. Harmony was much in his thoughts, both as a delight to the ear and a principle of life. That a play of his should be marred by clumsiness in the musical element would have greatly distressed him.

A matter no less urgent was the discovery and tuition of likely children, since so much depended on their abilities when they were given major roles. The blunder of a Hired Man in a small assignment was far less damaging than the miscasting of a boy in a big one. A lad called Richard Sharpe was entrusted by the King's Men with the title-role in Webster's *The Duchess of Malfi*. We hear no more of him: he did not stay on, as some other boys did, to be one of 'the principal actors' of 1623. It is unlikely that another company snapped him up after a success, for the King's Men were remarkably constant in their membership and, once established, generally stayed for life. One can imagine Sharpe meriting the remark made by Costard about the curate Sir Nathaniel who had been cast as Alexander the Great in the mummings in *Love's Labour's Lost*: 'You see how 'tis—a trifle o'er-parted.' And so the boy well might have been, with that load to carry amid men of great capacity and experience, Lowin as Bosola, Burbage as Ferdinand, and Condell as the Cardinal. (Taylor took Burbage's part in a revival after Burbage's death.)

Kindly to Richard Sharpe they probably were, since the relations of the Actor-Sharers with their apprentices are shown by many a reference to have been avuncular rather than tyrannical. But the nervous strain on boys highly promoted in the casting was inevitably harassing. We do not know what child was confronted with the colossal challenge of Shakespeare's Cleopatra. But Shakespeare, having created such a part, must have selected him with care and confidence and probably coached him personally in the speaking of his lines, which were very many and included some of the finest he ever wrote. But the boy was someone else's apprentice since, as far as we know, Shakespeare had none. He had no family home in London and the Actor-Sharers who engaged apprentices took them into their houses and made them one of the family. In that respect at least Shakespeare was the less burdened: he did not have to do homework as a tutor.

The boys engaged were called apprentices but they were not bound by strict terms of law. There was no Guild of Players resembling the sixty-one guilds of other trades mentioned in the Statute of Artificers of 1563 which barred the exercise of crafts by those not formally apprenticed. The actors' world was not thus organised on a national basis. The acceptance and training of the children was a matter for each company to arrange and we have certain knowledge that at least among the King's Men, and in the case of Edward Alleyn outside this fellowship, the relations of master and trainee were of a very friendly kind. Alleyn had a boy in his company called Pyk, known as Master Pig, whose letter sent while on tour to Mrs. Alleyn is of a most endearing kind. The child sent greetings to the maids who looked after him and to an old gentleman who was his rival for a good seat by the fire. It was signed by 'Your petty, pretty, prattling, parleying pig'—or rather more spoken than signed, since it came in Alleyn's script. No doubt Master Pig had a better memory for a part than a hand for writing. This fragment of correspondence indicates a friendliness in the home which may not have been universal but was common among the King's Men.

Among them Cooke was with Heminge as a child and later on named his daughter after Mistress Rebecca Heminge. Tooley had the good fortune to be a pupil of Richard Burbage. In his will, made four years after his master's death, he left ten pounds to

Burbage's sister Alice and twenty-nine pounds thirteen shillings to Burbage's daughter Sara: there was also a bequest of ten pounds for 'the wife of my good friend Mr. Cuthbert Burbage (in whose house I do now lodge) as a remembrance of my love in respect of her motherly care over me'. He also left five pounds to Mistress Condell. Rice was apprenticed to Heminge, who remembered him to the extent of twenty shillings in his will of 1630. Phillips, who died in 1605, left to his trainee, Samuel Gilburne, forty shillings, his mouse-coloured velvet hose, his white taffety doublet, a black taffety suit, a purple cloak, his sword, dagger, and base vial. To another apprentice, James Sands, he left money and musical instruments. When young Gilburne grew to man's size he could take the streets or the stage 'in full fig'.

Discipline there had to be together with a deal of hard work. Moods are volatile amid the demands of hasty theatrical production. Testamentary bequests and compliments, made long after old sores and grievances had been forgotten, may incline us to take too rosy a view of the apprentice's life and of his schooling by an important player with a big part to study and other cares in mind. But, on the whole, the available records suggest abiding friendships in the homes of the Actor-Sharers, some of whom had abundant children of their own to feed and educate.

The boys were taken on at an age as early as ten and were certainly hard at work when twelve. Ben Jonson's famous epitaph on Salathiel Pavy is proof of that.

> *Years he numbered scarce thirteen*
> *When Fates turned cruel,*
> *Yet three filled zodiacs had he been*
> *The stage's jewel.*

They had much to learn in addition to the practice of singing and of good delivery of speech. All actors of the period had to be dancers and fencers of approved capacity, and in addition to these physical activities there were graces to be learned. The boys had to master feminine make-up and the proper wearing of the voluminous women's dresses of the period. While in early training they were also used as general 'fags', fetching and carrying 'props', taking messages and so on. But there were compensations. An established boy-player could earn fifteen shillings a week, at least twice the money of a minor 'Hired Man'. But the crafty Henslowe apparently took the apprentice's wage and doled him out some pocket-money. The King's Men may have been more generous.

The whole system of juvenile employment in feminine parts worked well and without scandal. The Puritan opponents of the theatre kept up a discharge of violent, but unspecified, charges of immorality. The Book of Deuteronomy could be quoted against the boys. 'The woman shall not wear that which pertaineth to a man, neither shall a man put on a woman's garment: for all that do so are an abomination to the Lord thy God.' The intolerant Stubbs said of the actors that in 'their secret conclaves they play the Sodomites or worse'. But particular cases of this are not cited and no scandals attaching to individuals found their way, as far as we know, into the news of the town.

For a dramatist writing important roles and singing parts for boys there was the constant nuisance of too swift maturity. Cuthbert Burbage mentions this in his deposition already quoted. 'The boys growing up to be men . . . the boys daily wearing out.' More of those whom Hamlet called 'little eyases' (young hawks taken from the nest for training) had to be found and fostered. A constant nuisance was the attainment of puberty and the breaking of the voice. In *Hamlet* a long discussion of the author's and the actors' problems holds up the plot in a manner most serviceable to our knowledge of the Shakespearian theatre, but somewhat odd when we find the Prince scolding the clown-part players for gagging and fooling when there is 'some necessary question of the play to be considered'. Eager to declare his grievances about bad contemporary acting in England, Shakespeare was far from taking his own advice to get on with the story.

In this discourse on the state of the drama Hamlet is made to mention this trouble of the children growing up. Welcoming the players to Elsinore he remarks on a boy's rapid rise in height and adds the supplication: 'Pray God your voice like a piece of un-current gold be not cracked within the ring.' Later Shakespeare made a less than gentle allusion to a 'squeaking Cleopatra': with a voice suddenly breaking the squeaker would have become a barker or a growler. Producers in our time of plays which include child-ren's parts often encounter this difficulty in the case of a long run and have to re-cast the roles.

That Shakespeare himself suffered in this way is plainly shown by some lines in *Cymbeline*, Act IV, Scene 2. Cymbeline's two sons, Guiderius and Arviragus, are to sing the exquisite epitaph on Imogen beginning: 'Fear no more the heat o' the sun.' But Arviragus explains that 'our voices have got the mannish crack'. His brother says:

> *I cannot sing: I'll weep and word it with thee.*
> *For notes of sorrow out of tune are worse*
> *Than priests and fanes that lie.*

To this Arviragus replies, 'We'll speak it then.' One can imagine that Shakespeare, so fond of music, was indignant that so fine a song should have to be 'worded' only. Presumably the boys engaged were reliable in their parts and could not immediately be replaced because of the unfortunate arrival of 'the mannish crack'. Obviously the lines must have been inserted after the play had been written. Proper singing to music would be intended by the author and expected by the public: when that became impossible, an apology had to be made. It was neatly done. The presence of the playwright at the time of rehearsal or at some later performance is indicated; the explanatory lines have the Shakespearian ring and do not seem to have been scribbled in by one of the actors or the Book-keeper.

Any dramatist who keeps a keen eye on his play in performance has vexations to endure, and not only in the case of the child-actor who is too rapidly maturing. Slackness may set in among those of all ages; episodes may disappoint and need correction. Shakespeare, doubly a Sharer and eager for reasons of finance as well as of personal pride to have a full and satisfied audience for his plays, had his watching brief as well as his obligations of authorship.

CHAPTER IV

The Fellowship

HAMLET, jesting on his own readiness with a speech or a rhyme, said to Horatio that, with a forest of feathers and roses on his shoes, he would qualify for 'a fellowship in a cry of players'. To this he was given the answer that he was worth half a share. 'A whole one, I,' claimed Hamlet. In that he spoke for his author and actor too, if Burbage were the man: he also reminds us that theatrical shares were divisible property. In this use of the word fellowship Shakespeare may have meant only partnership: but the term has a warmer significance for us and one that was justified by the way in which the Chamberlain's and King's Men usually spoke of each other. The impression of a cohesive cordiality is strong and constant.

If there were regular meetings of the Sharers, as there surely must have been with some frequency amid the quick changes of programme, there were two groups at work. If Heminge presided over the counsels of the Actor-Sharers, Cuthbert Burbage was the natural choice to do the same for the House-keepers. He could give his whole time and attention to their problems since he had no parts to study and perform or rehearsals to attend, unless he chose to be a looker-on at the latter. This would have been resented. Directors and actors do not like rehearsal interlopers. The players would have wished him elsewhere, keeping a check on the accounts and on the conduct of 'the gatherers' who took the playgoers' money.

Appointing and paying these employees was one of the House-keeper's functions. The system was cumbrous. The members of the audience first paid one gatherer a penny to go in and then the extra pence to other gatherers according to the kind of gallery-seat that they wanted. The gatherers took the money in their boxes; hence our long-remaining term 'box-office' which is an absurd survival, since our old theatres have often only a few boxes and those only sold for a 'smash hit', while our new ones often have no boxes at all. Much of our theatrical vocabulary has remained unchanged since Shakespeare's time. The prompter still 'holds the book', parts are 'studied' by the actor, the entrances to cheap seats are 'the doors', and the money for costlier seats is taken at the 'box-office'. The man with the gathering box in Shakespeare's time was under vigilance, since the cash put into it was sometimes conjured out of it; or so it was alleged.

Shakespeare could attend both kinds of Sharers' meetings and my conjecture is that, with his sense of business, he did so as often as he could, since his earnings as an author were so much less than his share of the gathered income. There were some matters for joint consideration by the two groups, notably the allocation of the receipts. There were separate accounts for the two kinds of takings, the money collected at 'the doors' from those entering the standing-room in the Yard and the further payments for gallery seats already mentioned. The Swiss visitor, Platter, stated definitely that 'whoever cares to stand below pays only one English penny, but if he wishes to sit he enters by another door and pays another penny, while if he desires to sit in the cushioned seats, where he can be seen as well as see well, he pays yet another English penny at a third door'. This suggests three separate payments to three different gatherers, since De Witt's picture of the Swan Theatre marks an 'ingress' to the first gallery, sometimes called the orchestra, from the Yard.

Somebody also had to collect the sixpences paid by the fashionable and sometimes facetious gentry who wanted a seat on the stage. De Witt showed no such seats but there is abundant evidence of their use (and misuse) in some theatres and at some times. Dekker, describing the noisy and obnoxious playgoer of means in *The Gull's Hornbook*, published in 1609, wrote: 'Whether therefore the gatherers of the public or private play-house stand to receive the afternoon's rent, let our Gallant (having paid it) presently advance himself up to the throne of the stage . . . on the very rushes where the comedy is to dance . . . beating down the mews and hisses of the opposed rascality.' The standers in the Yard, dismissed as rascals and as 'penny stinkards' by such as Dekker's gallant, may have been rough and rowdy at times, but most of them were determined to get their pennyworth as lookers and listeners and might well mew and hiss the loutish fops on the stage who 'to make other fools fall a-laughing, mew at passionate speeches, blare at merry, find fault with the music, whew at the children's action, whistle at the songs and, above all, curse the Sharers'.

Dekker was a satirist writing to entertain and we cannot take his picture of a Jacobean audience as altogether factual. But the facts about the admission system are valuable. He makes further mention of the Lords' Rooms, which he calls boxes. In them, whatever their position, the charge for a seat could be a shilling. These rooms Dekker called 'but the Stage's Suburbs'. Their occupants were 'contemptably thrust into the rear' by 'a conspiracy of waiting women and gentlemen ushers and the covetousness of Sharers'. He added that 'much new satin is damned by being smothered to death there in darkness'. Growling at the Sharers was then as common a complaint as denouncing 'the management' has always been.

In *Shakespeare's Audience* Professor Harbage, working on the dimensions of the Fortune Theatre, of which we have the exact figures, and also of the human frame, decided that, with an allowance of 2·5 square feet per person, 818 standers could be accommodated in the Yard. He allotted to those sitting in the galleries 3·75 square feet per person and calculated the sitting capacity to be 1,526: thus there was a total holding of 2,344 if every place was taken, an occurrence probably rare. This compares with a capacity audience of 900 in London's moderately sized Haymarket Theatre and of 2,422 at the huge Palladium. In the pictures we have the theatres of Shakespeare's time do not look at all large; so either the crowding and cramping of the audience was drastic, as Professor Hotson maintains in his *Shakespeare's Wooden O*, or there has been some mistake.

But packed houses would be the exception. Professor Harbage allows amply for this and offers '1,250 as the average daily attendance at the Rose in the year 1595. This is my guess and I have the confidence to believe that it cannot be more than a few hundred off either way. It is to say that the Rose, an Elizabethan theatre of average size, was usually little more than half-filled.' He conjectures rather more twopenny seat holders than penny standers and less than a hundred threepenny patrons, with no allowance for a few shilling patrons in the Lord's Room and sixpenny gallants on Dekker's 'throne' of the stage. The 'house' with this reckoning was worth £8 9s. and he adds, 'This sum is plausible in view of the fact that £10 was the sum regularly received at this time for a performance at Court.'

Shakespeare and his fellow-Sharers may have had rather more to divide at the Globe, since the company was in a strong position when it was established there. And there would be more still at the Blackfriars, since we know that prices were higher in the covered theatres and the takings considerably greater. At the Globe each 'house' may have been worth ten pounds on average and the week's takings with six performances sixty pounds. The method of division between the two classes of Sharers is known. It is also known that there were disputes.

Cuthbert Burbage's statement to the Lord Chamberlain Pembroke in 1635 is precise as to past and present practices in the portioning of the receipts. 'The players that lived in the first times had only the profits arising from the Doors, but now the players receive all the comings in at the Doors to themselves and half the Galleries from the House-keepers.' It is plain that at first the House-keepers were getting the best of the bargain. However big the capacity of the penny Yard, and even if the gallery folk had first paid their Yard penny, the money taken for the higher-priced seats was likely to be larger and the Actor-Sharers could reasonably argue that they were the principal attraction and deserved better treatment. True, they needed the premises, but the premises were useless without them. When the dispute arose and was settled by a win for the players we do not know. But some contention there had been. The ratio of division would not matter so much when the groups of Actor-Sharers and House-keepers had largely similar membership: it was when House-keeper Shares began to be sold outside the company that ill-feeling would arise.

Agreement there was. Shakespeare, remaining a Sharer in both kinds, would be one of those resenting excessive takings by the House-keepers if outsiders were beginning to get hold of House-keeper Shares. He naturally wanted to see fair play for the actors among whom, whether he was doing much acting or not, he continued to be listed. In Cuthbert Burbage's statement already quoted we read that, when the Blackfriars Theatre was taken over 'with our money', the direction was 'placed with men players, which were Heminge, Condell, and Shakespeare'. Shakespeare is not spoken of as a dramatist, since dramatists were only earners of fees and poor fees at that, but as an actor. That was where the power and profit lay.

So the Actor-Sharers established their point. With Heminge as their leading counsellor they had ample business to consider, since they held both the stock of plays and the stock of costumes and properties: the first could be renewed cheaply, the second could not. It has been calculated that their capital invested in the wardrobe, armoury, and 'props' would run to eight hundred pounds. How was that capital raised? It is assumed that the players had to buy themselves into the Fellowship by purchase of a share and the shares were valuable, especially the House-keeper Shares which were selling at a hundred pounds apiece soon after 1630. It is hard to see how a Boy or a Hired Man, with their low wages, could possibly save enough to buy shares of any kind when the chance came of promotion to Sharer-status. I think it likely that some system of hire-purchase was practised. A Hired Man would be admitted to the Fellowship, beginning, perhaps, with the half-share mentioned by Horatio, on condition that he paid for it out of his share-takings month by month.

It has been suggested that the story of the Earl of Southampton's gift to Shakespeare of a thousand pounds 'to go through with a purchase which he had a mind to' was based on a present which would enable the Earl's friend to buy himself an Actor-Share and possibly also a House-keeper Share when the Chamberlain's Men were becoming well set in the early fifteen-nineties. What could be a more likely purchase on which to have his mind set? The sum of a thousand pounds has been regarded as impossibly large: but, if we knock off one nought, a hundred pounds would be a likely amount for Shakespeare to receive from a generous, though at the time far from wealthy patron, and to use for this coveted form of advancement. There was abundant evidence of favours received and of lavish gratitude in the dedication of the poem *Lucrece* to the Earl in 1594. Money is not mentioned, but 'the warrant I have of your disposition' points that way, especially as it is followed by 'what I have done is yours, what I have to do is yours, being part in all I have devoted yours'. 'Part in all I have' can well have had a financial application.

The Fellowship has been described, with ample confirmation of the facts known about the members' careers, as having a remarkable cohesion and loyalty based on mutual esteem. The departure of the droll Will Kempe was a lonely secession which may have followed some dispute as to the proper scope of 'clownage'. Shakespeare's clown parts were often small. Insertions in the Quarto and Folio texts of the names of the actor instead of the part that he had played occur occasionally and give us some of our regrettably small information about the casting of Shakespeare's plays. In this way we know that Kempe, already named as a principal player in 1594, played the servant Peter in *Romeo and Juliet*, probably in 1595. There is no satisfaction in that tiny role for a leading comedian. It is true that he had Dogberry in *Much Ado About Nothing* in 1599 just before he left the Fellowship and that offered larger and richer material for the winning of laughs. The Chamberlain's Men were still growing in repute and prosperity. Yet out he went to undertake his curious feat of dancing all the way to Norwich. That, however exhausting, was a solo performance, attracted plenty of attention and hospitality, gave him a chance to be his own reporter in a lively account of it, and so would gratify injured vanity. It is fair to assume that he would not have broken with his colleagues at that time except under pressure of a grievance which he found intolerable.

About this time Shakespeare was writing *Hamlet*, in which he included his observations on the drolls who took liberties with the text and guffawed at their own jokes. 'Let your clowns speak no more than is set down for them, for there will be some of them that will themselves laugh, to set on some quantity of barren spectators to laugh too . . . that's villainous and shows a most pitiful ambition in the fool that uses it.' Those are strong words and the audience, with Kempe away on his own, would have seen the point. Kempe may have been pitifully ambitious, at least in the eyes of the Fellowship. An anonymous reference to him made in 1590 called him 'the most Comical and Conceited Cavalier Monsieur du Kempe jest-monger and Vice-Gerent general to the ghost of Dick Tarlton'. (Tarleton, a pre-eminent Tudor Clown and Groom to the Queen, had died in 1588.) Conceited had not then the meaning that it has now and signified a witty man rather than one too big for his jester's shoes. But to call him Monsieur du Kempe and Cavalier does suggest some resentment of his pretentions. He was later dealing with Henslowe and he became a member of Worcester's Men. The mention of him as a fellow of Shakespeare and Burbage in the Cambridge University play *The Return from Parnassus*, somewhere about 1600, may refer to past association. News travelled slowly and perhaps Cambridge had not heard of the departure at the end of 1599.

Kempe was famous as a player and dancer in the jig, the short finale to a curious play, similar in kind to the farce which the programmes of the eighteenth and nineteenth century included with a strong drama or a tragedy. Thomas Platter saw one after the play of *Julius Caesar* in 1599 when he crossed the river to 'the playhouse with a thatched roof'. He related that 'at the end of the play two of the actors in men's clothes and two in women's performed a dance, as is their custom, wonderfully well together'. The playwrights resented this kind of sequel to their serious work. Dekker lamented the 'nasty, bawdy, jig' which followed 'a worthy tragedy'. Marlowe's prologue to the First Part of *Tamburlaine the Great* claims to be letting his audience escape

> *From jigging veins of rhyming mother-wits*
> *And such conceits as clownage keeps in pay.*

Shakespeare also resented the jigs and mentioned them several times with contempt. Hamlet sneers at the senile taste of Polonius. 'He's for a jig or a tale of bawdry or he sleeps'—a remark constantly echoed in the modern derision of 'the tired businessman' with his alleged craving for a leg-show and a 'blue' line. In *Love's Labour's Lost* Berowne, whose part is thought to contain a good deal of Shakespearian self-portraiture, exclaims:

> *Oh me, with what strict patience have I sat*
> *To see a king transformed into a gnat,*
> *To see great Hercules whipping a gig,*
> *And profound Solomon to tune a jig.*

There was much lack of sympathy with the jig-maker and a chance for bad feeling. Armin, who took Kempe's place and kept it, was evidently innocent of 'clownage' in excess. He was trusted with much better and rather different parts, if he took Feste in *Twelfth Night* and the Fool in *King Lear*. He may not have appeared in the final jigs if he had been taking a biggish Fool's part. At least he did not get on Shakespeare's nerves: he was more cultivated, himself an author and playwright, free of 'pitiful ambition' in his drolleries and more likely to maintain the 'fellowship' spirit than to destroy it.

The Chamberlain's-King's Men did not share out the task of writing after Shakespeare and Ben Jonson were established as soloists, although Shakespeare continued to help other men, including Fletcher. Elsewhere play-writing had been patch-work. A manager, and notably Henslowe, suggested a subject and then there was collaboration with selected writers. In 1598 Henslowe entertained with 'good cheer', and at a cost of five shillings, Drayton, Dekker, Chettle, and Wilson, and gave them an advance payment of a pound each for a piece called *Earl Godwin and His Three Sons*. Three of this party were by then approved and experienced writers and their names are familiar to us. The less known, Robert Wilson, shared a part in sixteen plays for Henslowe and was evidently a quick worker, since Meres paid a tribute to his 'learning and extemporal wit in this faculty', describing this readiness, perhaps too generously, as 'without compare'. Munday, reported to have failed as an actor and at one time busy as an anti-Catholic tractarian and pamphleteer, was another of Henslowe's regulars. Meres called him 'our best plotter', which suggests that in each collaboration one was responsible for laying out the story in terms of theatre: after the plotter had made his synopsis various sections were handed over to the members of the writing team. This method might easily lead to confusion. But clarity and consistency were not urgent requirements. At least this arrangement would guarantee speed in the production of a script if a replacement were quickly needed; three or four men writing simultaneously could usefully vamp up a play more quickly than one if time was the first consideration. The method of trusting a single dramatist certainly worked far better. But the blessing of Shakespeare's presence was exceptional.

Apart from Shakespeare's contributions, the business of choosing or commissioning plays had to be done by the Actor-Sharers. We may suppose them gathered in the tiring-room, allotting the scripts to be read, and considering suggestions: those made by Shakespeare for his next piece would be readily accepted, but Burbage would have a say in the matter with an eye to his own part.

He was not being unduly egotistical if he did so raise his voice. He could fairly claim that he was a principal agent in drawing the money and 'bringing them in'. The more cultivated members of the audience, who prided themselves on their taste in poetry, might consider their playgoing in terms of the author and suggest a trip across the river to see 'this new thing of Shakespeare's'. But a majority of those paying for a place at the play, and not the penny groundlings only, would want to see what Burbage was doing now, having heard the gossip after the opening and being, no doubt, informed that he was in grander form than ever.

Some conference of the Actor-Sharers there must have been and it is not in the nature of conferences to end quickly unless the chairman is unusually firm. We see John Heminge as presiding, and that capably and with devotion. Here was his life-work for nearly forty years. He has put his name third on the list of 'The Principal Actors in All these Plays' in the First Folio, following Shakespeare and Burbage. That does not indicate the importance of his roles: the placing, if not haphazard, may refer to the order of seniority in the company. Heminge was credited with a stutter by the rhymester who described the burning of the Globe in 1613, but this must refer to the natural incoherence of a grief-stricken man when that disaster occurred and not to a general impediment of speech. Such a hindrance to clear and powerful diction would not have been tolerated in an age when the acting was largely rhetorical. Heminge drew the just rewards of his long service. At his death in 1630 he held a quarter of the shares in the Globe and Blackfriars: some of these could have been Shakespeare's, taken over when the latter parted with his theatrical interests shortly before his death.

Heminge became the good uncle of the King's Men and even a father-figure of the profession. Fairly early in his life he was called 'Old Heminge' as though he had a paternal and protecting manner. He became the actors' champion outside his own Fellowship. In 1618 the London theatre companies, usually so keen in rivalry, united for negotiations with the Master of the Revels and Heminge was appointed as their representative, which proves a general confidence in his good sense. Henry Condell, who was an original shareholder in the Blackfriars but not in the Globe, joined Heminge in the editing of the First Folio, a task which would allow them only a limited amount of their normal activities while the collection and survey of the scripts were being made. The date of Heminge's birth is unknown, but he married in 1588: if he was only twenty then, he was fifty-five when the Folio appeared and that was a much greater age to an Elizabethan actor than it seems to us. When he died in 1630 he could look back on a full life. He had become a man 'of great wealth and power', as he was described some years earlier.

It was a life of kindness with a record of good citizenship. He and Condell were the men to whom the troubles of the team were brought. Two members, Alexander Cooke and John Underwood, who both died leaving a young and parentless family, made Heminge and Condell responsible for the care of their orphans; there was trust on the one side and a charitable benevolence on the other. Both these senior actors were churchwardens at St. Mary Aldermanbury in the City, in which parish they were living. By the time these cares were thrust upon them as willing wards of other men's children their own offspring must have been out in the world. A child about the house was nothing to them, since Heminge had fathered thirteen and Condell eight. The former's natural authority in his company of players is indicated in some lines written after Burbage's death, in which that actor's spirit is advised not to fear the rod of heaven since his companions already departed will be established as angels and 'old Heminge' will later on be God. This may be called excessive promotion for all members of the Fellowship, but shows some genuine reverence for the father-figure.

A word of sympathetic appreciation may well go to the wives of these actors. They bore and cared for very large families in houses with no conveniences and with all the water to be fetched from the nearest conduit, or bought from the professional water-carriers. To have piped water laid on to houses was then a luxury of the rich. They had boy-apprentices on their hands as well as their own numerous children. Life may have been eased for them by the fact that their husbands were kept out and about all day by their heavy rota of theatrical labours. The men were away part of the night too when there was need for a late rehearsal or there was a command to give an evening performance. However, domestic 'help' would cost very little and we know that Alleyn kept one servant and probably had more than one. But there was constant fear of plague. What happened then? The players, with their livelihood in London suddenly withdrawn, often coped with their loss by going on tour, but they could hardly trail a wife and a quiverful of children along with them as all available transport would be needed for themselves and their costumes, swords, and musical instruments. They were on their rounds with harassing fears about what was going on at home.

When they could afford it some of the actors moved to suburban homes which would not have to be deserted in times of a lethal epidemic. But when they were young men with young families they would be in their favoured areas just north of the City and on the Southwark shore, both areas liable to the terrible infection and to the ghastly scenes of corpse-disposal which Nashe has pictured so vividly. Shakespeare himself, if, as is generally supposed, he never brought his wife and children to London and only saw them on the annual holiday in Stratford mentioned in Rowe's life, had less to worry about. But the others, the married Londoners and their womenfolk, had plenty of occasion for anxiety and for the kind of scurried evacuations that so many families had to endure when another scourge hit them in 1939 and the subsequent years.

Certain features of this world of the Fellowship in which Shakespeare worked cannot be disputed. Its members had to be industrious and rose to be reasonably prosperous, since they were working efficiently in a rising market. Whatever their origins they became what we should call middle class, in which rank Shakespeare had been born. They had the bourgeois qualities and the virtues which have been constantly derided by the kind of artists who lack them. Churchgoers they had to be; attendance was compulsory by law. But some did more than answer the roll-call. Several took on the duties of churchwardenship.

Their cares in church management were heavy, for the wardens then were disciplinarians with the power to impose fines for all manner of offences, such as meat-eating on Fridays or burying a corpse without a woollen shroud (this astonishing ordinance was imposed to help the wool-trade and discourage the importation of linen). They could even fine the clergyman for slackness in his duties. Heminge and Condell, wardens at St. Mary Aldermanbury, where their memorial properly remains, were carrying these

burdens. It may have been a prudent move to have such ecclesias-
tical attachments at a time when the 'Square Toes' were continually
attacking the weekday occupation of the players. Even Henslowe,
whose financial procedures were of the kind now known in the
City as 'a bit swift', took care to be a churchwarden at St. Saviour's
on the Bankside. So did the actor Edward Alleyn, who succeeded
him in that office in 1610.

All we know of Heminge, which is a considerable amount,
suggests 'the uprightness of dealing which argues his honesty'
which Chettle had attributed to Shakespeare in 1592, when replying
to Greene's attack 'on the upstart Crow . . . in his own conceit the
only Shake-scene in the country'. Upright dealing was not
universal. Henslowe was accused in 1615 by the Lady Elizabeth's
Men of harsh money-lending and of having 'broken and dis-
membered five companies in three years'. The charge was headed
'Nine Articles of Oppression'. In the records there are no such
charges against Shakespeare's Fellowship. The boys may have had
their whimpers of resentment and the Hired Men may have had
their opinions about the Sharers' profits, but we have no parallel
to the grievances voiced by those who worked for Henslowe.

Opinion about theatre-life in the fifteen-nineties has been coloured by the mixture of scarlet in sin and grey in squalor revealed in the brief chronicles of Robert Greene's life. He had
consoled himself for a playwright's poverty by sneering at the
players, 'pranct with the glory of others' feathers'. At thirty-four
he died of a surfeit, it was said, of pickled herrings and Rhenish
wine. He was then in dismal lodgings attended by one of Doll
Tearsheet's fellowship and fatally distempered by the diet and
drinking linked with the name of Sir Toby Belch. No church-
wardenships for him. He had walked or staggered in the 'Boar's
Head' ambience. 'What company?' asked Prince Hal concerning
Falstaff. 'Ephesians, my lord, of the old Church', answered the
page. (Ephesus was to be replaced by Bohemia in the vocabulary of
the gay life.) That was the boisterous and self-destroying congregation of Greene and others who, with only a quill instead of players'
plumage, could hardly earn a night or two's supping and tippling
by turning out an act of a play and would probably be unable to
meet their debts to landladies and taverners by knocking off a
whole one. But the players, who had often to mime the revelling

Ephesians on the stage, had in their lives to be almost stoical, up in the morning for their practice and sober at night for their study of their next parts. The role of Falstaff is a long one to learn and, if Heminge was its creator, he had plenty to add to his labours as a Sharer.

The western suburbs were favoured by the players in their prosperity. Condell had a house at Fulham and Phillips a house at Mortlake. Lowin, who lived to a great age, became proprietor of an inn, 'The Three Pigeons' at Brentford; but his skill as an actor did not attend him as a caterer, if the tradition be true that he died in poverty. But he did not die young since he was certainly alive in 1652, then seventy-six years old, and may have been the 'John Lowen' buried at St. Paul's, Covent Garden, in March, 1669, when he would be ninety-three. Others made their investments further west; Shakespeare did so early and in gentlemanly manner at Stratford-upon-Avon; Cowley, an Actor-Sharer but not, apparently, a House-keeper among the King's Men, settled not far off in the Cotswolds. Shakespeare was not the only owner of a coat of arms: Richard Burbage, Heminge, Cowley, Pope, and Phillips all acquired these signs of gentility. What are now called status symbols appealed to them.

Some of the projects of the merchants in the Jacobean world were large and very profitable. But it was only a modest investment that Shakespeare's Fellowship could make. Outside its ranks much greater wealth was accumulated by Edward Alleyn, who rivalled Burbage in renown as a player and far outstripped him in wealth by going into management as a theatrical projector instead of working in an autonomous Fellowship. Although never a colleague of Shakespeare, at least when the careers of both were established, his affairs are worth notice as signs of the times and of the upward climb of an actor who was a shrewd business man. The money that he made was not dissipated in folly but put to the endowment of learning as well as to the handsome establishment of his family.

Alleyn's first wife had been Henslowe's daughter; the union brought him a valuable connection with the most crafty of the playhouse projectors. Alleyn was a triumphant investor in the Fortune Theatre and probably did better still with the menagerie of baitable bulls, bears, and mastiffs on the Bankside. With his father-in-law he became joint Master of the Game at Paris Garden in 1605.

There were large profits to be made in that form of show business, which then carried no stigma and had strong Royal support. Henslowe would appreciate that the wretched beasts, though they had to be bought and fed, did not, like authors and actors, require to be paid. Some of Alleyn's fortune went to the purchase of the manor of Dulwich for five thousand pounds and there were considerable further outlays on purchase of land and leases thereabouts. He built the Hospital and College of God's Gift in Dulwich, modestly attributing to the deity a generosity of his own. His acting was the triumph of a day; his benefaction 'eternised', to use a word of his time, the name of Alleyn of Dulwich.

For his second wife he married into the Church and wooed the daughter of John Donne, Dean of St. Paul's, with some serious misgivings on the part of the latter. But it was financially a good match for 'Con' Donne, since she was given a settlement of fifteen hundred pounds while her dowry was only five hundred pounds. She had a legacy of fifteen hundred pounds in trust at her husband's death in 1626, three years after the wedding. His end was occasioned by a chill caught while he was visiting some newly bought property in Yorkshire, evidence of the wide range of his investments.

The members of Shakespeare's Fellowship were not such magnates of the playhouse world. But they were able to go their middle-class way; one of them had a profitable side-line, for Heminge maintained his interest in a family grocery business. Shakespeare kept at least some of his attention on the value of land and tithes in Warwickshire. They avoided the troubles which came to others of their calling, especially the writers. It was then very easy to be apprehended for a small debt, participation in a brawl, or a political indiscretion. To write anything objectionable to the Court, such as scoffing at the Scotsmen who had seen advantage in coming to London in the reign of James I, was to make sure of punishment. Yet some writers went rashly into their stinging social comment. Ben Jonson was sent to the Marshalsea in 1596 for his share in *The Isle of Dogs,* a play judged 'very seditious and slanderous'.

Allusion has already been made to the frequent outbreaks of the too fiery spirits and to the readiness to draw a sword. Pens, too, could involve risk of disaster. Amid the recurrent follies of the too venturesome writers Shakespeare's companions steered mainly clear of trouble and there is no record of any imprisonment. They were once in danger for a political ineptitude. They received an invitation from Sir Giles Merrick, one of the Earl of Essex's supporters, at the time of the insurrection of 1601, to play Shakespeare's *Richard II,* a drama made dangerous by its inclusion of a successful deposition from the throne. That was a subject of which the Queen did not care to be reminded. The performance was on Saturday, February 7, 1601, and attended by the conspirators who, on the motion of Sir Charles Percy, had dinner together and then 'went all together to the Globe Theatre over the water where the Lord Chamberlain's Men use to play'. In August of that year the Queen, in a conversation at Greenwich with William Lambard, alleged that 'this tragedy was played forty times in open streets and houses'. This is a curious assertion and may be the wild exaggeration of an angry woman whose throne and even life had been menaced. But, even if we reduce the forty times to a few times, it indicates that the actors were not confined to formal stages and would go anywhere on invitation, even into the streets, if it paid them. The text and production used in the street must have been much cut and simplified, which further shows that the members of the Fellowship were ready for anything anywhere and that their work was not conditioned by stage-architecture.

They had protested that the play was 'stale' and would bring in nothing by another revival. But an offer was made to 'Phillips the player' of 'forty shillings extraordinary', i.e. beyond what money was taken by the gatherers in the normal way at the Globe performance. Forty shillings with only a small addition to be expected at 'the doors' for a 'stale offering', seems a small sum for so risky a proceeding when a Court Command Performance usually won them ten pounds. But the actors were politically naif at least on this occasion. At the subsequent inquiry it was a plea of innocent intentions that saved them from prison. Phillips, having agreed to the bargain, had to represent them and Heminge must have been glad to be out of the spokesman's office for once. Phillips did his job well enough to get his colleagues' innocence accepted. There were no long resentments at Court. The players were fortunately well established as the Royal favourites. Far from going to prison, they were called to appear again before her Majesty a fortnight later on Shrove Tuesday, the day on which the Queen signed the order for the execution of the Earl of Essex.

Whether Shakespeare was there at the time and agreed to the revival of *Richard II* we do not know. He might have had more sense of the political situation. If he was there, he had good reason for alarm: if not, he could blame his colleagues for a considerable folly. The escape was fortunate and other authors and companies, less generously treated when similar blunders were made, may have muttered about favouritism. However that may be, the Fellowship had learned its lesson and maintained its long service of the Queen and her successor with no suggestion of any further offence and with no pains or penalties. In their private lives they encountered no troubles of which we know. They were not street-fighters nor were they so ready to see or imagine an insult that they were drawn into duelling. Shakespeare's quarrel with Gardiner and Waite, which has already been mentioned, ended with legal sureties against violence and without the use of cudgels or swords.

Accordingly we can follow a progress of propriety as well as of prosperity, a comparatively calm life in a town elsewhere stormy and turbulent. The leaders were family men and of the incoming members only Nathan Field, a dramatist as well as a player, who had come from the Chapel Children to be an Actor-Sharer in 1616, had a reputation for a disorderly life. The players were no Puritans. That Shakespeare knew the tavern life to the full is obvious and they would have their celebrations, enjoying them the more because they were occasional and not part of a habitual sottishness. When a new play had been produced, the evening after 'a first afternoon' was an obvious occasion for one of those convivial wit-combats at the Mermaid Inn or elsewhere of whose good talk among 'canakin's clink' much was written by contemporary and subsequent poets. The Mermaid's apprentice, and later its proprietor, William Johnson, 'citizen and vintner', was one of Shakespeare's trustees when the latter added to his investments by the purchase of the Blackfriars Gatehouse in 1613. There is proof of close attachment and confidence there. But Shakespeare himself was too busy to be a regular reveller and this is supported by a scribbled note inserted in the third part of John Aubrey's *Brief Lives* and not appearing in the short biography of the poet in that lively book. This appears to record of 'W. Shakespeare' that he was the more to be admired because 'he was not a company keeper, lived in Shoreditch, would not be debauched and, if invited to, wrote: he was in pain'. This jotting may be taken more as an indication than a considered statement. But Aubrey's authority was not a bad one, since he talked with William Beeston, actor-son of Christopher Beeston who played with the Chamberlain's Men in Ben Jonson's *Every Man in his Humour* in 1598. Christopher does not appear in the Folio List of the Fellowship's principal players and he left them to pursue a successful career with other companies. But word of mouth passed down from him has therefore some authority; Shakespeare, we know, had been a fellow-player with Beeston in that comedy of Jonson's.

So it was a life without scandal. That Shakespeare had his raptures and certainly his suffering through entanglement with a Dark Lady is made plain by references, indirectly in some plays and directly in the *Sonnets,* to a dark 'daughter of the game' with eyes of 'pitch-ball' blackness, who tormented him and played him false. But, despite that distraction, the work went on, the memorising, rehearsing and acting, the training of the boys and the supervision of the Hired Men. There were two plays a year to be written and put into production, as well as the routine cares of the Housekeeper and the Actor-Sharer. There could be no time for regular attendances at long tavern nights either for him or for his colleagues; and, if Aubrey is to be trusted, Shakespeare had no such inclination. He was one of a Fellowship of family men who looked after themselves and their own. (Heminge sent a son to Westminster School and to Oxford.) They kept their heads, paid and made their way, and put their increasing money to sensible uses.

We need not idealise the lives of those so savagely arraigned for their 'abominable exercise of playing' and for enticing boys into an alleged school of vice. But, considering the general state of London's morals when King James was encouraging the most debauched, perverted, and unscrupulous members of his Court by special grants of titles, favours, and property, the conduct of the actors was exemplary. Satan, supposed by the Puritans to be their master, could find small mischief for hands already so full.

One thing must never be forgotten, our debt to Heminge and Condell. This is beyond calculation since, if they had not bothered, among their many tasks, to collect the thirty-six plays by Shakespeare which they printed in the First Folio, we should have no text of eighteen of them, including *Macbeth, Coriolanus, Cymbeline, Antony and Cleopatra* among the tragedies, and *Twelfth Night, As You Like It,* and *The Winter's Tale* among the comedies. In any theatre named after Shakespeare or built in his honour there should be a proper memorial to the Chief Sharers in the Fellowship and especially to those two. Donne's often quoted statement that 'no man is an island' had full relevance to the sea in which the Fellowship launched its projects.

CHAPTER V

Preparing

THE SHARERS, in preparing their next moves, had to be swift in counsel since there could be no expectation of a long run which would allow them to sit back and make far-reaching plans in a leisurely manner. That could never be their way of life. The mention of *Richard II* as a 'stale' play unlikely to do well in revival shows that by no means all of their chief dramatist's work could be relied on to live and to maintain a profitable place in their repertory. Yet the piece was at first a considerable success, since three Quarto editions were printed in two years, 1597 and 1598. There is contemporary evidence that *Romeo and Juliet* and the Falstaff plays were abiding favourites. There was another stand-by in *Titus Andronicus* which was in print from 1594 onwards with second and third Quartos appearing in 1600 and 1611. It was stated in both the latter publications that the piece was 'sundry times played', the usual phrase applied to pieces kept in readiness for revival. So in the reign of King James, some twenty years after its composition, this blood-soaked tale of horrors had not been staled in the public taste. The less than best, like *Pericles* much later on, could be substantial aids to the Fellowship when there had been a disappointment and a gap had to be filled. But the new work had to be written or found.

Since nothing remains of a documentary kind about the deliberations of the Sharers we can fairly make some conjecture on the probable course of the proceedings. Let us therefore imagine a session soon after the Globe Theatre had been opened in 1599. If rehearsals had filled the morning and a public performance the afternoon, the evening would be the only time for a meeting in committee: it could be held in the tiring-room or in some niche near by which Heminge used as his office and counting-house. Or there might be a move to the quiet corner of their favoured tavern.

Heminge is my candidate for the chair, with Burbage and Shakespeare beside him, since they were the members of most authority. To begin with it is pointed out that *Julius Caesar* has gone well and is likely to remain a useful asset. It might possibly have reached their ears by Bankside gossip or the grape-vine of the inns that a Swiss visitor to London, Thomas Platter, had been talking at his hostelry, 'The French Lily', in Mark Lane and also at a banquet at which the Lord Mayor entertained him and his fellow-voyagers. He had spoken well of the play and the actors, whom he was to praise in print later on. He had also enjoyed the jig. Mention of the latter is less pleasing to Shakespeare.

The pressing question is Will's next move. More history? Falstaff again? Or another king? Shakespeare is flattered, but disconsolate at the prospect of further delving in the chronicles of Hall and Holinshed. Can't he have a change? Somebody, perhaps Burbage, says that the Hamlet story has always been popular: revenge plays usually please: why not a new version of Hamlet by the best writer of the day? The notion is acceptable. Shakespeare has had it vaguely in mind and agrees to turn it over in a practical way. But there is some hard thinking to be done about that.

Meanwhile the meeting is reminded that they have a boy who can memorise and effectively handle a long and challenging part. His Beatrice has been deservedly a hit and proved his quality. Why not another comedy with him in view? It could be soon done by a hand so quick as Will's and with his fluency now at its fullest. That seems a reasonable possibility to Shakespeare. He remembers having read Thomas Lodge's *Rosalynde* and thought at the time that there was stuff in it with a good girl-into-boy part for this lad of talent. He is reminded that Armin has now joined them, replacing the 'difficult' Kempe, and there must be a good Clown's part to welcome him, give him the right chance, and make him start contented. Burbage inquires where he comes into all this. If Lodge's story does not yield a suitable role, Shakespeare promises to invent one and throw in some good fat speeches as well as a sour wit. (Jacques is not in Lodge's *Rosalynde*.)

Then Shakespeare agrees, while knocking this off, to let his mind really get to work on *Hamlet*. There may be something in Bernard Shaw's contention that the titles of *Much Ado About Nothing* and *As You Like It* were contemptuously chosen by a man yielding to demand and eager to get on with something better. There was to be yet another trifle written in the following year and sub-titled *What You Will;* there may have been word-play here, suggesting something willed on Will, who was ready enough to pun on his own name in his *Sonnets.* Again the brilliant boy, or another of brilliance if the first had grown out of these roles and had got 'the mannish crack' in his voice, would have a wonderful girl-into-boy opportunity. Shakespeare says that he is ready to carry on with a comedy or two while he is revolving larger and tragical matters in his mind. Burbage surmises with satisfaction that something good, perhaps the best of his career, may be coming his way since Will knows his worth and how to write for his particular powers.

Next they discuss other productions. They have just had two comedies of Ben Jonson and those 'Humour' pieces have served them well enough. But the fellow is so troublesome and is such a nuisance about the place. They never know what bother he will cause with his sword or his pen. (Three years later, after quarrels with other writers and conflicts with the law, he landed them with his Roman tragedy *Sejanus* and that did them no good.) Other difficulties are discussed and of course finance comes high among these. They are doing as well as can be hoped but the wardrobe is a continual problem. The public must have its finery and the finery is costly. Is anything coming along in the way of second-hand splendour? (Platter, like other visitors, recorded his admiration of the expensive and elaborate costumes of the actors, adding that the English noblemen used to bequeath or give away their robes and garments to their servants who could not wear such raiment without looking ridiculous and therefore sold them to the players for what they could get.) If there is no luck in that second-hand market, how much is to be allotted to the renewal of the stock? Heminge, as business manager, has his views on that.

Then questions arise as to the form shown by the Hired Men and the need for better enlistment and better training. Are the musicians good enough? Do they need to look round for new apprentice-boys since the children will grow out of their clothes and parts and become husky croakers instead of charming trebles with such damnable speed. I do not visualise long, rambling discussions. Here are men who have learned their job thoroughly and are kept working at full stretch. Such folk are not likely to be tolerant of long-winded and self-assertive egotists in committee. Ben Jonson had written for the Chamberlain's Men and was to write for them again, and at his best, with *Volpone* and *The Alchemist*. But, when the talk turns to him, there are dubious looks: he was never made one of the Sharers. That he would have liked to be one of them is a reasonable guess since they were a prospering society and Ben, intermittently successful as a playwright, was always living poorly on an author's fees and soon forced to write librettos for the Royal masques which he despised and dismissed as mere 'painting and carpentry', even though Inigo Jones was often the designer.

Talks of this kind there must have been. Making any kind of guess about Shakespeare's life is deemed unwarranted and even impertinent by some people. But in my opinion, if we are to understand him, we have inevitably to imagine him with his fellows in their workshop as well as alone at his desk. Some conference of the Sharers was inevitable at frequent intervals, if the players, work was to go on, and every dramatist whose life is closely integrated with that of one team of players must write with the actor in mind. If he is also financially interested, he will be eager to consider expenditure and the minor chores of management. I do not believe that Shakespeare's mind was above reckoning the price of Malvolio's gown of branched velvet or of some new out-lay by his fellow-Sharers on the copper-lace to which Alleyn was addicted and for which a groaning Henslowe paid the bill. That he could pass immediately from the calculations of costs and profits to complete immersion in the affairs and reflections of his tragic heroes is only further evidence of his myriad-minded genius. We do not demean the greatness of the poet by considering the common task of the Sharer: we enhance it.

The committee breaks up with a glass or two and its members go off with some homework in front of them. For they must meet tomorrow with more lines of a new play committed to memory and ready for the morning's drill of rehearsal. Writing a play is one thing and in the case of Shakespeare it may sometimes have been easy enough. But setting it on the stage with punctuality and efficiency is a very different problem. In the multitude of books about Shakespeare almost nothing is said about the burden of rehearsals and the nature of their direction. There is a reason for that. It is one of the great misfortunes of theatrical history in Shakespeare's period that we have so little evidence about time spent on preparing a production and the methods of organisation that were employed. But the matter is so essential to an understanding of Shakespeare's working life that an effort must be made to use what evidence there is. What was created has proved to be a possession for all time, little though the creator knew it. There is not only a strong temptation to visualise the stage birth of an enduring masterpiece; there is also an obligation on the historian to fill, if he can, this gap in our knowledge of production methods, since for production the plays were written.

We have fortunately some knowledge of the team and the tools with which Shakespeare had to work if he were conducting the staging of a play or with which, if he were away or disinclined for such a task, some other person did the work, plotting the moves of the actors, the comic 'business', the contribution of the musicians, and so forth. In daylight matinées there was no problem of lighting: the text proclaimed the hour and the weather, the darkness of night, and the radiance of the dawn. But when the company later moved to the roofed Blackfriars for half its work the director had his torches, lamps, and candles to consider. There was some masquing to be included with the action of the play. The business of getting the play on became more intricate and exacting.

One point I shall not consider, the architecture and lay-out of the Elizabethan and Jacobean theatres. There is a vast literature on this subject and there is certainly nothing like agreement, especially since Dr. Hotson has argued in *Shakespeare's Wooden O* for a 'theatre in the round', with spectators circled all about, with a series of 'mansions' on the central platform, and with a tiring-house below and not beside that stage. To enter this argument is to be lost in controversy. My view is that there was no fixed pattern of a theatre at that time. The players, Shakespeare's own fellows, were improvisers who could pull down a theatre in North London and put it up again on the Bankside. They were working in a rapidly growing and experimental industry: the materials of their playhouse were mainly wood and a few days' carpentry could alter the whole arrangement of the stage and its entrances.

How flexible these conditions were is proved beyond doubt by the structural orders given for the Hope Theatre which was built by Henslowe and Meade in 1613 to act as a double-purpose house on the Bankside. The builder, Gilbert Katherens, trained as a carpenter, was to pull down the old Bear Garden and to substitute 'a playhouse fit and convenient in all things for players to play in and for the game of Bears and Bulls to be baited in the same and also a pit and convenient Tire House'. The stage was to be on trestles and such that it could be lifted and taken away when there was to be 'the Game', i.e. baiting in the pit, instead of the play on the platform. If the stage was thus portable, what becomes of Dr. Hotson's under-stage Tire House? This would hardly be acceptable for a dressing-room or suitable for housing a costly wardrobe if it were soiled with blood and dung when the stage was put back on top of it. A Tire House 'fit and convenient' must have been somewhere behind or at the side.

There is no need to be involved at this point in the complicated disputes about the principles and details of Elizabethan theatre-structure. The architectural conditions of the Globe or whatever houses Shakespeare and his actors had previously tenanted were not the only consideration. The production in hand had to be a movable arrangement, since, if it were successful, it might be commanded for various palaces and great houses and taken on tour to university halls, town halls, and inn yards. What must be assumed is simply the presence of a platform, a tiring-room, a stage staff, probably very small, players of three grades (or four if 'supers' be included), musicians, costumes, and properties. About these we do know at least a few things for certain.

Considering the huge casts which in our editions stand at the head of most of Shakespeare's plays the number of players seems almost ridiculously inadequate. Platter stated that in the performance of *Julius Caesar* which he witnessed 'some fifteen' players were engaged. In the subsequent jig there were four dancers. These may possibly have had no part in *Julius Caesar,* but it is most unlikely that they were allowed to do nothing during the major part of the afternoon: we can assume that they did crowd work of which there is plenty in that play.

It is therefore plain that there was a great deal of doubling in the small parts and even of trebling in the smallest. The text of Shakespeare's *Julius Caesar* contains thirty-five speaking roles without counting 'supers' for the street, Senate House, and battle episodes. Naturally the leading actors would have their single important roles in all the plays, but the lesser men and boys had to be in and out, changing their costumes and appearances, and even their sex. The cast-list of the King's Men who appeared in Webster's *The Duchess of Malfi* is explicit on this point. Nicholas Towley (or Tooley) played Pescara and one of the Madmen, John Underwood played Forobosco and was also a Madman. A boy, John Tomson (or Thompson), was set down as taking 'The Doctor, Cariola, etc'. In *Julius Caesar* there must have been much scuttling about of the 'et cetera' players. It is true that Platter's reference to *Julius Caesar* does not specify Shakespeare as the author, but since 1599 was the date of Platter's visit and also that usually assigned to the play and since he crossed the river to the Bankside, site of the new Globe, to see it, there is an overwhelming probability that he was not witnessing another piece of the same name. In any case the speaking-parts in most of the plays of the period are twice as many as were the members and employees of a usual company.

The average number of actors whom Shakespeare had in view as he wrote would probably be at the most eight or nine Sharers, five or six Hired Men, and two to four boys: for such a piece as *A Midsummer Night's Dream* he would have had to make special arrangements for the fairies. The number of men available for the courtiers, Senators, citizens, and combatant soldiers appears to have been very small. Nowadays we expect in a Shakespearian production to see crowds filling the stage, plentiful as well as vocal in supporting or opposing the central characters. Yet the audiences of the Tudor and Jacobean theatres were plainly ready to accept token mobs and armies for the mass-demonstrations and the military alarums and excursions. In the Prologue to *Every Man in His Humour* Ben Jonson made sarcastic mention of the large words and small forces deployed in historical dramas, adding what seems to be a special allusion to the *Henry VI* trilogy in which the young Shakespeare had had a major if not a single hand.

> *With three rusty swords*
> *And help of some five-foot-and-half-foot words*
> *Fight over York and Lancaster's long jars*
> *And in the tiring-house bring wounds to scars.*

We need not take the number of three as wholly accurate; but the picture is there of ludicrously inadequate troops who hurry back into their dressing-place to daub themselves with imitation blood and then emerge again as battle-scarred. Jonson's view of the spectacular side of plays containing warfare might be dismissed as jocular or splenetic if he was alone in that opinion. But he was not alone. Shakespeare himself gave support to it in his own play of *Henry V*.

The speech of the Chorus preceding Act IV could not be more definite about the scarcity of the forces engaged.

> *And so our scene must to the battle fly,*
> *Where—O for pity—we shall much disgrace*
> *With four or five most vile and ragged foils*
> *The name of Agincourt. Yet sit and see,*
> *Minding true things by what these mockeries be.*

Jonson's three swords have risen to four or five; the rusty blades are no more impressive; called vile and ragged foils they are even worse. The mood is not sardonic, but indignant. There is confession of an effect that is laughable and the confession is painful.

Thus the Chorus declares in advance that the audience is to witness 'a brawl ridiculous'. If, as it may, the phrase 'vile and ragged foils' is meant to include the warriors as well as the weapons it further suggests incompetent performers in tattered fighting-gear. It is natural to wonder if the lines were indeed spoken. They may have been inserted in the text as the dramatist's lament and then judiciously cut in performance in order to save the faces of the wretched 'supers' thus damned in advance. However that may be, the statement about numbers is there. The members of the public would not be surprised by such a frank admission if they were accustomed to token parades of imagined hosts. They did not expect realism in the stage-craft and play-casting of their time. The Chorus in the Prologue had told them to multiply the tiny stage-armies by a thousand and to fancy a cavalry charge where no horses were.

> *Piece-out our imperfections with your thoughts,*
> *Into a thousand parts divide one man*
> *And make imaginary puissance;*
> *Think, when we talk of horses, that you see them,*
> *Printing their proud hoofs i' the receiving earth.*

In all forms of drama we are asked to make some concessions to the unreality of the actions feigned, withdrawing our incredulity. Audiences of later centuries came to expect much greater mobilisation of the swords and foils and did have not to concede so much. In recent English productions of Shakespearian battle-scenes, with specialists in stage-fights to assist the producer of the play, there have been some startling examples of combatant agility and audacious death-falls with as many engaged as can impressively fill the stage. Even so we are not cozened into believing that we are at Agincourt or Corioli. We are only admiring the amount of skilful direction and rehearsal that have carried us closer to the real thing. The Elizabethans who paid to see a play by Shakespeare were apparently as well satisfied with three men symbolising an army as we with thirty.

There were advantages for the Elizabethan Sharers in this acceptance of a convention whereby one man was a thousand. The number of supers to be paid was consequently very small and the amount of rehearsal needed was much reduced. It is obviously easier to teach a few men their movements and their sword-play than to keep in hand and integrate the scamperings and clashings of many. Shakespeare's cry of 'O pity!' proclaims his deep regret for the paucity of his troops on parade and suggests that he would have greatly enjoyed the spectacular effects obtained in the productions of succeeding centuries. But, as a man working in the profit-seeking theatre of his time, with no subsidies from an Arts Council to cover the losses incurred by sumptuous production, he had his reasons for putting up with 'brawl ridiculous'. Play must succeed play and his rehearsal-time was probably far less than our own. Thrift and convenience were both served by the tolerance of a phantom fighting-force or of a citizen-crowd which was only a citizen-handful. The man in charge, whoever he was, had his task much eased by an audience which was ready enough to piece out such imperfections with their thoughts. He could sadly reflect that his regiments were as few as they were ragged; he could comfort himself with the thought that his public knew no better and expected nothing more.

In any theatrical venture the best work of the players can be hampered and even ruined by incompetent staff-work in accommodating the audience and in setting the stage. In Shakespeare's front-of-house staff there were first the gatherers who took the money. Their activities had to be overlooked and their receipts checked. Then there was the sale of refreshments, the nuts, the apples, the bottled ale and possibly tobacco (the audiences contained constant smokers). The Inductions to Ben Jonson's plays, as well as the writings of the satirists and pamphleteers, contain abundant evidence about the habits of the playgoers. One of the boy-players who introduces Jonson's *Cynthia's Revels,* which in the year 1600 was acted by the Queen Elizabeth's Children of the Chapel, describes 'an auditor' as speaking thus:

'Having paid my money at the door, with much ado, here I take my place and sit down: I have my three sorts of tobacco in my pocket and my light by me and thus I begin. (At this he breaks his tobacco.) By this light I wonder that any is so mad as to come to see these rascally tits' plays—they do act like so many wrens or pismires—not the fifth part of a good face amongst them all—and their music is abominable. . . . By this vapour, an t' were not for tobacco, I think the very stench of 'em would poison me, I should not dare to come in at their gates—A man were better visit fifteen jails or a dozen or two of hospitals than venture to come near them.'

The playwright's mockery of the players, not of the important Sharers but of the Hired Men and 'rascally tits', was an Elizabethan habit which must have won some easy laughs; Jonson also laughed at himself, 'the poet', in his Inductions. We must take the custom into account in considering Shakespeare's complaint about his 'ragged foils'. The contemptuous auditor at *Cynthia's Revels* was an example of that kind of jesting. He is seen as a tiresome fellow, but he has paid for a good seat. He has brought his comfort in his wallet. He has three types of tobacco in hand and his lighter with a sparking flint; so he has no need to make further purchase of that kind on the spot. But others may have come less provided. Many would have a thirst and might long to quench it before the afternoon or evening was over. Thus there was scope for salesmanship.

The performances were evidently not all as brief as Shakespeare's mention of 'the two hours' traffic of our stage' suggests. Jonson in the Induction of *Bartholomew Fair* wrote of two and a half hours as the likely length of the session that was beginning. Nor was the acting always continuous; Platter's description of his playgoing in

London is precise about the service of refreshments. During the performance, he wrote, food and drink are carried round so that people can buy what they like according to their willingness to pay. If there was no interval, this would have added to the clatter among an audience containing some noisy members and there is abundant witness to the tiresome conduct of these and to the interjections made. The trouble came more from the rowdy bucks rather than from the penny groundlings who wanted their money's worth of the tragical and comical, blood and laughter. It was to the players' advantage to have as much as possible of the catering done before or during a break in the performance.

If good profits were obtainable from the catering, the Sharers, presumably the House-Sharers in this case, would see to it that the servitors did not miss the opportunity. To supervise the gatherers and the waiters, there must have been a House-Manager. Heminge, if he were in general charge of the business management, as well as frequently an actor of important parts, could not be bothered with that and must have had his deputy to watch these details keenly and to prevent leakages. The front-of-the-house administration was doubly important. The public was not to be deterred by too much interference with its minor pleasures: at the same time sufficient order had to be kept to satisfy the serious 'auditors' and give the play and the players a fair chance in a theatre which was not to become a rough-house.

Behind or around the stage there were three types of assistant. The Stage-keeper was a cleaner and general utility man. We meet this character in person before the start of *Bartholomew Fair*. He enters to ask patience: the first player due to be seen 'has a stitch new fallen in his black silk stocking'. (Mention of silk stockings indicates yet again the lavishness of the players' wardrobe: no dull woollens for them.) But the mending will occur 'ere you can tell twenty'. The Stage-keeper then enjoys a soliloquy of some length explaining that he is a veteran job-holder since he 'kept the stage in Master Tarleton's time'. (That famous comedian died in 1588 and *Bartholomew Fair* was produced in 1614.) Then the Book-holder arrives with his Scrivener to check this talkative and intrusive Stage-keeper who protests that the 'understanding gentlemen o' the ground' had asked his judgment. This is sharply met by the Book-holder who says: 'Your judgment, rascal! For what? Sweeping the stage or gathering up the broken apples for the bears within ? Away rogue, it's come to a fine degree in these spectacles when such a youth as you pretend to a judgment.' The Stage-keeper, with his seniority thus flouted and his proper functions flung in his face, gives up his chatter and goes. He has been told to know his place, a humble position taken over by Puck at the close of *A Midsummer Night's Dream,* even before the play has ended.

> *I am sent with broom before*
> *To sweep the dust behind the door.*

But disposing of the refuse cannot have been the Stage-keeper's only work. Somebody must have been responsible for the properties and hangings such as 'the silk curtains to hang the stage here' and 'the fresh pictures that use to beautify the decayed, dead arras in a public theatre', mentioned in the Induction to *Cynthia's Revels.*

The players' wardrobe was guarded and mended, in the case of that laddered silk-stocking, by the Tire-man. Since 'back-stage', like the stage itself, was a workshop for men only such hurried needle-work had to be done by a man except when there was time to send garments out for repair. Because the costumes were so valuable, the senior Tire-man had a post of responsibility: theft or misuse of garments had to be strictly avoided. That he had assistants with further duties is shown in the Induction to one of Jonson's later plays *The Staple of News,* acted after the accession of King Charles I. Here the Book-holder, speaking 'within', says: 'Mend your lights, gentlemen.' Then: 'Enter the Tire-men to mend the lights.' (*The Staple of News* was acted at an indoor theatre.) The speaker of the Prologue then adds: 'Nay, start not ladies. These carry no fireworks to fright you, but a torch in their hands to give light to the business.' The minor Tire-men could be used for more than wardrobe purposes and, when Shakespeare's company took over the roofed Blackfriars Theatre, they were probably in charge of the necessary torches and candles.

The Book-holder was a man of consequence in a theatre company. During the performance of a play he was the prompter, situated probably in the tiring-room at the side of the stage with some sort of opening at eye-and-mouth level through which he could watch and assist the players. In a hard-pressed repertory, with a new play and revivals mixed, his aid may have been much used. The system, now practised in some countries, of full-time prompting by a Book-holder hidden below and in front of the players and reading the text just ahead of the speaker would not be feasible with the groundlings pressing up against the projecting platform. Also it would be very difficult, if the prompter were away in the tiring-house. In *Romeo and Juliet* (Act I, Scene 4) Benvolio speaks of a 'without-book prologue, faintly spoke after the prompter', which could indicate that the whole prologue was being read out a word or two in advance of the player appointed to speak the lines: but the words may quite as well suggest only an occasional prompting when the player made one of the usual signs of drying-up and was evidently at a loss. That there was no continuous prompting is suggested by the remark in Shakespeare's *Coriolanus* (Act V, Scene 3):

> *Like a dull actor now*
> *I have forgot my part and I am out*
> *Even to a full disgrace.*

Shakespeare, it seems, was not sympathetic to the player who 'dried': disgrace awaited him.

But the Book-holder had far more to do than prompt the faltering player. He received from the dramatist his hand-written text of the play or 'the book', as it was and still is called, and then arranged with the scrivener for at least one whole copy to be made, no easy task if the author's hand-writing was difficult. Then either the original or the copy was submitted by the Book-holder to the Master of the Revels for his 'allowance', the official and valuable permission to perform. The Book-holder got his copy back with orders to remove any hint of subversive political suggestion or of a profane and irreligious tendency.

With the allowance gained the Book-holder then made further arrangements with the scrivener and his assistants and it is obvious that with such a constant flow of new plays the scriveners must have been swift at deciphering ill-written scripts and rapid also in their own use of a quill. There was much to be done. Not only the entire play had to be transcribed; the actors' parts had also to be separately copied on long scrolls with the cues marked. No player would have a text of the whole play, since that was far too precious, but the members of the company may have heard a summary of the action or attended a preliminary reading and explanatory talk by the playwright so that they could begin to study their lines with some comprehension of what the piece was about, how it developed, and the significance of their parts. Then the Book-holder had to prepare a further aid for the players called 'The Plot'. This was an abstract of the whole play made scene by scene. It listed the entrances and exits of the characters in each episode with the names of the actors cast for these characters. This document, which must have been easily legible to serve its purpose, was pasted on a board and hung up in the tiring-room as a guide to the players, who had to keep their eyes closely fixed upon it since it served as their call-boy.

The Book-holder, in addition to the work already described, had to be as good as his alternative name of Book-keeper. He kept the books, not in the accounting sense, but as the guardian of valuable property. Apart from the musicians, one can see a threefold grading behind Shakespeare's stage, with the Stage-keeper as the least important and most easily replaceable member of the staff. The Tire-man had his precious wardrobe to watch and to enlarge when the Actor-Sharers were in funds and were ready to invest in new costumes; so he had to be a man of proved honesty as well as a capable director of his assistants who, as has been seen, were employed not only as dressers for the actors and menders of damaged goods, but as stage-hands looking to the properties and lights where lights were needed. Of more importance still was the Book-holder, who was not only in charge of the precious scripts but had also to send them up to the Master of the Revels for allowance and then to make any alterations commanded. This involved emending the part-scrolls as well as the whole text.

Further the Book-holder had to see that competent scriveners were available for copying plays and writing out on separate scrolls the parts for the actors. A careless Book-holder could do great harm to the Fellowship by failing to carry out the cuts and amendments ordered, by inability to get the copying promptly executed, and by letting scripts pass out of the theatre into the hands of the play-pirates. A dramatist like Shakespeare, whose work was well worth pirating, had to be constantly in touch with a Book-holder whom he trusted. Henslowe, too, with his general control of the Fellowship's affairs, had to make sure that the occupant of this office was well enough paid and of such dependable probity that he would be proof against selling manuscripts to other companies or to printers in search of material likely to appeal to the buyers of poetry- and play-books.

The extent and the methods of literary and theatrical piracy in Shakespeare's time have a specialised literature of their own. It is sufficient here to quote the statement of Heminge and Condell in their foreword to the First Folio that the public had been 'abused with divers stolen and surreptitious copies, maim'd and deformed by the frauds and stealths of injurious impostors'. The Folio was to provide the texts of the plays 'cured and perfect of their limbs and all the rest absolute in their numbers as he (Shakespeare) conceived them'. This need not be taken as censuring the Book-holders who had served the Fellowship. There were other sources of leakage. The Actor-Sharers could be trusted. But it was always possible for a small-part and poorly paid Hired Man, especially if he had a grievance, to get hold of a scroll and do some copying or memorising of its contents and pass these on to the 'injurious impostors'. Hence came the 'maim'd and deformed' texts to be found in what are called the Bad Quartos. From a source of this kind, it has been supposed, came the First Quarto of *Hamlet* by way of the Hired Man who had played the part of Marcellus. The Book-holder could not prevent every effort at 'frauds and stealths'.

Entry of a book at Stationers' Hall provided copyright of a sort in the printing of a script. But there was no such protection in the use of a play-text for acting and that presumably is why so many of Shakespeare's plays, including some of the most popular, were kept from the printers until the First Folio appeared. Plays when paid for were the property of the company and had to be closely guarded. Consequently the Book-keeper's locked chest was one of the Fellowship's great assets, and, if the theatres were suddenly closed by an outbreak of plague, one can see it being carefully removed to someone's home and not left in an empty and deserted theatre. If a tour were substituted for the abandoned London season, the Book-keeper may have taken it as a precious part of their luggage. When fire was destroying the first Globe the rescue of the play-chest was an essential part of the salvage work. We can only guess what was in it; but it is more probable than possible that some of Shakespeare's then unprinted work could have disappeared for ever without prompt action by the Book-holder when that calamity occurred.

In this matter of guarding papers against piracy a similar state of affairs existed in the United States less than a hundred years ago. There was no copyright then for British work. Annexation of rights had inflicted enormous losses on Charles Dickens. Later Gilbert and Sullivan were victims of a similar robber in the theatre. The exploitation of their first great success *H.M.S. Pinafore* had proved extremely profitable to the American pirates. When this was followed by a production of *The Pirates of Penzance* great precautions were taken by Richard D'Oyly Carte, by the librettist, and by the composer to keep the text and the score in their own hands. The conductor of the orchestra, Alfred Cellier, used to take the band-parts back to his hotel and lock them up in a safe every night. The practisers of 'frauds and stealths' could go to the theatre and roughly memorise as far as possible the words and tunes: but Sullivan's scoring could be kept a secret. Cellier was thus in the same position as a Book-keeper of the Elizabethan stage. But he did not have to act as supervisor of scriveners and as prompter too. The Book-holder's lot, like that of the Gilbertian Sergeant of Police, was, 'taking one consideration with another', by no means a happy one. As prompter he was surrounded by excitable playwrights (Jonson was explicit about their tantrums) and by possibly forgetful actors. Worse still, he had at the gate the injurious impostor 'maturing his felonious little plans' for procuring a profitable script.

CHAPTER VI

Getting The Play On

IN CONSIDERING the problems of rehearsal and production there is first the matter of vocabulary to be settled. In the days of the great English actor-managers the direction of the rehearsals was usually conducted by the leading actor himself with the aid of his stage-manager, moves and business being marked in the prompt-copy of the play. Sir Arthur Pinero, a dramatist who had been an actor, liked to direct the rehearsals of his own plays, and Bernard Shaw, who had not been an actor, liked to give his own instructions. But the European habit of having a specialist, who was to unite the writing, the acting, and the choice of setting, came into the English theatre, or at least into the *avant-garde* wing of it, at the beginning of the twentieth century and his work, if well done, was found so valuable that this third party to the play became constantly employed and given his credit on the programme.

At first he was called the producer; but in America the producer of a play was not the conductor of rehearsals but the man responsible for the business arrangements, who saw to the necessary finance and theatrical premises. He was the modern successor to the old projector. Accordingly, the man in charge of rehearsals had to have another title and he was called the director. Gradually this title has been substituted for that of producer in England and it is now customary to read on programmes that the play has been 'directed' by so-and-so. The phrase 'produced by' has been steadily dropping out. Therefore in discussing the Shakespearian theatre I shall think of the plays as produced by the Actor-Sharers and directed in rehearsal by the person whose identity is now to be discussed. Was he the author, the principal player, or a third party?

Allardyce Nicoll, whose authority as a historian of the theatre stands so high that it is an audacity to contend with him, states flatly that there was no such person. In the first chapter of his book *The*

87

Theatre and Dramatic Theory (1962) he asserts that 'because the Elizabethan playhouse had more or less established companies familiar with each other's skill, because this playhouse had no scenery or lighting, and because the age had a characteristic style of its own, the theatre needed no producer or director'. He ends the paragraph in which this sweeping statement is made with the confident dismissal of any directing authority: 'In Shakespeare's playhouse there was no demand for any single person to take command.'

But there is much to put against this view. There were many occasions when scenery of a kind was used. In a play of Robert Greene's, *The Looking Glass,* the author asks for 'a brave arbour' to rise from the ground, and there was also 'an arbour' in Kyd's *The Spanish Tragedy.* Both these plays were presented in Shakespeare's early years in London and before the influence of the masque, which was scenic in the extreme, had begun to affect the theatre. There were arrases to be hung and thrones and other furnishings to be moved and that is scenery of a kind whose disposition must be settled by someone. The Children's companies played indoors and must have had artificial lighting problems. Brief masques were introduced into later plays with large demands on spectacle and needing the apparatus to produce 'strange wonderments'. There must have been somebody in charge. The familiarity with each other's skill could not bring a god safely down from the sky any more than it could bring arbours up through trap-doors. Battle-scenes and crowd-scenes had to be organised and such organisa-tion must have required guidance from above the battle and outside the tumult. The armies and crowds were no doubt very small, mere token regiments and rabbles. Even so, somebody brought them into action and out of it. The musical effects had to be arranged, rehearsed, and synchronised with the spoken word. The happy and successful anarchy supposed by Allardyce Nicoll is incredible to me. I agree with Bridges-Adams that 'we have good ground for believing that the Elizabethan stage was not bare but on the contrary that it was often elaborately dressed and handsome to the eye'. Such dressing commands a dresser.

Allardyce Nicoll admits the existence of 'a functionary' of a directing kind in the Italian Renaissance theatre. The first example is 'associated with performances at ducal courts, performances given not by professionals but by amateurs in playhouses wherein the pictorial artists of the time amused themselves with scenic experiments'. At Mantua a book was written to give counsel on such productions. The second instance of a directing functionary is taken from the professional work of the Italian 'Commedia dell'-Arte' whose most experienced member 'had to conduct rehearsals and give advice on the conduct of the various scenes'. The director of operations was known as a *concertatore* or *guida*. It is claimed that the Italian theatre was so different from the Elizabethan in scope and style that any idea of similar methods in London is baseless. But many actors, as well as milords, were travellers at that time and Europe was not in another world. The English had felt the full impact of the Renaissance. And in any case an acted play is a concerted thing and must have some *concertatore*.

If the *concertatore* does not appear in Elizabethan writing, the *guida* does—in the English form of guider, and it is used of the theatre as Shakespeare knew it. There is a significant passage in *The Gull's Hornbook* by Thomas Dekker. When he is describing the ill-mannered rowdies who could afford to take sixpenny seats on the stage, interrupt the actors, and make a mock of their performance, he added that sometimes a fellow of this kind 'would presume to be a guider and stand at the helm to steer the passage of the scenes'. That somebody did stand at the helm and act as steersman during rehearsals is an inescapable deduction from this picture of a boisterous mimic and from the use of the very name which the Italians had given to the director of the antics and the 'business' of the Italian comedians.

Moreover Italy was not the only country from which guidance about guiding could be drawn and in this case it was neither actor nor author but a third party, holding a strong controlling position, who had been at work in the medieval theatre.

A paper on 'Shakespeare as Man of the Theatre' was read by Professor J. Isaacs to the members of the Shakespeare Association and published with other lectures by the Oxford University Press for that Association in 1927. In it there was valuable information about the methods adopted in big theatrical performances and celebrations in other countries. The writer mentioned a portrait of a continental director in a miniature painted by Jean Fouquet in 1461. This guider 'wore a long clerical robe and cape, with a tiara-like hat on his head, and held a prompt-book in his left hand, while with a baton in his right he was directing a beautifully organised medley of late medieval religious performers'. 'We have the greater faith in the accuracy of this representation,' added Professor Isaacs, 'since Fouquet is known to have assisted in preparing a theatrical welcome for the entry of Louis XI into Tours in 1461. A little later we hear of Jean Bouchet, whose success as producer of a Passion Play at Poitiers in 1508 caused his services to be demanded all over France and Belgium.' Apparently this *régisseur* had supreme authority; no complaints were to be made, particularly at rehearsals, and there was a ban against the haunting of taverns during the days of performance.

This description of the medieval religious drama included a reference to the Mayor and Corporation as exercising guidance in similar performances in England. That the English mystery plays were directed by local politicians does not suggest to us nowadays either sensitive direction or technical efficiency. But in the fifteenth century the 'worshipful persons' who administered civic affairs were usually themselves members of the craft-guilds who were staging the plays and organising their 'progress' on wagons through the streets. So their knowledge of and attitude to the arts could be that of experienced and enthusiastic people. The professional theatre of Shakespeare's time was partly an heir of tradition and partly an eager innovator. It took over something of the old equipment. Even on the open stages the players may have used the scenic 'houses' of the medieval play-cycles. But in the London theatres there is no news of independent directors who were neither actors nor authors, but a third party to the play. That Shakespeare's Fellowship and their rival companies did have a functionary of this order is unlikely since we hear nothing more of him than this allusion to a man at the helm. Dekker's remark does not postulate a directing specialist. It could apply to a playwright or a leading player who took on the job of steersman.

These alternatives must be considered in relation to the available descriptions of the procedure. We may naturally turn to Shakespeare's own 'plays within plays' in search of information. In the case of the touring company which arrived in Elsinore, so opportunely for Hamlet's device to catch the conscience of the King, the First Player is in charge and is evidently the guider. Hamlet deals directly with him in his demand for a quickly written speech of some twelve or sixteen lines to be inserted in the text of *The Murder of Gonzago*. Their arrangements were so simple and elastic that this could easily be done. A travelling team would cut its numbers for economy. It was unlikely to bring with it the authors of the plays which they took on tour. So there is nothing to be gained from that episode since it has no relevance to conditions in a London theatre.

The mummery at the end of *Love's Labour's Lost* is no more helpful. The King of Navarre would have Don Armado present the Princess of France with 'some delightful ostentation or show or pageant or firework'. The resulting 'eruption', as it is called, is a pageant of the Nine Worthies and can hardly be described as a play. Armado and Holofernes, the schoolmaster, who are both going to appear in it, cast the parts. A paper is handed to the King; this is a programme explaining which worthy is to be impersonated by each of the various participants. The 'eruption' is hardly to be honoured with the word 'production'. It turns into a ridiculous scramble and muddle in which the socially exalted audience adds to the confusion by behaving in as boorish a way as do the guests at the wedding revels of Duke Theseus in *A Midsummer Night's Dream*. If Dekker's description of the sixpenny gallants is not exaggerated, Shakespeare's own public would not be surprised by these discourtesies.

In the play or 'eruption' offered by the 'hempen homespuns' for the ducal marriage-night in *A Midsummer Night's Dream* we can assume that the proceedings are a farcical version of something, though not of all, that occurred in the professional theatre. From the start Quince the Carpenter is in charge as Book-holder and in this case he also appears to add to that man's functions the task of guider. Also he has the chores of a Stage-manager since he draws up 'a bill of properties such as our play wants'. He arrives at the first rehearsal in his own home carrying 'the scroll of every man's name which is thought fit, through all Athens, to play in our interlude before the duke and duchess on his wedding-day at night'. He is then requested by Bottom the weaver to 'say what the play treats on, then read the names of the actors, and so grow to a point'. Quince announces the play as 'The most lamentable comedy and cruel death of Pyramus and Thisbe', which is approved by

Bottom as 'a very good piece and merry'. The author's name is not mentioned; nobody seems to care about him. When the list of possible entertainments for the wedding-night is read over by Duke Theseus and the Pyramus play is 'preferred' there is no mention of the author's name in the case of the three rejected pieces. The humble position of writers in the Tudor theatre is thus indirectly indicated.

It is reasonable to suppose that there is here at least a rough outline of normal procedure in the professional theatre. There was a meeting at which the actors were told the subject and story of the play and allotted their roles: at such a meeting Heminge, with the Book-holder beside him, was likely to preside, but, if the author were, as in Shakespeare's case, one of the company, he would certainly have had his say about the casting and the way of handling his piece. The naming of the parts does not satisfy Bottom, cast as Pyramus the hero; he wants to play both Thisbe the heroine and the Lion too. While this adds to the amusement of the episode and establishes the exaggerated enthusiasm and bustling self-importance of Bottom, it may contain a side-slap at one of Shakespeare's own actors who was apt to snatch at more and larger roles or at a dissatisfied player of Clown and Fool parts who wanted more than was set down for him.

Quince appoints himself to the role of Thisbe's father with Starveling as Thisbe's mother, but these parts disappear since it is necessary to have Starveling and Snout to impersonate Moonshine and Wall. If Quince had appeared briefly as Thisbe's father, he would have had to abandon his role of Book-holding and prompting. He is prompter at the rehearsals and he must also be regarded as speaking the prologue, though the text does not state this. There was no other player left to deliver the explanatory introduction.

The Pyramus play is there for farcical purposes and we cannot take its arrangements as reliable evidence of what went on at a professionals' rehearsal. But it does suggest that the Book-holder was a man of authority. It is Quince who has to tackle the problems of production and the 'two hard things', obtaining a moonlight effect and procuring a wall. He himself suggests the appearance of Moonshine as a character while he accepts Bottom's advice 'that some man or other must present Wall', and then, duly loamed and plastered, indicate the necessary chink in it with his fingers. Quince in the end is thus actor (as Prologue), guider, prompter, and holder of general responsibility.

The impression one gets from the numerous worries of Quince and from an estimate, admittedly made on slight evidence, of the theatre in which Shakespeare began his career, is that Johannes Factotum is an apt phrase for any theatre-worker at the time. 'The profession', if this view be realistic, was not made up of persons with exactly defined duties. An actor with a knack could furbish up old plays or write new ones. A Book-holder might do more than serve as warden of the company's scripts; he had to make a list of the properties required and hold the book as prompter during performances. As compiler of 'The Plot' for the use of the players he might perhaps devise and insert suitable business, thus acting in some sort as a general guider. That is the kind of loosely co-operative and frantically busy atmosphere in which I visualise Shakespeare first recruited and then growing in utility and rising in power. Something new was always being wanted and something new was always being somehow provided. The young actor-playwright would at first have to do what he was told, take a part, write, and learn how to direct a performance.

The Plot supplied to the players for their instruction was an outline of entrances and exits and not a producer's script with details inserted. That, at any rate, is what we learn from the few surviving specimens; none of them, unfortunately, is the Plot of a Shakespearian play. We have a good example in the Plot, or Platt as the Book-keeper or scrivener wrote it, of a piece by Richard Tarleton of the Queen's Men, a favourite clown of Queen Elizabeth. He died in 1588, and the Plot which we possess was probably arranged for a revival a year or two later made by Strange's Men who afterwards became the nucleus of Shakespeare's company under the protection of the Lord Chamberlain. Some of the actors mentioned were Shakespeare's colleagues for many years to come.

The piece, entitled *The Second Part of The Seven Deadly Sins,* is a descendant of the old Morality plays. There is an introductory episode in which King Henry VI is found asleep 'in a tent being plast on the stage' and is visited by 'Pride, Gluttony, Wrath, and Covetousness' coming in from one door, and by Envy, Sloth, and Lechery entering from another. The Sins are driven away by a Lieutenant, a Pursuivant, and a Warder, whose parts were taken by

Richard Cowley, Jo Duke, and R. Pallant. (Cowley's name appears in the First Folio among the names of 'the Principal Actors in all these plays' and Duke was still with the Chamberlain's Men when Ben Jonson's *Every Man in His Humour* was produced by them in 1598.) Another R. Pallant played a woman's part for the same fellowship, then the King's Men, in a revival of *The Duchess of Malfi* in 1619. If this R. Pallant was a boy-player, as is likely, he may have been son or even grandson of the Pallant mentioned in this Plot.

The Plot divides the play into three acts, each of which begins with a conversation between Henry VI and a monk called Lidgate. Then the dominant Sin of the following act 'passeth over'. The passers are in turn Envy, Sloth, and Lechery. Then a short play on each of these three themes is outlined with the exits and entrances of the characters, followed by the names, in full or abbreviated, of the actors. The first episode begins with music and dumb show. The music was the trumpet-greeting given to royalty called a sennet. Here is the abstract of the first act as provided for the players:

'Enter King Gorboduk wth Counsailers. R. Burgadg Mr Brian Th. Goodale. The Queene with Ferrex and Porrex and som attendaunts follow. Saunder. W. Sly. Harry. J. Duke, Kitt. R. Pallant. J. Holland. After Gorboduk hath consulted with his lords he brings his 2 sonns to several seates. Ferrex offers to take Porex his Corowne. he draws his weapon. The king Queene and Lords step between them. They thrust them away and menasing ech other exit. The Queene and Lords depart hevilie. Lidgate speaks.

Enter Ferrex crownd with drum and coulers and soliders one way. Harry. Kitt. R. Cowley. John Duke. to them at another dore Porrex drum and collors and soldiers. W. Sly, R. Pallant. John Sincler, J. Holland.

Enter queene with 2 counsailors Mr. Brian Tho Goodale. to them Ferrex and Porrex several waies with drums and powers. Gorboduk entering in the midst between. Henry speaks.

Alarums with excurtions. After Lidgate speakes.

Enter Ferrex and Porrex severally Gorboduk still following them. Lucius Damasus Mr. Bry T. Good.

Enter Ferrex at one dore. Porrex at another. The fight. Ferrex is slayne. To them Videna the Queene. to her Damasus. to him Lucius.

Enter Porrex sad with Dordan his man. R. P. W. Sly. To them the Queene and a Ladie. Nich. Saunder. and Lords R. Cowly Mr. Brian. To them Lucius running.'

The Plot of Act I is more detailed than that of Act II while the Plot of Act III is extremely curt, which suggests that the Book-holder or whoever drew up the Plot was tired or rushed. The players are told when to come and go; there is little advice as to the kind of acting needed, but in Act I the words 'hevilie' and 'sad' give some instruction for the movement and facial expression required. Later there is only a bare statement of entrance and exit and of an essential property, the severed head in a dish. Exhibiting the results of decapitation was to remain a common tit-bit of the blood-soaked plays; Shakespeare himself conformed to this practice, to the embarrassment of directors in our time and with no appeal to audiences with less voracity for horrors. The actors needed for this play do not exceed the usual number of fifteen or so. The exact total is difficult to settle owing to the confused way in which family names, Christian names, and initials are jumbled together. The Book-holder was evidently a man with no time to spare. In the cast of the Second Act Pope appears as Mr. Pope, just as Brian had been Mr. Brian. This must presumably be a tribute to seniority or a dignity conferred on Senior Sharers. Both were older than Burbage. Pope and Brian had been with an English company who visited Denmark and Saxony in 1586, and both retired from the stage soon after 1600. One character is named as Will Foole; he may have been Kempe.

If a Plot of this kind was not greatly amplified by the guider and if the players simply delivered their lines with no more direction than is given, the result was likely to be extremely crude. It is possible, of course, that Tudor performances, even at a later date and of plays which we regard as masterly in writing, were much cruder than we imagine. But we must surely assume that the outline given in the Plot, an abstract made, perhaps hurriedly, by the Book-holder, was considerably filled in during rehearsal by some supervising person. There was, no doubt, much reliance on well-known tricks, as there must be in any repertory company which has to maintain a steady sequence of what it hopes will merit the trade name of 'attractions'. The 'alarums with excurtions', mentioned here and so often elsewhere, may have been a well-practised formality to whose frequent repetition the audience was accustomed. But the processions in triumph and the fights would become tedious if they were not freshened up with new uses of grouping and of colour, of athletic exhibition, and of a skill in combat which was not just a slap-sword routine. The players whom we meet thus early in *The Seven Deadly Sins* were remarkably cohesive; some of the team's membership did not greatly vary over a decade and a half; a few remained longer. If they only repeated their moves and fights without novelty and invention they could hardly have increased their popularity and renown, as in fact they did. But innovation needs direction by an original mind and by some person possessing a lively sense of theatre together with the capacity and authority for training actors to carry out his purposes.

The idea of a theatre in which functions were not strictly marked out and in which all, or at least those of the inner circle, were ready to lend a hand in several capacities suggests that direction of a production was not always the business of the same person, whether he were author, principal actor, or, less likely, a third party, the guider. We have no certain proof that Shakespeare did direct his own plays, but there is some indirect evidence to suggest the probability of this: and if he did, as well as writing and taking on minor roles, as later tradition maintains that he did, the burden of amplifying the elementary 'plot', keeping the peace with the senior actors, appeasing the dissatisfied, and training the boys and the Hired Men was surely enough for any man's physical stamina and nervous energy.

So much for the actor as director. What of the playwright? There is evidence that authors who were not actors did supervise the staging of their plays. It is certain as may be that Ben Jonson undertook direction of his own work. So apparently did other dramatists. That it was the habit for the writers to school the actors, or such as would take their schooling, is indicated by the remarks of a foreign observer. Professor Isaacs, in the paper already mentioned, quotes the statement of a German writer, Johannes Rhenanus, who adapted an English play in 1613. In his preface Rhenanus wrote:

'So far as actors are concerned they, as I noticed in England, are daily instructed, as it were in a school, so that even the most eminent actors have to allow themselves to be instructed by the Dramatists, which arrangement gives life and ornament to a well-written play, so that it is no wonder that the English players (I speak of the skilled ones) surpass and have the advantage of others.' There are tributes from other countries which show the high esteem in which English actors were held in Europe. Further evidence comes from John Aubrey in his piece on Shakespeare in *Brief Lives*. He said that 'B Jonson was never a good actor, but an excellent instructor'. Stage-experience of our own time confirms that the best actors are not necessarily the best instructors and that the teaching of acting, as of other subjects, is a craft independent of personal expertness or leadership in the subject that is taught. Aubrey was often inaccurate and was fonder of gossip than of verification when he jotted down his somewhat random biographies, but he claimed to have his information about the Elizabethan theatre from 'old Mr. Beeston, who knew all the English poets whose lives I am taking from him'. Aubrey added that Beeston was 'master of the play-house', whatever that may mean. This William Beeston was, we know, an actor of the Restoration period. He was the son of Christopher Beeston, who had been for a while a member of the Chamberlain's Men. Statements coming down through the actors can be taken as evidence worth considering. Furthermore, Jonson's own allusions to the dramatist ranging and raging at large in the tiring-house plainly show that the writers were liable to be much, and even furiously, involved in life behind and around the stage.

We can derive a picture of a play in production and during a first performance by further reference to the Induction of Jonson's *Cynthia's Revels*. The second of the children who are quarrelling over the speaking of the Prologue tells the third to 'quit the stage then and take a place; the play is instantly to begin'. The third child replies: 'Most willingly, but I would speak with your author. Where is he?' He receives this answer:

'Not this way, I assure you, Sir, we are not so officiously befriended by him, as to have his presence in the tiring-house, to prompt us aloud, stamp at the book-holder, swear for our properties, curse the poor tireman, rail the music out of tune, and sweat for every venial trespass we commit.'

This is plain proof that, while Jonson disclaims his own tumultuous presence in the thick of this particular production, he could very well have been there and that other writers of a tetchy temperament would appear in the tiring-house and 'create', as the actors say. That Shakespeare, with his reputation for mildness and good temper, thus habitually stamped and swore is unlikely. But, since Prologues and Inductions so often contained remarks about the coming performance and its limitations in terms of frank self-mockery, Jonson may have been laughing at his own outbreaks in the tiring-house. Incidentally there is confirmation here that the Book-holder had his place in the tiring-house and did his prompting from there.

Jonson made a similar mention of the poet rampant off-stage in the Prologue to *The Staple of News* where among the characters are Tattle and Mirth as well as the speaker of the Prologue.

Prologue. '. . . The truth is, there are a set of gamesters within, in travail of a thing called a play, and would fain be deliver'd of it: and they have entreated me to be their man midwife, the prologue; for they are like to have a hard labour on't.

Tat. Then the poet has abused himself, like an ass as he is.

Mirth. No, his actors will abuse him enough, or I am deceived. Yonder he is within (I was in the tiring-house awhile to see the actors drest) rolling himself up and down like a tun in the midst of them, and purges, never did vessel of wort or wine work so! his sweating put me in mind of a good Shroving-dish (and I believe would be taken up for a service of state somewhere, an't were known), a stewed poet! he doth sit like an unbraced drum, with one of his heads beaten out; for that you must note, a poet hath two heads, as a drum has; one for making, the other repeating! and his repeating head is all to pieces; they may gather it up in the tiring-house; for he hath torn the book in a poetical fury, and put himself to silence in dead sack, which, were there no other vexation, were sufficient to make him the most miserable emblem of patience.'

Jonson wrote his Inductions to get the audience in a laughing mood at the start of a comedy, but there would have been no point in the jesting if it were not based on some facts of fretfulness and fury among 'stewed poets' who directed or confused the players and had a place among them in the tiring-house.

That Shakespeare was the guider of the work in which he first had a writer's hand is unlikely. The direction of the three *Henry VI* plays needed experience and authority, so eventful is their movement and so large the sweep of action and of conflict in that harassed reign. But, when he had acquired some standing in the Fellowship, had learned to use his effects, and had the confidence of the company, his natural concern for his own work as a dramatist would prompt Johannes Factotum to include direction with his other labours. Moreover, as a player he was on the spot to write in lines if needed or to do the cutting, if necessary, for himself.

Mention of hurriedly written insertions brings to mind one of Maurice Baring's ingenious and amusing *Diminutive Dramas*. It provides very briefly a glimpse of a rehearsal before the production of *Macbeth*, a rehearsal which might almost be called 'an eruption'. One or two of the cast are absent and have sent their excuses. The youngster playing Lady Macbeth has threatened not to go on as Juliet later in the day if a suggestion to cut the sleep-walking scene is made. (The fellow makes a fair point when he asks how he can rub his hands when the stage-direction tells him to carry a taper.) Burbage has been knocked about in a run-through of the fighting, is in a bad mood, and complains that he has not enough in the last act. After 'She should have died hereafter', he wants a touching soliloquy about their once happy domestic life: he must have something sympathetic or the audience will not stand it. Shakespeare, who is playing the tiny part of Seyton (he had been cast as Duncan but was not up to it) is meek, affable, and ready to oblige. So he hurries off to scribble 'Tomorrow and tomorrow and tomorrow'.

Burbage says, with some excuse, that this stuff has nothing to do with the case, insists that the reference to a poor player is an insult to the stage, and throws up the part in a fury. Baring did not add that, like many temperamental players who throw up parts in rehearsal, he was soon back to catch it before it fell into other and eager hands. It has always seemed to me that one part of Baring's jesting fancy may have come quite close to the actualities of a Shakespeare play in preparation. The dramatist may have inserted some of his most memorable speeches on the spur of the moment and, sad thought, he may also have cut some that would have been no less memorable, because there was too much already or because an actor disliked them or could not manage them.

The text of the plays in the First Folio carries, for the most part, strangely few stage-directions. Prompt-copies must surely have contained far more of these. But Heminge and Condell were preparing a volume expressly for 'the great variety of readers, from the most able to him that can but spell'. The final injunction in their Preface is 'Read him therefore and again and again'. Their labours were not intended to benefit other companies with a compendium of prompt-copies. They may therefore have cut out many of the Book-holder's additions to the author's scripts, leaving only the essentials for play-reading. But it is noticeable that in the latest plays there is more instruction to the players and to a director who may not have been the author himself. Granville-Barker, in his volume on *Coriolanus*, the fourth in his valuable series of Shakespeare Prefaces, has noted this and suggested that the text of this play 'speaks pretty plainly of a manuscript to be sent to London and of a staging which the author did not expect to supervise himself'. He mentioned especially the instruction to Coriolanus before he yields to Volumnia (Act V, Scene 3): 'Holds her by the hand silent.' If 'the book' came up from Stratford, for a production with the author absent, this kind of order to the player inserted in the text would be a natural assistance to Shakespeare's deputy.

The increase in stage-directions of this kind is far more noticeable in *Henry VIII*. There has been much argument about Shakespeare's authorship of part or all of this play: the fact that Heminge and Condell, with their intimate knowledge of the Fellowship's affairs, included it in the Folio, seems to me to be conclusive evidence that they regarded it as Shakespeare's work in general and knew that his hand was much more responsible for this piece than it was for *Pericles* which, though very popular and obviously Shakespearian in its last two acts, they chose to leave out. If we accept a retirement to Stratford in Shakespeare's last years, it is very likely that he wrote *Henry VIII* there or rewrote a draft by John Fletcher with no prospect of being himself its director. Hence

the detailed instructions for the several important processions in
the play and for Queen Katherine's Vision; hence also the advice
to the players of a kind and a fullness unusual in the Folio texts.
Moods, as well as movements, are firmly indicated. The King sits
'reading pensively' and twice enters 'frowning', once 'with the
Nobles smiling and whispering'. Cromwell 'stands amazed'.
Wolsey and Buckingham look at each other 'full of disdain'.
Salutes are to be made 'gracefully'.

If John Downes who listened to and recorded the Restoration's
theatre talk is to be trusted, Shakespeare did take some personal
part in the direction of *Henry VIII*. A report had reached Downes,
by way of D'Avenant and Betterton from 'Old Mr. Lowin', that he,
Lowin, who played the King, 'had his instructions from Mr.
Shakespeare himself'. That Lowin was proud of this guidance and
that Joseph Taylor was supposed to make the same claim of
Shakespearean coaching is evidence that the poet's capacity as a
director was much appreciated by the players. It may be that
Shakespeare, having sent the text of *Henry VIII* up from the
country for another to direct, later saw a performance when visiting
London, as he surely would be eager to do, and then gave Lowin
some notes for the improvement of his work as the King.

The texts of the plays contain advice to the players apart from
any stage-directions inserted. It has been argued and widely agreed
that the punctuation of the First Folio is based on the need to
instruct the players in the right pauses to make in the delivery of
their lines. The speeches of the characters sometimes include
descriptions of changing mood which could have been put in
stage-direction form. Lip-biting and trembling as signs of anger
are mentioned by Desdemona.

Why gnaw you so your nether lip?
Some bloody passion shakes your very frame.

Othello had to respond physically to that, just as Queen Gertrude
in *Hamlet* had to play up to the Ghost's announcement that 'amaze-
ment on her sits'. Such items in the speeches were pointers not only
for the player but for the director, whoever he was, to see that
the desired effect was realised by the actor.

If Shakespeare were overworked or away in the country, one of the senior actors would take on the guidance of rehearsals. If the actor-managers in the centuries to come could, with the aid of an experienced stage-manager, direct an elaborate production as well as play the leading roles, Burbage could have done the direction of a piece in which he was protagonist; he could indeed have done it more easily since he had no great crowds of 'supers' to organise and no acres of canvas, with numerous changes of scene, to overlook. But it would be wrong to imagine a Shakespearian production as being as simple as the Plot of *The Seven Deadly Sins* would suggest. That came before the great rise in the theatre's reputation and standards during the end of the Elizabethan and the beginning of the Jacobean epochs. The writing of plays improved enormously as we can tell from Shakespeare's own work, and it would be natural for the acting and the direction to be continually gaining in quality, with the players ceasing to rant and conforming to Shakespeare's ideal of a true-to-nature acting. Later there was the improvement of spectacle that indoor performance, artificial lighting, and the increased resources of the Blackfriars Theatre could provide.

The introduction of masques demanded further preparation; the standard of masquerade at the Jacobean Court was high in decoration and may have been elegant in performance if the masquers remained sober, which we know from one chaotic occasion they did not. The theatre-men could not spend the vast sums which King James and his keepers of the purse managed to find for these richly dressed dances, *tableaux vivants,* and mimings often enriched with sets designed in the Italian style by Inigo Jones. In these his Danish Queen took an extravagant delight. Three thousand pounds, a fantastic sum in the money of the time, was spent by the Queen on the decoration and dresses of one Court masque alone. Dramatists turning out whole plays for a few pounds could reasonably curse the Royal munificence in these antics. The players had to add to their labour and their costs by keeping up with the fashion and introduce amid their performances what Bacon in his Essay on *Masques and Triumphs* called the 'petty wonderments'.

These were not so petty for busy actors to arrange. Since *Cymbeline* and *The Tempest* are late play Shakespeare may not have been there to direct them. Whoever took his place had to cope with 'Jupiter descending on an eagle amid thunder and lightning' in the first and provide magic with a lavish banquet suddenly disappearing 'by a quaint device', also amid thunder and lightning, in the second. Thunderstorms might not be so difficult; the drums looked after them. They were a constant feature of the theatrical weather on the stage of the time. But gods and eagles in mid-air demanded precise rehearsal and security measures. As the plays became more ambitiously staged, the time given to rehearsal must have grown longer.

How long were the rehearsals? We have no clear information. If the estimate of fifteen new plays a year as the output of Shakespeare's company be correct—and Henslowe, as was explained, worked much faster than that—this would allow a little over three weeks. But that assumes incessant work with no breaks for bad weather in winter or a holiday pause. During the six weeks of Lent performance was in theory forbidden, but, as was seen, there were evasions of that edict: and, if the theatres were closed to the public, the players could use the time, privately if not on their stages, for preparation. So we may surmise that the maximum rehearsal-time could have been three weeks. But frequently it might for various reasons have been less; and these were not whole-day rehearsals but carried on in the mornings and sometimes evenings with the new parts to be studied at the same time. There were enormous new roles to be memorised while the leading men were playing equally long ones in the afternoons.

The happiest rehearsals may have been those held at the office of the Revels in Clerkenwell. For the Christmas and New Year celebrations in Whitehall the players were no longer having to pay their own way. Sir Edmund Tilney, the Master of the Revels, could sanction and provide the outlay for a production more ample than was possible in the public theatres. For a while they worked in conditions of unusual comfort and amenity which must have been especially welcome if the winter was a hard one. The Revels Accounts include considerable expenditure on heating and lighting for the actors' chamber and payments to a head-porter and his underlings. For Court performances there was special scenery made, including 'mansions' of painted canvas to be set at the side of the actors' platform or arena.

Clerkenwell, in the last weeks of the year, was alive with actors coming and going to rehearsals: costumiers and wig-makers were bringing in their creations: painters and carpenters were busy with their colours and their tools. The idea that Shakespeare's plays were performed with the minimum of decoration may be partly true of the open Globe and it is probably true of performances given on tour, when as little as possible would be carted round in an age of bad roads, highway thieving, and limited transport. The Revels Accounts show that Court performances demanded expense on costumes and as much spectacle as possible. It is most unlikely that a Court audience, in which personal display with the height of masculine dandyism and feminine splendour was everywhere about, would put up with a naked stage or with actors playing the parts of Kings in garments obviously more suitable for the tag-rag commons.

Shakespeare, if he were acting in and directing his own plays, had to work constantly in that bustling workshop where so much depended on winning Tilney's approval. He was often the author especially preferred. Between November, 1604 and Shrove Monday, February 11, 1605 there were Court performances by the King's Men of *Othello*, *The Merry Wives of Windsor*, *Measure for Measure*, *The Comedy of Errors*, *Love's Labour's Lost*, *Henry V*, and *The Merchant of Venice*. We know that *King Lear* was given at Whitehall on December 26, 1606 'before the King's Majesty' and this is its first recorded performance. That does not prove it to be the first performance of all, but both this production and that of *Othello* on 'Hallamas Day', November 1, 1604, 'in the Bankuetinge House' may well have been what we call 'first nights'. *King Lear* seems a stern choice for what we call Boxing Night: but other times, other tastes.

Maurice Baring's light-hearted little sketch was mentioned because of the possibility of last-minute additions to the text by Shakespeare. The suggestion that rehearsals were not only stormy but ill-attended need not be accepted. The work of the players was well disciplined. We know that in Henslowe's case there was a system of fining unpunctual or disorderly actors and these fines were extremely high considering the wages paid, a shilling for being late and two shillings for total absence. The penalties extended to three shillings for failure to be on the spot and properly costumed at the time of the public performance; intoxication could involve a fine of ten shillings, which was more than a Hired Man's weekly payment, and total absence except with sickness proved could involve a ruinous impost of twenty shillings. Shakespeare's company would not have needed so strict a regimen, if the team-spirit were strong and loyalty general. But discipline would be there and one who was both dramatist and director would have every reason to enforce it.

CHAPTER VII

Quality Of Player

❦

THAT SHAKESPEARE was an Actor-Sharer for the Chamberlain's
and King's Men for some twenty years is as certain as may be: it
involved the labours as well as the rewards of play-selection and
play-direction. How much time he gave to personal appearance as
an actor and with what success is far from sure. Contemporary
mentions of his performance as a player are few and the allusions
made after, and long after, his death are slight and more of a gossipy
than a convincing kind.

But to build up a plausible view of Shakespeare's acting is not
impossible. The record begins in 1592, when Shakespeare was
twenty-eight, with Robert Greene's angry and often quoted
reference in his 'Groat's Worth of Wit', to 'an upstart Crow,
beautified with our feathers, that with his Tyger's hart wrapt in a
Player's hyde supposes he is as well able to bombast out a blanke
verse as the rest of you: and beeing an absolute Johannes Factotum
is in his own conceit the only Shake-scene in a countrey'. It is true
that Shakespeare's name is not directly mentioned, but the sneer at
a bombasting Shake-scene, combined with a quotation from
Henry VI, Part III, make obvious the target of Greene's attack.
The authorship of the *Henry VI* trilogy has been attributed to
several hands, but Heminge and Condell included it in the First
Folio as Shakespeare's work. This and the play on the name make it
hard to believe that Greene had anybody but Shakespeare in mind.
Henry Chettle in his reply to Greene in the same year, three months
after the latter's death, stated that Greene's attack on 'divers play-
makers' had been 'offensively by one or two of them taken', and
therefore since 'on the dead they cannot be avenged' it lighted on
him, Chettle, to write in their defence. He then championed one of
them, generally taken to be the 'Shake-scene' of Greene's special
vituperation. 'Myselfe', wrote Chettle, 'hath seene his demeanor no
lesse civill than he excelent in the qualitie he professes: Besides,

divers of worship have reported his uprightness of dealing, which argues his honesty and his facetious grace in writing, that aprooves his Art.'

Chettle, by distinguishing between 'the qualitie he professes' and the 'grace in writing' must be referring to the double occupation of Shakespeare the player-poet. He contradicts Greene's picture of a bombasting 'ham' actor and claims excellence instead. The attribution of civility and honesty fits in with the general view of Shakespeare's 'gentle' character, and the 'divers of worship', who have spoken well of this new arrival in the front rank, presumably include the Earl of Southampton and other men of rank with an eye and an ear for the early work of a genius.

So far then we have a contradiction as to the merit of Shakespeare's acting. But, since Greene was a jealous author infuriated by the success of others and by the greater esteem and rewards won by the players whom he abusively calls Apes, Puppets, Antics, and Painted Monsters, we need not take seriously his contempt for a bombasting Shakespeare. Chettle's verdict, since he is acting as apologist for men wronged, may be over-kind, but it has the ring of a sincere admiration.

In 1594 came the mention of Kempe, Shakespeare, and Burbage as recipients of Court payments. Since Shakespeare is mentioned with two other leading actors in his company the implication is that he is named as an Actor-Sharer and not as a dramatist. In 1598 Shakespeare acted with the Chamberlain's Men in Ben Jonson's *Every Man in his Humour*. The cast-list printed in 1616 in the Folio of Jonson's plays states that the 'Principall Comoedians were Will Shakespeare, Ric. Burbage, Aug. Philips, Joh. Hemings, Hen. Condel, Tho. Pope, Will Slye, Chr. Beeston, Will Kempe, Joh. Duke.' That Shakespeare is put at the head of the list and before Burbage is curious. It may indicate that he had the leading part or it may be only a tribute to his leading position among the Actor-Sharers.

In 1603 he comes second in the cast-list of Jonson's classical tragedy *Sejanus*. This time Burbage heads the list from which Pope, Kempe, and Beeston have dropped out with Joh. Lowin and Alex. Cooke as replacements. That Burbage is now the top name suggests that the previous placing of Shakespeare in that position was due not to seniority as a Sharer but to the importance of his part in

Every Man in His Humour. In the same year John Davies of Hereford in his *Microcosmos* wrote:

> *Players, I love yee, and your Qualitie,*
> *As ye are Men, that pass time not abused:*
> *And some I love for painting, poesie.*

In the margin Davies wrote in after 'And some' the initials W.S. and R.B.

Burbage was a spare-time painter and Shakespeare an industrious poet. But the latter seems to be mentioned here as an actor, not an author. In 1605 in *The Civill Wars of Death and Fortune* Davies again referred to Burbage and Shakespeare together as 'Stage Plaiers' who had been criticised for small faults and had not been praised or 'guerdon'd' according to their deserts. In *The Scourge of Folly* (1610) Davies wrote:

> 'To our English Terence, Mr. Will Shake-speare'.
>
> *Some say (good Will) which I, in sport, do sing,*
> *Had'st thou not plaid some Kingly parts in sport,*
> *Thou hadst bin a companion for a King;*
> *And, beene a King among the meaner sort.*
> *Some others raile; but, raile as they thinke fit,*
> *Thou hast no rayling, but, a raigning Wit:*
> *And honesty thou sow'st, which they do reape;*
> *So, to increase their Stocke which they do keepe.*

This is deplorably cryptic. What were the kingly parts sportingly taken? Had Shakespeare offended King James by some light portrayal of a monarch in one of his own or another man's plays? Nobody seems to have found an answer: but plainly Davies took Shakespeare's acting to be important. The last line presumably alludes to the increasing prosperity as well as mounting reputation of the King's Men.

Finally there is the appearance of W. Shakespeare in the First Folio at the head of 'The Principall Actors in All These Plays', with Burbage second. The placing is probably a compliment to the author. There is no doubt that, in public estimation, Burbage was the leading man and main attraction. But the general impression to be derived from the allusions to and mentions of Shakespeare's acting, from Chettle to the Folio, is of a player of approved skill and considerable status. Certainly there is the suggestion that Shakespeare continued for some time to be an actor appearing frequently and even conspicuously after he had become a prolific and most popular playwright. In 1603 he was in the midst of his finest and, one would think, most taxing authorship. But there he undoubtedly was, studying, rehearsing, and playing a part, the second largest part if we go by the cast-list order, in Jonson's *Sejanus*.

That this happens to be the last appearance of Shakespeare's name in a cast-list does not prove that this was his last appearance as a player. Cuthbert Burbage, in his statement made to the Lord Chamberlain in 1635 concerning the lease of the Blackfriars Theatre which the King's Men took over in 1608, said that those chiefly responsible were 'Men Players, which were Heminge, Condell, Shakespeare, etc.' This shows that Shakespeare then was regarded as an Actor-Sharer. If performance on the stage, at least from time to time, was necessary to keep that profitable status, it is likely that Shakespeare would meet the conditions and supply the service. In any case actors do not lightly give up acting; old applause echoes invitingly in their eyes. 'Farewell performances' are often '*au revoirs*'. We can reasonably surmise that Shakespeare had some reluctance to abandon appearing on the stage and speaking his own lines as he believed they should be spoken.

Some have believed that he wrote the part of Prospero for himself and came back to the stage to deliver the eloquent and poignant farewell to 'revels'. It is a pleasant fancy with no supporting evidence. Burbage would regard Prospero as his natural assignment, but might have passed it on; he might also have privately decided that Prospero could be regarded as a poor part, at least at the beginning of the play when the audience may agree with the inattentive Miranda that he is tedious and difficult to listen to. When Alastair Sim played Prospero at the Old Vic in 1962 he very ingeniously injected some entertaining comedy into the role. Shakespeare would have admired the skill if not the idea.

Subsequent comment on the author's acting begins favourably with Aubrey who was probably using Beeston's talk when he stated that Shakespeare was 'an Actor at one of the playhouses and did act exceedingly well'. He added the opinion, already mentioned, that Ben Jonson was never a good performer in that kind but excellent in schooling others. But Nicholas Rowe (1674–1718), dramatist, Poet Laureate, and first editor of Shakespeare, took a less kindly view. His statement that Shakespeare was 'received into the Company at first in a very mean rank' is probably true. Then follows the slighting remark, 'Though I have inquired, I never met with any further account of him in this way than that the top of his performance was the Ghost in his own *Hamlet.*'

The Ghost's part is by no means small or unimportant, but it could be more easily combined with direction of rehearsals than could another role, say that of Horatio, who is frequently reappearing. There is a slight puzzle here. The Ghost's lines are least susceptible to the natural style of acting which Shakespeare, through Hamlet, recommends to the players. When Shakespeare was counselling them to observe 'the modesty of nature' and avoid the booming of a town-crier, was he himself taking the rhetorical and sonorous part which seems to demand an unearthly and unnatural voice and eeriness of intonation?

> *Thy knotted and combined locks to part*
> *And each particular hair to stand on end,*
> *Like quills upon the fretful porpentine. . . .*

Can a man 'use all gently' in delivering the spectral rhetoric? Perhaps Shakespeare did undertake the part in order to humanise it since it was the least human in the play. Or did he enjoy himself, despite the advice to the players, with a growling declamation of

> *O horrible, O horrible, most horrible!*

Whatever the answer we can accept Rowe's information that Shakespeare did play the Ghost, but need not be too much impressed by the claim that he did nothing bigger or better. The view conveyed by Rowe that he was never much of an actor contradicts not only Aubrey's tribute of excellence, admittedly based on hearsay, but also the high praises of John Davies who must have seen Shakespeare act and linked him with Burbage in his approbation.

That Shakespeare took the tiny part of Adam in *As You Like It,* is a report that comes to us from the antiquary, John Oldys (1696–1761), author of a life of Shakespeare which has not survived and of some contributions to what Sir Edmund Chambers called

'The Shakespeare Mythos', that is the accumulation of legend in the eighteenth century. Oldys mentioned that 'one of Shakespeare's younger brothers who lived to a good old age, even some years, I compute, after the restoration of King Charles II, would in his younger days come to London to visit his brother Will, as he called him, and be a spectator of him as an actor in some of his own plays'. (We have no record of any younger brother living to a great age which somewhat invalidates the story.) This brother, said Oldys, was 'so stricken in years and possibly his memory so weakened with infirmities' that he could give little help to inquirers. What he did remember was a faint idea '. . . of having once seen him act a part in one of his own comedies, wherein, being to personate a decrepit old man, he wore a long beard, and appeared so weak and drooping and unable to walk, that he was forced to be supported and carried by another of the company, who were eating, and one of them sang a song.' Obviously this refers to Orlando's Adam, that 'good old man' and model of the perfect servant, who did not sweat for 'meed' and asked for no promotion. It is likely enough that, if Shakespeare were himself directing *As You Like It*, which has twenty speaking parts as well as 'Lords, Pages, and Attendants', he helped the company by taking on this trifle which would not much interfere with his general guiding of the rehearsals.

The trend of the evidence appears, on the whole, to show that Shakespeare was a better performer than has been generally supposed and sometimes had more substantial roles than the Ghost and Adam. Rowe's remarks may have created a wrong impression and it must be remembered that Rowe also said of Shakespeare's acting that it was 'not extraordinary'. To deny superiority to the normal in any kind of work is not to dismiss it as inconsiderable.

Two passages in the *Sonnets* have been taken as evidence that Shakespeare despised the theatre and acting. In Sonnet 110, he wrote:

> *Alas, 'tis true I have gone here and there,*
> *And made myself a motley to the view,*
> *Gored mine own thoughts, sold cheap what is most dear,*
> *Made old offences of affections new;*
> *Most true it is that I have lookt on truth*
> *Askance and strangely: but, by all above,*

> *These blenches gave my heart another youth,*
> *And worse essays proved thee my best of love.*

And in Sonnet 111 he returned to his grievance:

> *O, for my sake do you with Fortune chide,*
> *The guilty goddess of my harmful deeds,*
> *That did not better for my life provide*
> *Than public means which public manners breeds*
> *Thence comes it that my name receives a brand;*
> *And almost thence my nature is subdued*
> *To what it works in, like the dyer's hand:*
> *Pity me, then, and wish I were renew'd. . . .*

But these by no means explicit expressions of self-pity have to be set against a long and prosperous career in the world of 'motley' and of abiding friendships made in it. If the two sonnets were written about the same time they could well be the result of a single disappointment or fit of weariness. A temporary disagreement, a long day of acting one part and rehearsing another, with a bad house for the former and some incompetence and confusion at the latter, could easily provoke the revulsion of a nature which felt for once subdued, like the dyer's hand, to its materials.

Shakespeare had his social ambitions and satisfied them with the grant of a coat of arms to his father and his own acquisition of the principal house in his home town. Before that success he could very well, on one of the bad days which come to any man in any profession, have envied the Earl of Southampton or the Earl of Pembroke, if either were the man addressed, for their life of elegance and leisure. The players were constantly under fire from the Puritans and their status, even the high status of the Chamberlain's Men who were on the fringe of the Royal Establishment, was never wholly secure. Any tactless blunder could put a player in trouble and even in gaol. When the Earl went to the Tower in 1601, fortunate to escape the headsman and the fate of Essex, Shakespeare might have not been so envious of a lord's position and so much concerned about a 'branded' name. Brand or no brand, he continued as a player and there is no other evidence that he regretted it.

But he did think of the art of the theatre as something fictional, transient, and illusive; that was reasonable, for in many of its forms it is. His favourite word for expressing this mood is shadow. That was the trade-name for the covered rear-part of his stage under 'the heavens' which were the canopy above the platform in an open theatre. He also applied the word shadow several times to the players and their work. 'If we shadows have offended,' says Puck in the epilogue of *A Midsummer Night's Dream* when he makes his modest and unnecessary apology for

> *this weak and idle theme,*
> *No more yielding but a dream.*

In the same play Duke Theseus, who frequently shows bad manners by interrupting the well-meant endeavours of the 'hempen home-spuns' in their charade, has the grace for once to reflect upon actors in general and to make the striking observation that 'the best in this kind are but shadows, and the worst are no worse, if imagination amend them'. So, thinks Shakespeare, the best are but shadows, even Kempe and Burbage, the other prominent Actor-Sharers, and myself among them. Burbage, if he played Macbeth, which is extremely probable but not in fact supported by any written record, was later to say

> *Life's but a walking shadow, a poor player*
> *That struts and frets his hour upon the stage*
> *And then is heard no more.*

The shadowy art is not less than life if life be a shadow too. But for Shakespeare's Cleopatra, when for a moment she becomes strangely philosophical in the praise of her dead lord, life at its best can be richer than any artist's creation.

> *Nature wants stuff*
> *To vie strange forms with fancy: yet t' imagine*
> *An Antony, were nature's piece 'gainst fancy,*
> *Condemning shadows quite.*

The shadow appears again, defeated in this case by natural, physical man, who in the fine figure of an Antony, has out-ranged the dim world of shades.

Simon Shadow, one of Falstaff's tattered conscripts in *Henry IV, Part II,* is a faint copy of the proper soldier and evokes more play with the word. 'Shadow will serve for summer—prick him, for we have a number of shadows to fill up the muster.'

But to consider the actor as a shadow of reality and to remind even the heads of the craft that the best in this kind have an insubstantial life is not to despair of the profession. Shadows are great contributors to the beauty of the world. In Clarence's dream of doom in *Richard III* beauty is mingled with terror.

> *Then came wandering by*
> *A shadow, like an angel, with bright hair.*

Shadows, in vision, in life, or on the stage, had a powerful fascination for Shakespeare. He knew too that the word itself makes a magical sound.

The commentary made by Hamlet on the acting of the time is plain proof that there were at least two styles of performance to be seen. There was the 'larger than life' method employing a town-crier vocalism and tearing passions to tatters with the copious gestures and the face-pulling which would help the tragedian to 'out-Herod Herod' in ferocity. The censure of melodramatic roaring and posturing must have been a hit at another company. This team could only have been the Admiral's Men, managed by Henslowe, since in 1598 the Privy Council had for a while restricted the licence to play to only two adult companies, the Chamberlain's Men and the Admiral's. If Hamlet's remarks on acting were written at the end of 1599, or the beginning of 1600, a probable date for the composition of the play, they would have had the pungency of reference to near neighbours as well as keen rivals. The Admiral's Men were at the Swan Theatre, close to the Globe, at this time.

But the criticisms of monstrous over-acting would not be aimed at Edward Alleyn, the one-time leader of the Admiral's Men, since he had made a temporary retirement. He had prospered and need not be kept to the routine in order to pay his way. This displeased the Queen at whose request, which would be a command, he returned to work with Henslowe and the Admiral's Men later in 1601 when the new Fortune Theatre was opened north of the river. Shakespeare would hardly want to make offensive criticisms of one who had been a colleague of many of the Chamberlain's Men in their early careers as Lord Strange's Men. Alleyn was two years younger than Shakespeare, but he was said to have been 'bred a stage-player'. He started to work as actor before he was eighteen and was the talk of the town in his early twenties when he played 'the leads' in Marlowe's *Tamburlaine, Faustus,* and *The Jew of Malta.* While Shakespeare was beginning his own stage life he must have watched Alleyn with the admiring eyes of a stage-struck newcomer determined himself to succeed in this quality.

In 1592 Nashe had written that no actor who ever lived 'since before Christ' could 'perform more in action' than 'famous Ned Alleyn'. It is not a very sensible remark since Nashe was not a Methuselah twice-over, who had watched the stage for sixteen hundred years. But it voiced the popular view. The 'ham' acting against which Shakespeare protested would be that of the company which Alleyn had for a while left and of Alleyn's successor in the big roles who might be absurdly showing that, while he was out-Heroding Herod, he could also out-Alleyn Alleyn.

It has been suggested that Hamlet, in denouncing the passion-tearing style of acting and yet praising the First Player for his delivery of 'The Rugged Pyrrhus' speech, is inconsistent. The first speech which the First Player has to deliver is itself a parody of the turgid style of the hack writers who set out to make terror rampant on the stage and to give the audience the shivers by soaking their language in 'coagulate gore' and 'bisson rheum' (blinding tears). Antiquated and far-fetched terms of speech and elaborate classical allusions are packed both into the Player's preliminary speech and the subsequent play. To describe thirty years of marriage thus:

> *Full thirty times hath Phoebus' cart gone round*
> *Neptune's salt wash and Tellus' orbed ground,*
> *And thirty dozen moons with borrow'd sheen*
> *About the world have times twelve thirties been,*
> *Since love our hearts, and Hymen did our hands,*
> *Unite commutual in most sacred bands*

is not to ask for the modesty of nature and a quiet realism in the delivery of such pompous sweepings from the classical lexicon. The First Player had to let fly and intone and is praised for the skill with which he can appear to show

> *his visage wann'd*
> *Tears in his eyes, distraction in's aspect,*

despite the unconscious efforts of his anonymous dramatist to make sincere acting impossible. Shakespeare, an actor himself, sympathises with the actor who thus triumphs over the resounding balderdash which he has to speak. The point surely is that the actors next door, Shakespeare's fellows in the quality of playing and rivals in the commerce of the craft, might do very well if they were not condemned to 'cleave the general ear with horrid speech' by the plays in which they had to appear. When the First Player, after receiving Hamlet's strictures on abominable imitations of humanity, says that his men have reformed their methods 'indifferently' he is curtly told to reform them altogether. The implication is that the Chamberlain's Men could effectively use more natural methods because their writers did not load them with unnatural rodomontade. Discretion could be shown in performance since their writers were discreet in their dialogue.

There is evidence that Burbage was regarded as no ranter but a plastic actor who could mould himself to a natural impersonation of all his roles. In an elegy written after his death it was said that his characters, especially Hamlet, Old Hieronymo of *The Spanish Tragedy* by Thomas Kyd, Lear, Othello, and 'more beside' had 'lived in him' and would die with his death. Richard III might have been mentioned along with these. The prophecy that these roles were perishable goods was false but the tribute to the actor was not unduly flattering. 'Hung be the heavens with black,' wrote Middleton after Burbage's death and the Earl of Pembroke, one of the 'incomparable pair of brethren' to whom the First Folio is dedicated, declined to go and see a play at a party given for the French Ambassador. The chosen piece, he wrote, 'I so tenderhearted could not endure to see so soone after the loss of my old acquaintance, Burbage'. A major light had been dimmed in the life of London. Burbage must have realised in his performances the restrained style of acting which Shakespeare, speaking through Hamlet, approved and desired for his great parts: otherwise the partnership could not have lasted as it did.

Both Burbage and Alleyn, to judge by their sovereignty over the public, must have been owners of the personal magnetism which is essential to a star actor. Star-quality, as it is called, demands more than technical efficiency: it may even go with technical faults and physical handicaps. The genius of Edmund Kean blazed from a tiny body. Sir Henry Irving had his pecularities of speech and movement. What matters is authority, the power to make the public look and listen whatever the player may be doing or saying on the stage. Bad parts and bad plays may not be made good parts or good plays by a superlative actor, at least in the eyes of a detached critic; but they are made attractive and even irresistible to the average playgoer who is more than involved and is in some degree hypnotised by the man or woman whom he is seeing and hearing. The same thing occurs occasionally in the preacher's pulpit or on the political platform. A speech by Mr. Lloyd-George in his prime was nothing much to read in a report. To hear and observe him playing on an audience was a different experience altogether. He was an actor and an actor of star-quality.

That Shakespeare's own acting had anything like this magnetic quality is unlikely. The tributes to his character emphasise civility and friendliness. He evidently did not impress his companions or the playgoing public as the owner of a dominant or striking personality. One cannot see him as a talked-about London figure, which Burbage and Alleyn did become and which the clowning Tarleton had been in the past. Ben Jonson, though reported a failure as an actor and often failing to please the audiences with his plays, became a notable character, sovereign among the wits and tavern-talkers. Because after 1619 he had a pension from King James, Ben has been called the first of England's Poet Laureates, though the title was not made official until its award to John Dryden. Jonson had an abundant physical energy as well as great mental vigour and Shakespeare, though 'well-shaped' according to Aubrey, was probably not of a strength that would have kept up with Jonson's on the latter's journey to Edinburgh. There must have been a rough star-quality about Jonson's personality and table-talk. Living on for twenty-one years after Shakespeare's death, he died poor but abidingly prominent, and was buried in Westminster Abbey.

One has to see Jonson as a protruding personality. It was said that when Sir Henry Irving entered the Garrick Club at supper-time after one of his performances, the company rose from their seats to salute the first of actors. Perhaps the tavern-talkers of Jonson's later years did not rise to greet their Ben in reverence at 'The Mermaid' or 'The Devil', but they would know that a Presence was there. They may have felt the same about Burbage; he would loom. Imagination sees Shakespeare's entrance to the company as lighter, less protrusive and less noticed, but when he had started talking he could delight the listeners by scoring against weight. Thomas Fuller (1608–61) cannot have seen the meetings of the two unless he attended the taverns before he was eight years of age, but he probably wrote of Shakespeare with good information when he left his famous description in *The Worthies of England:*

'Many were the wit-combates betwixt him and Ben Johnson, which two I behold like a Spanish great Gallion and an English man of War; Master Johnson (like the former) was built far higher in Learning; Solid, but Slow in his performances. Shake-spear, with the English-man of War, lesser in bulk, but lighter in sailing, could turn with all tides, tack about and take advantage of all winds, by the quickness of his Wit and Invention.'

Shakespeare conquered by speed, not flamboyance.

Of that quality Burbage obviously had much, keeping it well-disciplined for stage purposes if he were to please his principal authority, but a quality always there. It was natural for Shakespeare as an actor to work within that modesty of nature which he prescribed for good performance. None was ever less moderate in perspicacity of vision and in power to communicate the amazing world of his mind's eye. But he did not stand out upon the stage; if he had done so, there would have been more linking of his name with that of Burbage. Only Davies so united them in admiration. We may fairly think of him as a reliable actor of medium as well as minor parts, an excellent stand-by for the supporting roles which really do support, a 'trouper' loyal and diligent always, whether writing, acting, or directing. Without authors to write plays there can be no glory of the actor, but the stage owes its primary lustre and attraction for the general public to the First Players of star-quality. To be a capable Second Player, or even Third, one who can plod on and 'keep the passion fresh', is an achievement of great and constant value to a company. If Shakespeare from time to time saw the actor's life as a parade of shadows, he continued, among 'the best in this kind', to fall in and keep step, Second or Third and sometimes, to use his favoured term, quite a tiny shadow in the grouped silhouette of the Fellowship.

CHAPTER VIII

Training and Touring

꽃꽃꽃

SHAKESPEARE the actor could not begin a stage career without serious application to the player's part of the work. The preparation of the play may often have been hasty if something new was suddenly needed or a special performance was unexpectedly required, but the preparation of the young player meant a steady and strict training by his seniors in movement, the proper carriage of unusual costume, singing, instrumental music, stage-fighting, and of course, and most thoroughly, in speech and gesture. Assuming that Shakespeare was never a boy-player and came in first as a Hired Man he started under some handicap when compared with the children who had been schooled in the work since the age of ten or eleven and so he had to face strenuous years of learning his craft. There is no proof that he was a distinguished musician or that he specialised in the use of one instrument. But it is obvious from his plays that he, like most men of his period, had a keen ear for harmony and realised the importance of music in a stage-production. He would play his part in that and later in seeing that the cues for drums and trumpets in the battles and melody for his songs were well provided. The various capacities of a good actor were listed in a publication by 'T.G.' called 'Rich Cabinet', issued in 1616.

'Player hath many times many excellent qualities: as dancing, activity, music, song, elocution, ability of body, memory, vigilancy, skill of weapon, pregnancy of wit, and such like: in all of which he resembleth an excellent spring of water, which grows the more sweeter and the more plentiful by the often drawing out of it: so are all these the more perfect and plausible by the more often practice.'

This makes it plain that the apprentice had plenty to learn and had to undergo physical as well as histrionic and vocal training in a comprehensive way.

It is worth noting that skill in 'memory' is included as one of the essentials. The parts to be studied with no time to spare were often of vast length and, since the boys' companies tackled plays of full size and great difficulty, their powers of memorising must have been tested in most exacting ways. The learning powers of the young are quick, but their tasks were severe. Let anyone read, for example, Ben Jonson's *The Poetaster,* a satire on the theatre of his time put in a Roman setting. It is typical of Jonson's classicism and flow of words: for boy players the text must seem to us long and diffuse; it demands a mastery of speaking complicated prose as well as of verse. Yet the piece was successfully performed in 1601 by the Children of Queen Elizabeth's Chapel. The important parts of the various poets and of the boisterous and militant Tucca would be formidable loads for matured actors of experience. But they were coped with by the 'little Eyases'.

There was obviously in some companies much 'drying-up' and improvising to make up for a fault of memory. An expressive term for this was 'thribbling'. Richard Brome, who began a stage career as servant to Ben Jonson and was a successful author of comedies for the Caroline stage, wrote of a nobleman who was organising a play and was quite ready not only to tolerate but to be amused by a player who 'dried' and 'thribbled':

> *My actors*
> *Are all in readiness and I think all perfect*
> *But one, that never will be perfect in a thing*
> *He studies: yet he makes such shift extempore,*
> *(Knowing the purpose that he is to speak to)*
> *That he moves mirth in me above the rest,*
> *For I am none of those Poetic Furies*
> *That threats the actor's life, in a whole play*
> *That adds a syllable or takes away.*
> *If he can thribble through and make delight*
> *In others, I am pleased.*

Shakespeare, if he rarely took the longest parts, had less occasion to be a thribbler and we know from *Hamlet* that he strongly disliked the gaggers in Clown parts who added more than a syllable and that he elsewhere deplored the imperfect actor who forgot his lines. Brome makes it plain that many authors were on

Shakespeare's side and threatened the actor's life with the rage of a poetic fury for lapses of memory and hastily substituted words. If Shakespeare censured the thribbling type, he must have been careful never to offend in this way in his own performance.

In his *Shakespeare* Mr. M. M. Reese describes as 'an outstanding infelicity' in the film version of *Henry V* the implication that the players were incompetent muddlers dependent on the prompter and blundering about in a state of confusion. That picture of an Elizabethan production provided comedy in the film, but not, in all probability, accuracy in its picture of Shakespeare's company. The Chamberlain's Men were then, or later became, the leading professionals of their day. Although their audiences could be turbulent, it is certain that Shakespeare insisted on disciplined work and valued the proficiency described in *Rich Cabinet*. It can be argued that the reference in *Henry V* to the 'vile and ragged foils' indicates scarcity and incompetence of 'supers', but that need not convey the idea of a general and frequent confusion among the senior players, whether Sharers or Hired Men. Appearances at Court could not be chaotic.

There was regular training in speech of an eloquent, oratorical style with full use of stylised gesture and this method of delivery could become an empty routine which destroyed truth and naturalism in the drawing of a character. Shakespeare, probably trained to the rhetorical pattern in his early career, reacted against it and he evidently had Burbage on his side. Together with a formal system of utterance there was a formal method of movement and of walking across the stage. This was called by Shakespeare strutting, a word he used on several occasions. The *Oxford English Dictionary* defines strutting as 'a manner of walking with stiff steps and head erect, affecting dignity or superiority, a stiff self-important gait'. Hamlet linked strutting with bellowing and the 'abominable imitation of humanity'. Ulysses in *Troilus and Cressida* (Act I, Scene 3) speaks of the

> *Strutting player whose conceit*
> *Lies in his ham-string and doth think it rich*
> *To hear the wooden dialogue and sound*
> *T'wixt his stretch'd footing and the scaffoldage.*

This strutting and stamping on the boards was then denounced as 'to-be-pitied and o'er-wrested seeming'. Macbeth spoke of the actor's strutting and fretting, and links this kind of carriage with 'a poor player'. Shakespeare evidently disliked stiff or pounding footwork. I have seen it suggested that the word 'ham' applied to an actor goes back to the strutter whose conceit was in his ham-string and does not come from the use of ham-fat in make-up or from ham-fistedness, signifying clumsiness in general, which I believe are the usual interpretations of this term.

To the question 'What happened in case of illness?' I can find no answer in the records of the time. Plague closed the theatres and that was final and fatal as far as performance in the centre of London was concerned. But, when there was no plague, there must have been cases of an individual player being attacked by a fever or suffering a physical injury by some accident, a fall or thrust in a combat-scene, which would make it impossible for him to appear. We do not hear of understudies. With the small numbers of actors employed and amid the pressure of short-run or repertory productions it would have been most difficult to arrange for efficient deputising and for constant readiness to take over an absentee's part. Even in the fairly opulent conditions of modern theatrical work in a capital or large city there are sometimes disasters owing to thrift in the provision of understudies. If one player has been engaged to understudy two parts of some size and the players of both parts are simultaneously smitten by an epidemic of influenza or some other malady, it has been known, fortunately very rarely, for the prompter to come on and read the part from 'the book'.

Was that one of the duties for which the Book-keeper in Shakespeare's theatre had to be prepared? Working with a manuscript, perhaps written with the professional clarity of a scrivener and perhaps only the 'foul' papers of a not easily legible dramatist, he was always at a disadvantage compared with the modern owner of a typewritten copy. But repertory companies in our time, whose arrangement of understudying must be sketchy, are known to get through somehow. Players who ought to be in bed manage to stagger on to the stage. In the last-minute learning of a part by an assistant stage-manager there are remarkable feats of rapid memorising aided by a certain amount of improvisation, while the other players ingeniously cope with missed cues and awkward pauses.

That 'the curtain must go up' is the rule of the profession and in the open Elizabethan playhouses with no curtain the play had to go on. A second clown could gag his way through if a Tarleton or Kempe were suddenly out of the cast; that ability was expected of him and perhaps enjoyed both by the player and the audience, though not by the author if he were Shakespeare. But, if a Burbage had been smitten by a germ or suffered damage to his ham-string, there could have been terrible moments. Can one see a Book-keeper, scroll in hand, plunging through crime to battle as Macbeth? If there was some sort of half-prepared understudy he would, in Brome's phrase, 'make shift extempore' because he was 'knowing the purpose he is speaking to'.

The training recommended in *Rich Cabinet* included 'vigilancy, memory and such like'. Brome's character was moved to mirth by actors at a loss for their lines and the mannerless bucks who were ready to 'mew' at the Elizabethan actors at the best of times must have enjoyed a festival of mockery when the Book-keeper appeared as Hamlet, Lear, or Macbeth, or when some half-fledged deputy went thribbling through those gigantic roles. Without evidence, we can only think that it did not happen often and that a limping or a fevered Burbage struggled on.

During Shakespeare's lifetime there was a recurrent necessity for the London acting companies to go on tour when plague hit the town. This pestilence was never wholly absent, but the latent menace was so constant that it must have been taken for granted as a normal part of their city life. Acute trouble to their finances as well as acute danger to their lives came when the roll of plague deaths rose to forty or fifty a week. Then the theatres were closed by order and their income stopped abruptly unless they could make money 'on the road'.

The years most harmful to the players were 1592–4, 1603, and 1609, during which there were nearly fifty thousand deaths in a town with a population only about four times that number. The estimates are of eleven thousand fatal cases in 1593, thirty thousand in 1603, and four thousand in 1609. Apart from plague-enforced travelling, there is abundant evidence in municipal records that Shakespeare's company frequently made other journeys, going west as far as Barnstaple, penetrating north-west as far as Shrews-bury, eastward to Saffron Walden and Ipswich, and touring Kent and Sussex with stays at Rye and Dover. The university towns of Oxford and Cambridge were both visited and the road to Bath was several times taken with stops at Marlborough. It is obvious that halts were not always dictated by the attraction of the takings: there had to be stages in the slow and toilsome journey and those who put up for the night in a small town would play there for what they could get as part-payment of their inn charges.

Londoners on tour had no monopoly of their craft as they went about the country, since the noblemen in various districts had their own teams of players who visited the towns in their localities. Shakespeare's own Stratford was constantly visited during his boyhood by the players carrying the protecting names of the Earls of Worcester, Leicester, Warwick, Oxford, Derby, Berkeley, and Stafford, also by the Queen's Men and the Countess of Essex's company. So the young Shakespeare could see plenty of theatrical fare and observe the life of the strolling player on his rounds long before he decided that this was to be his world. The men from the capital had the advantage of the latest plays written and played by poets with familiar names; they were probably more skilled performers and would be regarded as a special attraction. They could be announced by crier or written bills, as touring companies long continued to be, 'direct from the leading London theatres'.

The late summer months were a favourite time for such tours. In winter a full day's journey would begin and end in the dark and there was a perpetual risk of highway robbery. On sodden roads a well-laden wagon might be bogged down and all travel would be made slow and disagreeable by the usual English rains. But in the plague year of 1603 the King's Men certainly had to face these conditions in midwinter, 'now that the fields are dank and ways are mire', as Milton wrote of 'sullen days'. The players had moved to the suburb of Mortlake from the infected centre of the town and in December they were summoned to Wilton House, beyond Salisbury, in Wiltshire, the home of the Earl and Countess of Pembroke, patrons of the arts and at that time host and hostess to King James.

That Shakespeare was with the company when they made their wintry journey to Salisbury and Wilton House in 1603 is suggested by a piece of information which unfortunately lacks documentary support owing to a missing letter. This came from William Cory, the Victorian Cambridge scholar and Eton Master who wrote the words of the 'Eton Boating Song' as well as a poem called *Heraclitus* which appears in many anthologies. He recorded that in

1865 he was told by Lady Herbert of Wilton that they had in the house a letter from the second Countess of Pembroke to her son who became Lord Chamberlain in 1615 and was a fellow-recipient with his brother Philip of the First Folio's dedication. The mother's letter asked the son to bring King James from Salisbury to see *As You Like It*, adding 'we have the man Shakespeare with us'. The letter has never been found, but the story sounds likely enough. The King had been driven out of London by the plague in 1603 and kept Court at Salisbury; his Queen stayed for some weeks at near-by Wilton House. Why not send for the King's Men? And why should not Shakespeare be with them? Cory's authority is that of a man of reliable and scholarly character and letters do unfortunately get lost.

It was a visit well rewarded in money as well as in the honour of the call. Heminge was paid thirty pounds for 'the paynes and expences of himself and the rest of the company' in making the journey and presenting 'one playe'. Unfortunately the Chamber account does not specify the play. The sum received was far above the usual takings on tour. Typical of these were forty shillings at Cambridge, twenty at Rye, thirteen and fourpence at Dover, twenty at Bath, and six at Marlborough, a stopping-place on the Bath Road. Marlborough would hardly pay for their beds and a meagre supper, but the horses, as well as the men, had to be rested. (These 'dates' were all made in 1597, except that at Cambridge which was in 1595.) In the year of the Wilton visit the King's Men had taken thirty shillings at Bath, twenty at Shrewsbury, forty at Coventry, twenty-five at Ipswich, and forty at Oxford.

There are many local records of these town payments; but we need not suppose that these were the only sums taken by the actors. A civic payment did not preclude other money accruing for extra performances or for special seats at a civic entertainment. Fees for visits to private houses would not be recorded in municipal accounts. Since the players stopped at inns and had to pay for their keep, unless entertained at a big house, as presumably they were at Wilton, they could not have existed on the sums mentioned, even if they cut their man-power down to the lowest possible strength when touring. Inevitably they would keep their numbers down and so give performances with less equipment and with more doubling and trebling of parts than was the case in London. Since the command to visit Wilton was rewarded with the unusual sum of thirty pounds there was probably a full turn-out of the King's Men.

Conditions of travel were rough. Accounts of accommodation at Elizabethan inns vary from cordial approval to angry condemnation. The risk of robbery on the road is made evident in a pamphlet, of which a single copy has fortunately survived, called *Ratsey's Ghost*. A 'gentleman of the road', with the curious name of Gamaliel Ratsey, sounding at once biblical and verminous, together with some attending rogues, throve on highway piracy until the leader was caught and hanged at Bedford in 1605, the year in which the account of his knaveries appeared. Its anonymous author relates how Ratsey and his crew

'. . . still hazarding their several haps, as they had several hopes, came by chance into an inn where that night there harboured a company of players; and Ratsey, framing himself to a humour of merriment, caused one or two of the chiefest of them to be sent for up into his chamber, where he demanded whose men they were, and they answered they served such an honorable personage. "I pray you," quoth Ratsey, "let me hear your music, for I have often gone to plays more for music's sake than for action; for some of you not content to do well, but striving to overdo and go beyond yourselves often times, by St. George, mar all: yet your poets take great pains to make your parts fit for your mouths, though you gape never so wide. Other-some, I must needs confess, are very well deserving, both for true action and fair delivery of speech; and yet, I warrant you, the very best have sometimes been content to go home at night with fifteen pence share apiece. Others there are whom fortune has so well favored that, what by penny-sparing and long practice of playing, are grown so wealthy that they have expected to be knighted, or at least to be conjunct in authority and to sit with men of great worship on the bench of justice . . ." '

The last remark may well have been directed at Shakespeare whose thrift and industry had enabled him to acquire the status and property of a gentleman, though he was not a knight or a magistrate. Ratsey, claiming some taste in the arts, confidently acting as a dramatic critic, and finding some of the actors of the time to be worthy of his approval, called for music from the players thus met on the road. This shows that they carried their musical instruments with them. There followed an abundance of singing, dancing, and revelling at the inn and for it the jovial highwayman 'made the players taste of his bounty'. So they parted happily. A week later Ratsey, who had disguised himself for professional reasons with a false head of hair and a beard, was not at first recognised when he met the players at another inn. He demanded a play and was well pleased. The account continues:

'. . . Ratsey . . . very liberally took out his purse and gave them forty shillings, with which they held themselves very richly satisfied, for they scarce had twenty shillings' audience at any time, for a play in the country. But Ratsey thought they should not enjoy it long, although he let them bear it about them till the next day in their purses; for the morning being come, and they having packed away their luggage, and some part of their company before in a wagon, discharged the house, payed his bill, and followed them presently. Ratsey intended not to be long after, but having learned which way they travelled, he, being very well horsed and mounted upon his black gelding, soon overtook them; and when they saw it was the gentleman who had been so liberal with them the night before, they began to do him much courtesy and to greet his late kindness with many thanks. But that was not the matter which he aimed at. Therefore he roundly told them they were deceived in him—he was not the man they took him for. "I am a soldier," said he, "and one that for means hath ventured my fortunes abroad, and now for money am driven to hazard them at home; I am not to be played upon by players; therefore be short, deliver me your money; I will turn usurer now; my forty shillings again will not serve without interest." They began to make many faces, and to cap and knee, but all would not serve their turn. He bade them leave off their cringing and compliments, and their apish tricks, and dispatch; which they did for fear of the worst, seeing to beg was bootless; and having made a desperate tender of their stock into Ratsey's hands, he bade them play for more, for, says he, "It is an idle profession that brings in much profit, and every night where you come, your playing bears your charges, and (leaves you) somewhat in your purse. Besides, you have fiddlers' fare—meat, drink and money. If the worst be, it is but pawning your apparel, for as good actors and stalkers as you are have done it. . . ." '

Ratsey, having got his money back with interest, mockingly told the actors to play for a fortnight as Ratsey's Men. Then the scoundrel added some interesting remarks to his act of robbery: '. . . "And for you sirs," says he to the chiefest of them, "thou hast a good presence upon a stage; methinks thou darkenest thy merit by playing in the country. Get thee to London, for, if one man were dead, they will have much need for such a one as thou art. There would be none in my opinion fitter than thyself to play his parts. My concept is such of thee that I durst venture all the money in my purse on thy head, to play Hamlet with him for a wager. There thou shalt learn to be frugal—for players were never so thrifty as they are now about London—and to feed upon all men, to let none feed upon thee; to make thy hand a stranger to thy pocket, thy heart slow to perform thy tongue's promise; and when thou feelest thy purse well lined, buy thee some place or lordship in the country, that growing weary of playing, thy money may there bring thee to dignity and reputation; then thou needest care for no man, nor for them that before made thee proud with speaking their words upon the stage." "Sir, I thank thee," quoth the player, "for this good counsel. I promise you I will make good use of it, for I have heard, indeed, of some that have gone to London very meanly, and have come in time to be exceeding wealthy." "And in this presage and prophetical humour of mine," says Ratsey, "kneel down—rise up, Sir Simon Two Shares and a Half; thou art now one of my Knights, and the first knight that ever was player in England. The next time I meet thee, I must share with thee again for playing under my warrant, and so for this time adieu." '

There is much useful information here. Twenty shillings is referred to as an exceptionally good reward for a country performance. The mention of fifteen pence as the height of one man's share suggests a company of sixteen, but there is no reason to suppose that Ratsey was working with a close reckoning of the arithmetic, since touring teams were sometimes by no means as large as the London ones. This company had one wagon. So some must have ridden or walked. Thus they moved at a pace which could be easily overtaken. We are further told that such venturers, with their luck out, might have to sell the costumes. This statement is confirmed as accurate by the unhappy fate of Pembroke's Men in the plague year of 1593. Then Henslowe wrote to Alleyn that this company 'cannot save their charges with travel, as I hear, and are fain to pawne their apparel for their charge'.

Ratsey's references to *Hamlet*, a play of the King's Men, and to those who have come meanly to London and made money, with a second allusion to buying a place in the country, seem to bring us close to Shakespeare. The jest about 'Two Shares and a Half' would apply to those who were both Actor-Sharers and House-Sharers, as were Burbage and Shakespeare, and the mention of a supreme player of Hamlet's part must point again to Burbage. But Burbage was obviously not with the touring men whom Ratsey gulled and robbed. Who was the man whom this piratical arbiter of stage excellence designated as fit to play Hamlet for a wager with Burbage? It could possibly be Shakespeare, since the other remarks point to his presence in the company. But Hamlet had not been his role in London. If he was on tour he may have been doubling or trebling the Ghost with other parts. Of course we cannot certainly apply the story to a calamity among the King's Men on tour. It has been plausibly argued that Shakespeare toured as little as might be since he could be better employed at his writing-table. The absence of Burbage from a company which was taking Hamlet on tour indicates that there could be two teams of the Fellowship if the London theatres were open, the No. 1 company staying in town and the No. 2 and less expensive company taking to the road.

That Shakespeare did go on tour might be further revealed by references in his writing to particular places which so busy a man, with his roots in Stratford and London, would not be likely to visit except for professional reasons. He was not much given to particular descriptions of scenery or locality and so this source of evidence does not yield much. Mentions of the Cotswold and near-Cotswold country include Gloucestershire's 'high wild hills and rough uneven ways' and 'Berkeley Castle with its tuft of trees' (*Richard II*, Act II, Scene 3). He was unlikely to mention a particular tuft of trees unless it had struck his eye as conspicuous when he had been there and it has been suggested that before he went to London he joined the Earl of Berkeley's private company of players. If he did go to Berkeley Castle from Stratford, for that or any other reason, he would traverse the high, uneven, and then rough-roaded Cotswolds. But this does not provide evidence of touring in later years.

Nor do the comments of King Duncan and Banquo on the climate and bird-life of Inverness compel us to think that Shakespeare had himself sniffed the nimble and delicate air with which Macbeth's stronghold is complimented or had done some bird-watching round the castle walls. Laurence Fletcher, the Scottish actor and favourite of King James, brought by the King to join the King's Men, could have mentioned agreeable weather in that town and there were castles enough in England to afford observation of the nesting choices of the swift, if Shakespeare's martlet be that bird and not the house-martin.

That Shakespeare visited Bath is likely enough. His company was known to have included that town in their travels of 1593, 1597, and 1603. Its springs of warm and curative water and their value to the tourist industry were described by Edmund Spenser in the second book of *The Faerie Queene*:

> *Behold the boiling baths at Cair Badon,*
> *Which seethe with secret fire eternally,*
> *And in their entrails, full of quick brimstone,*
> *Nourish the flames which they are warm'd upon;*
> *That to their people wealth they forth do well,*
> *And health to every foreign nation.*

In the last two sonnets (Nos. 153 and 154) Shakespeare played with the idea put forward by a late Greek poet Marianus who had fancifully suggested that Eros (Cupid) laid down a torch which was turned to a hot spring. Whether Shakespeare's 'little Latin and less Greek' ran to adapting the Greek or a Latin version of the poem is conjectural; there could have been an English version and some of the more learned citizens of Bath may have liked to perpetuate in their own language the fancy of their medicinal pools being the creation of the Love-God. The two sonnets are repetitive and both include the statement that the poet went, when sick, to a hot bath in search of a cure and both link this with his incurable passion for his mistress:

Cupid laid by his brand, and fell asleep:
A maid of Dian's this advantage found,
And his love-kindling fire did quickly steep
In a cold valley-fountain of that ground;
Which borrow'd from this holy fire of Love
A dateless lively heat, still to endure,
And grew a seething bath, which yet men prove
Against strange maladies a sovereign cure.
But at my mistress' eye Love's brand new-fired,
The boy for trial needs would touch my breast;
I, sick withal, the help of bath desired,
And thither hied, a sad distemper'd guest,
*   But found no cure: the bath for my help lies*
*   Where Cupid got new fire,—my mistress' eyes.*

The following sonnet says much the same and a mention of bath occurs again. The repeated stress on the word bath suggests a reference to the place as well as the waters and, since first Lord Strange's and then the Chamberlain's and the King's Men took in Bath when on their circuit in the west, it is a reasonable surmise that Shakespeare, perhaps distempered with rheumatism or some other 'strange malady' by the rigours of touring, tried the cure when his company 'thither hied'. The treatment may not have been so disappointing as both Sonnets suggest since the poet was expressing a pain of the heart as well as of the limbs, his incurable enslavement by the eyes of 'raven black' as they are described in Sonnet 127, the ebon eyes which flash from the white face of the Dark Lady of the Sonnets.

It may be significant that Falstaff, when describing his own valour, explained that he had 'fought a long hour by Shrewsbury clock' (*Henry IV, Part I*, Act V, Scene 4). Why mention the clock unless its prominence had struck Shakespeare's eye during a visit? There was such a visit of Lord Strange's Men in 1593 and, since this company then contained many of Shakespeare's associates, including Heminge, Kempe and Burbage, before the formation of the Chamberlain's Men, he may have been with them. But the clock-tower is a shaky structure on which to hang any conclusions.

Far better evidence of Shakespeare's presence on a tour is provided by the cliffs of Dover. For once the dramatist does give a detailed account of the scenery and of the human workers perilously engaged. Edgar's speech in *King Lear* (Act IV, Scene 6) must be based on personal observation:

> Stand still. How fearful
> And dizzy 'tis to cast one's eyes so low'.
> The crows and choughs that wing the midway air
> Show scarce so gross as beetles. Half-way down
> Hangs one that gathers samphire, dreadful trade!
> Methinks he seems no bigger than his head.
> The fishermen that walk upon the beach
> Appear like mice; and yond tall anchoring bark
> Diminished to her cock, her cock a buoy
> Almost too small for sight. The murmuring surge,
> That on the unnumbered idle pebbles chafes,
> Cannot be heard so high. I'll look no more,
> Lest my brain turn, and the deficient sight
> Topple down headlong.

The aromatic and saline leaves of the rock-haunting samphire were valued for their use in pickles and sauces. Shakespeare seems to have been struck by the countless stones of a pebble beach. He calls them unnumbered here and again in *Cymbeline* (Act I, Scene 6) there is the same adjective used of stones on a shore.

The King's Men were at Dover in the late summer of 1606 and took forty shillings there. They returned to London by way of Maidstone where they and some trumpeters together received forty five shillings. *King Lear* was produced on December 26 at Whitehall, probably its 'first night' or soon after that occasion, since this was the first mention of the play. So it is reasonable to assume that Shakespeare was with the players at Dover and wrote the cliff-scenery passage either then or just after.

By putting this somewhat scrappy evidence together and in proportion it may be decided that Shakespeare was sometimes, and perhaps often, a touring player. The detailed picture of the cliffs at Dover surely suggests that he had been there and had been deeply impressed by their height and the risks of the cliff-hangers seeking samphire. This description, which is not dramatically necessary to the scene but gives it notable colour, coincides with the date of *King Lear*. If he was there it shows that as late in his career as 1606 he was willing to face the hardships of the road and the labour of performing on frequently changing 'fit-up' stands in town halls or any other available premises. That he wrote much on tour is difficult to believe: to jot down impressions and ideas and an isolated passage or two was feasible, but to find the desk and the peace for writing would be very difficult amid the chatter and the jostle of players at an inn, with the nuisance of constantly packing up and moving on, and with the worry of acting in continually different and possibly primitive conditions. To carry with him a script of which there was only the one copy on which he was working was to run the danger of a sad loss. The picture of the strolling player's life given in the Ratsey story does not indicate a chance for any writing except that of a note-taking and casual kind.

Against this can be set the ability of a skilled and experienced journalist to produce first-rate reports for hasty transmission by telegram or telephone amid crowds and clatter and even physical danger, if he has been despatched to one of the world's 'trouble-spots'. These hasty messages may emerge not only as capable and graphic summaries of what occurred but also as excellent examples of clear and vigorous writing. So it can be held that Shakespeare, when he had learned the knack, could turn out even the best of his poetry in the least favourable surroundings. If, as Maurice Baring playfully surmised, he could during the hubbub of a difficult rehearsal add a passage so striking as to be memorable and continually quoted, he might have done the same during the daily scramble of a tour with one stop after another. But my own conjecture is that Dover, with its chalky bastions, its choughs, and its samphire, were stored in the mind or on a scrap of paper and that the real work of writing *King Lear* took place in a room at his Cripplegate lodging between the end of the tour and the Christmas season of rehearsals at Clerkenwell and of performances at Court in the autumn and winter of 1606. But, while Shakespeare was jogging along on a horse beside the players' property-wagon, there was plenty of time during which the ideas could flow in for future decanting at journey's end.

But 1606 was not the only chance of taking that dizzying view. The Dover passage in *King Lear* could have been based on well-stored memories of a visit in the autumn of 1597 when the Chamberlain's Men were paid thirteen shillings and eight pence at that town, a sum less than the twenty shillings received at Rye and sixteen at Faversham. It was obviously not a promising 'date', but they returned to it and did much better. If Shakespeare was engaged in the tour of 1606, with *King Lear* in preparation, such thoughts as came to him on the road were not of traveller's joy. He was seeing the world, through the powerful glass of his imagination, very darkly indeed. Comedy had for some years been out of mind and the Dover road did not induce a return to it.

CHAPTER IX

At The Desk

❧

IF THE figure of Shakespeare so far drawn is only roughly true, he had small opportunity for lolling and yawning at his desk. Time and tranquillity there could be when he was at Stratford on early holiday or in later retirement. There too, as well as in London, I see him as no loiterer with his pen: one who has acquired speed of writing retains the knack. In London he was in the thick of things, at the beck and call of busy colleagues. He was spared the modern nuisance, as well as occasional convenience, of the telephone, but messengers could fetch him to the theatre when crisis came and his counsel was precious. Interrupted or not, the author-actor-manager was not slow in authorship. There is much dispute about the dating of some plays, but there is fairly general agreement about the work done in one pre-eminent period of five years.

Between the beginning of 1597 and the end of 1601, if this agreement be accepted, Shakespeare, amid all his other duties of the playhouse, wrote *The Merchant of Venice*, the two parts of *Henry IV*, the 'newly corrected and augmented' version of *Love's Labour's Lost*, if not the early draft as well, *Henry V*, *Much Ado About Nothing*, *Julius Caesar*, *The Merry Wives of Windsor*, *Troilus and Cressida*, *As You Like It*, *Twelfth Night*, and *Hamlet*. The revision of one comedy may have been slight work and knocking off *The Merry Wives* a rapid but necessary response to a royal command that he should promptly present the fat knight in love. (There are two eighteenth-century traditions that he did this as 'a rush job' for the Queen's pleasure, one report giving it a fortnight and another ten days: we have no contemporary evidence of this, but the play has the air of speed and fatigue with its repetition of the same situation.) The rest are supreme achievements in all three modes of the time, historical, comical, tragical. Never after was there to be such a marriage of abundance with excellence. The quality might grow; the quantity could not.

It is not surprising that Heminge and Condell in their short First Folio address to 'the great variety of readers' said that the mind and hand of Shakespeare 'went together'. 'What he thought he uttered with that easiness, that we have scarce received from him a blot in his papers.' That is all the direct evidence we have about Shakespeare's work on paper, but we have a fair amount of information about the methods of providing plays for the players in general use during his lifetime. With that we can form some picture of Shakespeare at the desk and passing the product to the players.

The first question to be faced is the relation of our printed texts to what Shakespeare actually wrote. How far were they tampered with in the process of rehearsal and revival? Into the accuracy of Shakespeare texts and the various values of the Quartos and the First Folio there has been long and intense research with a super-structure of occasionally conflicting opinion. To the work in this kind of Sir Edmund Chambers, Sir Walter Greg, A. W. Pollard, J. Dover Wilson, F. P. Wilson, R. B. McKerrow and others much is owed. Previous to their examination of the playhouse and printing-house procedure there had been acceptance of Dr. Johnson's pessimism about the authenticity of the generally accepted texts. He had maintained that Shakespeare sold his plays 'not to be printed but to be played' and that 'they were immediately copied for the actors'. Both these statements can hardly be disputed. But Johnson's further opinion that they were 'multiplied by transcript after transcript, vitiated by the blunders of the penmen or changed by the affectations of the players' needs qualification. That the transcripts were numerous seems to be untrue: that they were faulty is uncertain. The best of the book-holders and scriveners, such as Knight and Crane who worked for the King's Men, were reliable and careful and are not to be dismissed as 'vitiators'. Nor do most modern editors agree that the majority of the texts which we possess are 'compilations made by chance of stealth out of the separate parts written for the theatre', which elements were described by Johnson as 'minutely broken' and 'fortuitously reunited'. What are called 'assembled texts' did draw upon the actors' separate part-scrolls, but in the good Quartos the scrolls were used, if at all, with discretion.

Pollard's separation of the Shakespeare Quartos into the Bad and the Good has been widely accepted. The Bad are the first printed versions of *Romeo and Juliet, Henry V, The Merry Wives of Windsor,* and *Hamlet.* These inadequate and corrupt texts may have been based on stealthy and crude shorthand reporting in the theatre made by men capable of rapid jottings for other companies. (The word stenography, which is the Greek for narrow writing, was in use in England in 1602.) Or they may have been worked up from the memories or part-scrolls of Hired Men who could be bribed. The Sharers would not be connivers at theft. The fact that some parts, e.g. that of the Host in *The Merry Wives of Windsor,* are much closer than others to the later Quarto and Folio versions suggests some of the sources on which pirating printers and envious rivals in the playhouse could draw. All these sources might have been used at once and the results jumbled together. More important is the conclusion that the printers of the Good Quartos and the editors and printers of the First Folio were using playhouse scripts either in Shakespeare's own hand or copied by responsible scriveners from the manuscripts which he handed in. So Dr. Johnson's idea of a text far removed from Shakespeare's original by careless errors and interpolations has been much discredited.

Completely discredited, some would say. But unless there was in Shakespeare's time a reverence for authorship by no means common in the theatre since then, Dr. Johnson's suspicions could have some reason behind them. For two centuries after 1660 the texts were not only hacked about but rewritten with plots radically altered. Some were made into librettos for musical pieces, e.g. the version of *The Tempest* by Dryden and D'Avenant with a score by Henry Purcell, which was thought worthy of a revival at the Old Vic theatre in London in 1957 and made a delightful entertainment. This practice has continued into our time and none can fairly complain that the gay and tuneful version of *The Taming of the Shrew* called *Kiss Me Kate* was any kind of outrage. Shakespeare himself could hardly grumble, since he drew freely on other men's plays, probably in this very case of Petruchio and his Kate. As far as plots were concerned, there was freedom to purloin. It was all in the playhouse game. But he could have been justly indignant at the the shameless perversion of his work during the seventeenth, eighteenth, and nineteenth centuries by Nahum Tate and his followers, even David Garrick, who would give a sugary ending to the bitterest of tragedies.

But, apart from cuts which might be needed to fit the playing-time and did not alter the story, there appear to have been no major alterations of Shakespeare's work until the Civil Wars closed the theatres and broke the continuity of playhouse tradition. Yet the suggestion that 'the affectations of the actors' had corrupted the dialogue is not to be altogether overlooked simply because much of the Johnsonian case against the purity of the texts has been disputed and on the whole disproved. Eighteen of Shakespeare's plays were never printed until 1623, which means that these texts had been lying in the playhouse book-chest for ten, twenty, or even thirty years. If they were plays that failed to please and so were not revived there would be no occasion for the insertions made by actors and for the impromptus of the comedians to creep in: if the plays were popular and intermittently, even constantly, restaged, it is likely enough that some of the players' 'affectations' could have been scribbled in and kept their place.

This may be especially true of the droll's parts. It would not be strange if injected lines which proved effective and raised a laugh were added and retained. It is also possible that some of the word-play and verbal quibbling which we least enjoy was not Shakespeare's. Stage directions did become imbedded. When Benedick in the Church Scene in *Much Ado About Nothing* says 'How now, interjections?' in the middle of his dialogue with Claudio and Leonato it is a reasonable surmise that 'interjections' was a book-keeper's note to prompt the supers who made up the congregation. Against this, however, must be set the assertion of Heminge and Condell that, in preparing their Folio text, they had done the necessary scouring and tidying and were now offering the reader Shakespeare's texts not 'maim'd and deform'd' but 'cured and perfect in their limbs' and 'absolute in their numbers as he conceived them'. Yet, despite their good intentions, the problem of sifting the Bad Quartos and of editing the eighteen unprinted plays, written probably in various handwritings by various scriveners, was so taxing that obvious mistakes and passages so confused as to be almost unintelligible did survive. Accordingly we cannot be certain that the curing process removed all growths upon the body of the plays. It would indeed be astonishing if no such blemishes remained.

For those who wish to examine in detail the relative sources and values of the Quartos and the Folio and to assess the genuineness of the texts as we know them there is enough material in the writings of the scholars mentioned and in the numerous editions of the plays in separate form to keep the student occupied for many years. What has been much less discussed and what concerns the purpose of this book is the form in which Shakespeare passed his plays to the players and the methods and conditions of his authorship. How, in short, did Shakespeare use pen and paper when he was not engaged in the toils of rehearsal, direction, performance, and the administrative duties of the Actor-Sharer and the House-Sharer?

The common practice of the dramatists, as was earlier explained, was to confer about a subject with a manager or the Actor-Sharers of a Fellowship of Players. The majority of playwrights were team-workers and they might contribute only one or two acts on a theme agreed: thus would be collected a series of rough, and perhaps very rough, drafts which had to be collated, either by the most trusted author or by the company's Book-keeper. Men writing independently produced their own first drafts which were known at the time by the seemingly impolite term of Foul Papers. Then, in the case of an experienced dramatist, these might need and receive little or no alteration. But there had of course to be at least one copy made, for no company would risk the total loss of the play which could occur if a single manuscript disappeared or was destroyed. The Fair Copy was made by the author himself, if he had time and good enough penmanship. Otherwise the Book-keeper might do it. We know that one of the Book-keepers of the King's Men had the qualification. If there was none such, the Foul Papers went to a professional scrivener.

Knight was both Book-keeper to the King's Men and a transcriber; he made a copy of Beaumont and Fletcher's *Bonduca* which was played in 1613 with Burbage, Condell, Lowin and Richard Robinson in the principal parts. He added the information that the first Book used by the actors had been lost and that he had used for his transcription the Author's Foul Papers 'which were found'. There is evidence here of the hazards to which manuscripts were subject. In this case the Fair Copy had vanished and the rough draft had to be looked for and was fortunately discovered.

The Book-keeper marked his Fair Copy and prepared it for rehearsal with such stage-directions as he thought were necessary in addition to the author's own notes of this kind. He thus provided a Prompt Copy, to which the director of rehearsals would add more. Before production was under way the Book-keeper sent the Fair Copy to the Master of the Revels for 'allowance'. With the Foul Papers to hand he could make out the summary called the Plot and arrange for the copying of the actors' parts on their scrolls. When there was urgent need of a quick production these scrolls might be got ready before the 'allowance' had been gained. In 1624 the Master, then Sir Henry Herbert, returned to Knight, as Book-keeper, the text of 'Woman's Prize or the Tamer Tamed' by Fletcher with his objections. Herbert wrote testily that, while Knight had already made some desirable cuts, there was more to be done. He added 'Purge their parts, as I have the Book'. This command would be unnecessary if the parts had not already been written out unpurged.

A considerable number of original play-manuscripts of the period have survived; unfortunately none of them is by Shakespeare. Of the forty extant some are in the hand of the author, others have been copied by the scrivener. One of Massinger's and two of Heywood's are holographs, that is to say documents wholly written by the person in whose name they appear. Some show considerable signs of play-house preparation, others few or none. In the case of the latter, production may have been intended—otherwise the trouble of making a Fair Copy would not have been undertaken—and then dropped on second thoughts.

A playwright in labour appears in the correspondence of Robert Daborne, an actor-dramatist who at one time worked for Henslowe. His letters were kept and have been preserved in the Alleyn Collection at Dulwich. In 1615 Daborne was ill and wrote from his bed, begging for an advance of one pound for a play called *The Bellman of London*. (His immediate poverty was relieved to this extent and he evidently escaped later on to a life of comfort and a loftier occupation, since he was Dean of Lismore when he died in 1628.) In the case of *The Bellman* he had read aloud his play by instalments from his Foul Papers while seeking the acceptance of Alleyn and his company. Acceptance was gained, but he was behind time with his Fair Copy: he promised to 'perfit the book', which would be used as a Prompt Copy. He sent this second draft in sections, 'three acts fair written' and then two more sheets and again two more sheets, sitting at his work 'till past twelve'. In the end, with Henslowe accusing him of breach of promise to deliver the goods, Daborne passed over the text of the last scene not 'copied fair' but in its Foul Paper form.

Henslowe was evidently not wasting money by employing a scrivener to make the Fair Copy of Daborne's piece: sick or well, this author had to 'perfit' the job himself. But certainly scriveners were engaged for Shakespeare's work, though not perhaps with regularity in the early part of his career. The King's Men in their prosperity used Knight and Crane. Crane had certain mannerisms in his presentation. One of them was to name all the characters in a scene at the head of it, though all did not enter at once and even though it began with a soliloquy. This served as a useful reminder to the actors to be ready. So the specialists have been able to estimate by the appearance of this and other mannerisms in the printed texts which of the Fair Copies by Crane had been used in preparing the First Folio. Greg decided that the Folio text of *The Merry Wives of Windsor* was taken from a transcript by Crane 'probably of Foul Papers'. He also found Crane's work in the unsuccessful *The Two Gentlemen of Verona*, of which no performance is known in Shakespeare's lifetime. It must have been lying about for thirty years if Crane worked on it just before 1623. The Folio texts of *The Winter's Tale* and *The Tempest*, neither previously issued in Quarto form, were also attributed to Crane by Greg. That they are the first four plays in the First Folio may signify that their copying was one man's work.

If Shakespeare followed the usual practice of his fellow-playwrights he first discussed the elements of a play with the Actor-Sharers. When he was accepted as their leading writer he would hardly meet much opposition to his suggestions. With their approval gained, he wrote the play in Foul Papers and then read the result to the company. Then he made his own Fair Copy or passed this task over to the company's scrivener: but he would not immediately hand it on if he wanted to make alterations in the original. Rewriting to 'perfit' the whole play meant more manual labour and would naturally be avoided by a man otherwise busy. In his maturity he could be so sure of himself that he considered the Foul Papers to be fair enough and left the transcription of the Fair Copy for the immediate attention of the scrivener.

It seems churlish to grumble at anything done by Heminge and Condell since our obligation for their work of salvage is so great. Yet we can lament the brevity of their preface to the First Folio and wish that it had been more explicit about the Shakespeare manuscripts. Incidentally, it is hard to see why certain scholars deny to these two the writing of the foreword, to which they put their signatures, and attribute it to Ben Jonson or another. One hesitates to go against the authority of such scholars as Greg and Chambers, both of whom favour Jonson. But surely the men who set their names on the Folio as editors, without challenge at the time, were capable of penning a preface. Greg calls them 'men so far as we know without experience in literary composition'.

There seems to be some intellectual snobbishness here. The actors of the time were not university wits, but they had had their Elizabethan schooling which, with no university career added, had served Shakespeare well enough. They were moving in a whirl of fine speech and in a world of language used to the full. The clown Kempe was able to write a vivid and literate account of his dancing journey to Norwich and his successor Armin wrote several books and a play. Nathan Field, of the King's Men, was a playwright whose comedies pleased. Alleyn, a good letter-writer, endowed education. Heminge had to communicate with the Court and do business with the Lord Chamberlain's and the Revels Office; he must have been able to use a pen. To regard him and Condell as unable to make the Folio dedication to the Earls of Pembroke and Montgomery and the address to the readers and to do so with some flourish and grace of style is an unwarrantable injustice to their own Fellowship and to their profession as a whole. Jonson contributed and signed his own memorial verses for the volume: he had no need to 'ghost' for the editors in prose. Why should we accuse the editors of false pretences? What they had edited, they could introduce.

The cause of my regret for an omission lies in the vagueness of the statement about Shakespeare's manuscripts in which Heminge and Condell said there was scarcely a blot. It is difficult to see whether this means that they possessed the plays, or most of them, in the author's own Fair Copy or that they had his Foul Papers which were so little 'foul' as to be as good as Fair. Some of the texts, we are told with Greg's authority, were Fair Copies in the hand of the scrivener, Crane; did the editors have Shakespeare's first drafts as well as Crane's transcriptions and were the former written with such assurance that blottings out and corrections were absent or extremely rare?

While full trust must be given to the editors' tribute to Shakespeare's facility, it is very hard to believe that he never altered or rewrote. When the editors stated that 'we have scarce received a blot in his papers' we may naturally imagine some bias of courtesy to a loved companion, especially in the introduction of a tributary volume. By comparison with the work of others, they may have meant to say, Shakespeare's manuscripts were remarkably clean. A section of the manuscript of the jointly written play *Sir Thomas More* called Hand D has been allotted to Shakespeare's pen because it certainly has some smack of his style and some usage of words that he favoured. If the attribution be correct, then he did scratch out lines; these papers are not unblotted.

That Shakespeare wrote with the ease mentioned by Heminge and Condell must have been the case. That he could have written with such unlaboured fluency that what he passed on to the players was his first draft in every line is well-nigh incredible. There must have been times when he stuck, wrote a passage, disliked it, and altered or abandoned it. He was not just turning out dialogue that would do; he was composing superb poetry. It is likely that he was unaware, or little aware, of that: he was writing for the actors and not with an eye on 'all time'. None the less, we must allow him some of a poet's eagerness to tinker with his work, using second and third thoughts to amend the first impulsive outpour.

Others of the highest poetic rank and quality have pondered over a single word and returned again and again to the redrafting of a brief lyric. If at the end the manuscript went clean to the printer, it was not because the first draft was thus perfect. Shakespeare, before he sent in what were called his Foul Papers, may have been sifting pieces set down here and there amid the press of theatre business and then collecting them and touching them up when he had a clear day or night before him. Revision could be as swift as creation and both processes could grow still more rapid as his command of the job increased with steady practice. We need not take literally the unblotted papers of which we are told.

Shakespeare went to work with his quill and with sheets of paper the size of our foolscap, if we judge by the manuscript play-books of the period. That is reasonable, since these were of a uniform kind. The custom was to use both sides of a folio page which contained about fifty lines on both sides. Since many of the dramatists were poor men, those who were paid a pound for an act had reason to be thrifty with their raw materials. The page was divided by folding into four columns. On the left was the speaker's name; the middle two sections were used for the verse: the prose could stretch over into the fourth column where there were also entered stage-directions and exits. Then the sheets were put together by stitching or by piercing and fastening and assembled with a vellum cover. And so to the Book-keeper.

To ask how fast the writing went is an idle question. Speed of creative writing must vary with the moods of the creator, as it varies with the talents of different men. Webster confessed to costiveness at the desk. There is testimony to Shakespeare's fertility and facility not only in the First Folio editors' statement that his mind and hand went together but also in Milton's tribute to the way in which Shakespeare shamed 'slow-endeavouring art' with the 'easy flow' of his numbers. Leonard Digges, stepson of Thomas Russell, one of the overseers and beneficiaries of Shakespeare's will, wrote laudatory verses for the First Folio and left others which were included five years after his death, in the Second. The latter included a list of the Shakespearian characters who packed the house, Falstaff, Prince Hal, Beatrice and Benedick, Brutus and Cassius, Othello, and Lear. The lines may have been written for the First Folio and then dropped because offensive to Ben Jonson with their reference to his 'tedious though well-laboured Catiline' and 'irksome Sejanus'. After Ben's death that could be said. Digges also alluded to Shakespeare's 'ease'. 'To contrive a play' was no labour to him.

These references are general. As to the speed of output in individual cases we have only the much later reference to ten days or a fortnight spent on *The Merry Wives of Windsor*. Several critics have made their guesses. John Masefield in *William Shakespeare* (p. 134) wrote of *Macbeth:* 'I have little doubt that nearly all the first two acts were written in one marvellous day.' It may have been so. This is the judgment of a poet who knows how the mind and hand

may race together. *Macbeth* starts at a thunderous gallop and without the more deliberate crescendo of the other great tragedies. But
Masefield, commenting on the shortness of this play and the
commonly held view that we have in the Folio only a cut acting
version (there was no Quarto edition) says that it was snipped by
'fatal scissors' at the Globe with a resulting loss of seven hundred
lines. This number can be confirmed by comparing the length of
Macbeth with that of the other tragedies. If so much of *Macbeth*
was pared away, that was for us 'the most unkindest cut of all'.
With this allowed for, the start as Shakespeare wrote it may not
have been so headlong in its course. If the beginning was longer
the argument for a torrential speed of writing is weakened. Yet one
does feel that *Macbeth* comes out of the Highlands like a river in
full spate, not only dark as peaty waters but 'whummlin' down',
as the Scots would say.

Another estimate of fantastic speed was made by Dr. Leslie
Hotson in his book on *The First Night of Twelfth Night*. He argued
that this masterpiece of comedy was hurriedly prepared for a Royal
command performance at Whitehall on the twelfth night of
January, 1601, at which the Duke Virginio Orsino, just arrived in
London from Italy, was to be gloriously entertained. 'In ten or
eleven days,' wrote Dr. Hotson, 'the play must be written and
licensed, the parts cast and memorised, the production perfected in
rehearsal, and performed. And this was the festive season of
Christmas, between the company's regular daily performances.'

Dr. Hotson need not have included the other 'regular performances'. During the usual intensive rehearsal at Clerkenwell of a
whole series of plays for the after-Christmas revels at Court the
routine at the Globe could be laid off: it was no season of the year
for playgoing in an unroofed theatre on short, dark, and cold or
wet afternoons. But even if the players were not hurrying across
London from wind-swept matinées and so came fresh to their
strenuous and possibly all-night rehearsals at the Revels Office, I
find this surmise incredible. Shakespeare might have applied to
Illyria the conjectured speed of writing which he was later to
bestow on Inverness, but this was, as Dr. Hotson emphasises, to be
a very special occasion for very important people. There could be
no 'thribbling through'. The actors would have to be word-
perfect and how could they be sure of that with their part-scrolls

coming along in bits and pieces? Then there would be new and sumptuous costumes needed or old ones to be cleaned and refurbished. Also there was the preparation of the moves, business, and music.

Dr. Hotson supports his contention with other examples of prodigious speed, reminding us that the prolific Lopé de Vega boasted 'that more than a hundred of my comedies have taken only twenty-four hours to pass from my brain to the boards'. But the comparison between the Spaniard's output and the Shakespearian perfection of phrase and fancy in *Twelfth Night* is unpersuasive. Even if their author charged through Illyria at full speed, the actors could not go lunging pell-mell into their preparations for such a night as Dr. Hotson proceeds vividly to picture. If the name Orsino had to be given to a character described in the play as noble, free, valiant, learned, stainless, and gracious, that change could easily have been made in a play already in hand, without dashing off a new one.

The reader of Shakespeare can make his own guesses about the varying pace at which various plays were written. If the tradition about the hasty composition of *The Merry Wives* is true, it is obvious that prose came quicker than poetry, since that play is nearly all in prose. One's natural inclination is to think that the poorer (or less excellent) writing came less rapidly or even sluggishly. *All's Well That End's Well* has, for me at least, an air of weariness about it. There is little suggestion of the impetuous work which strains against the dam of fatigue and which demands to be released. But it can be argued in reply that Shakespeare wrote most rapidly when least interested and was in this case wearily saying to himself all's well that ends somehow. Every author with a large output must at some time in his life mutter 'To hell with all this' and scribble in order to get done with what has turned upon the desk from an excitement to a drudgery.

If John Masefield's opinion about the first two acts of *Macbeth* is an accurate conjecture and if there were no passages roughly penned and revised before those two galloping acts were stitched together and sent in, then Shakespeare could write with a concentration of genius that leaves one astounded, if not incredulous. That the episodes on the heath and at Forres came like the wind is easily acceptable, but once at Inverness every line is so close-packed with depth of meaning and appropriate word-music that immediate and unpondered composition is hard to credit. This does not imply long sweating and boggling over the perfection of each phrase, but time to take breath, to rest the hand, and let fancy wander from the written sheet into new reaches of metaphor and image.

> *He's here in double trust:*
> *First, as I am his kinsman and his subject,*
> *Strong both against the deed; then, as his host,*
> *Who should against his murderer shut the door,*
> *Not bear the knife myself. Besides, this Duncan*
> *Hath borne his faculties so meek, hath been*
> *So clear in his great office, that his virtues*
> *Will plead like angels, trumpet-tongued, against*
> *The deep damnation of his taking-off;*
> *And pity, like a naked new-born babe,*
> *Striding the blast, or heaven's cherubin, horsed*
> *Upon the sightless cou, iers of the air,*
> *Shall blow the horrid deed in every eye,*
> *That tears shall drown the wind,—I have no spur*
> *To prick the sides of my intent, but only*
> *Vaulting ambition, which o'erleaps itself,*
> *And falls on th'other.*

Did that just tumble on the page? If so, John Masefield's 'marvellous day' was not a marvel but a miracle. Whenever I re-read *Macbeth* I think of lines little noted because what lies around has proved more notable. After the second disappearance of Banquo's Ghost Macbeth says:

> *Can such things be*
> *And overcome us like a summer's cloud*
> *Without our special wonder?*

The music of it is so apt to the sky-scape of the simile. Did that also just tumble out? If so our own 'special wonder' is the more intense.

That the mind and hand went together seems not to be wholly true of some of the later writing. There were times when the mind was surpassing the power of the pen to keep up with it. The brain was outrunning the hand. The nimbleness of thought and the forge-like power which Falstaff found in sherris-sack were at work in Falstaff's creator with or without physical stimulation. The sign of that is the telescoping of metaphors and similes like railway-carriages after a shattering accident. Defeated Antony exclaims against the defection of his followers:

> *The hearts*
> *That spaniel'd me at heels, to whom I gave*
> *Their wishes, do discandy, melt their sweets*
> *On blossoming Caesar and their pine is bark't*
> *That overtopt them all.*

The racing mind has in four amazing lines mixed hearts and heels, fawning dogs and melting sweetmeats, flowers and forestry. There is a similar high-pressure of crowding images in *Coriolanus* and *The Winter's Tale* which imposes great difficulties on the actor who must, while embodying the furious passion of the character, disentangle for the audience the tangled skein of similes. Such passages must have come turbid with their vehemence from the brain to the desk: a writer taking his time, and thinking more of his players, would have combed them out.

Against the idea of consummate ease and reckless speed must be set Ben Jonson's lines in his First Folio verses in which he maintains that he

> *Who casts to write a living line must sweat*
> *(Such as thine are) and strike the second heat*
> *Upon the muses' anvil*

and says of Shakespeare 'such wert thou'. Jonson's further insistence that 'a good poet's made as well as born' certainly invites us to visualise a Shakespeare toiling at his poetic forge while he strikes and re-strikes the malleable metal. But I agree with Dover Wilson who in *The Essential Shakespeare* (p. 71) sees a latent jealousy at the back of this picture of a patient and perspiring Shakespeare. Jonson was known for his diligence at the desk (witness the comment of Digges, already quoted, on his 'tedious, though well-laboured Catiline') and could not entertain or could hardly endure the idea of another whose hand could go tearing on without revision. Dover Wilson points to the collapses in Shakespeare's plays whose 'huddled finales' and sudden declines into feeble concluding couplets suggest the gasping of one who has run himself to exhaustion. After the superb reflective soliloquy spoken by the doomed Richard II in his cell at Pomfret we have as wretched an end as any hack might have been ashamed to scribble. Says the Earl of Northumberland:

> *The next news is, I have to London sent*
> *The heads of Oxford, Salisbury, Blunt, and Kent;*
> *The manner of their taking may appear*
> *At large discoursed in this paper here.*

When Lord Fitzwater brings news of further decapitations and several heads dispatched to the capital the triumphant Bolingbroke commends him thus:

> *Thy pains, Fitzwater, shall not be forgot*
> *Right noble is thy merit, well I wot.*

If Shakespeare did not finish at Pomfret and wrote this himself he had been running till he dropped. 'To Hell with all this' was never more clearly written between the lines. On the other hand he may have been working over an old and poorly written play, as he sometimes did to obtain a convenient framework of plot and then may have forgotten or neglected to rewrite fragments of the old script because he had been hustled by the players or had grown careless with fatigue.

Dover Wilson reminds the reader of a passage in Jonson's volume of notes and brief essays called *Timber* or *Discoveries*. Jonson died in 1637 and since this book appeared after his death it must have been put together well after the appearance of the First Folio. It contains his well-known saying of Shakespeare 'I loved the man (on this side idolatry) as well as any', and also his criticism of Shakespeare, master of 'ease' and praised for his unblotted lines. 'Would he had blotted a thousand,' snapped Jonson, adding his opinion that 'he flowed with that facility that sometimes it should be stopped', and the rather grudging concession that 'there was ever more in him to be praised than to be pardoned'. This description of excessive fluency flatly contradicts Jonson's own earlier picture of a careful recaster of his lines.

In *Discoveries* also Jonson wrote of an author whom he does not name:

'I have known a man vehement on both sides; that knew no mean either to intermit his studies or call upon them again. When he hath set himself to writing, he would join night to day; press upon himself without release, not minding it till he fainted: and when he left off, resolve himself into all sports and looseness again; that it was almost a despair to draw him to his book: but once got to it, he grew stronger and more earnest by the ease.'

Dover Wilson believes that this probably refers to Shakespeare because it so well explains the slackening off after the fierce energy of magnificent writing. It is a likely surmise about the mind and hand which raced together until both were faint with weariness. Also it fits in with John Masefield's glimpse of the 'marvellous day' which sent Macbeth to his doom in a blaze of unforgettable words.

Shakespeare's comments on the methods of a writer are few, but they suggest on the whole a fast-running pen. The familiar account of the poet's 'fine frenzy' (*A Midsummer Night's Dream*, Act V, Scene 1) is certainly not applicable to a plodder. The poet is likened to the lunatic and lover with their 'seething brains'; while his imagination 'bodies forth the form of things unknown', the frenzy of the mind's eye would not tolerate slow composition. Against this, the character called Poet in *Timon of Athens* (Act I, Scene 1, a part of the play marked with Shakespeare's style) is made to say

> *Our poesy is as a gum which oozes*
> *From whence 'tis nourisht*

which suggests a sticky and sluggish motion. But two lines later it

> *like the current flies*
> *Each bound it chafes. . . .*

The ooze has suddenly been accelerated. Stickiness returns to mind when the poet explains that his

> *Free drift*
> *Halts not particularly but moves itself*
> *In a wide sea of wax.*

A moment later the drift has soared into the sky and

Flies an eagle flight, bold and forth on.

There is some contradiction in this mixture of metaphors. The daring aerial sweep has replaced the ooze. I take the eagle's use of pinions to be the more revealing image and 'bold and forth on' the usual temper of Shakespeare at the desk.

Authors are frequently plagued with the question, 'How long did it take you to write that book?' The query is absurd unless it is applied only to hours spent with pen and paper and measured by a stop-watch. Any creative writing, of story, play, or poem, may have been long ago conceived and carried in the womb of the mind. The length of this pregnancy is often something which the parent can hardly remember. Some of Shakespeare's plays may have been as rapidly planned as penned. I cannot imagine a long gestation of *The Merry Wives* or of *The Taming of the Shrew*. But for the great tragedies I can suspect a long pre-natal growth in embryo. When I said something of this kind to J. B. Priestley, he answered that Shakespeare had been writing *Hamlet* all his life, with which I agree. It was not a long life, for the author was only thirty-six or so when he sent in the Foul Papers of that play for 'allowance' and performance. Thoughts that 'lie beyond the reaches of our souls' had come up at intervals and lingered in the recesses of the mind. But once the birth-pains were at work, the hand of 'one joining night to day' and 'not minding it till he fainted' was at liberty to speed, 'bold and forth on'. The time-sheet so important to the fellow-actors needing a play, and that promptly, has no relevance to the true natal history of a masterpiece.

CHAPTER X

In the Study

❧

DAYS OF fierce application to the desk, when the free days were there for total immersion in writing, must have stretched into the night. When *Macbeth* began to flow, one sees it in total flux, not ceasing on the midnight. The many references in the plays to the boon and balm of sleep have prompted the opinion that Shakespeare was an insomniac, vexed with a too eagerly active mind which would not cease to pulse and revolve in its own cell. He who cannot sleep may work on and on, hoping to relieve the trouble: but this attempted cure sometimes proves to be a further aggravation. 'Macbeth hath murdered sleep' could be true of Macbeth's creator. The apothecaries of the time had their remedies, the 'drowsy syrups' and the

> *Many simples operative, whose power*
> *Will close the eyes of anguish.*

It is significant that it is the Doctor in *Macbeth* who says

> *Our foster-nurse of nature is repose*
> *The which he lacks. . . .*

and then talks of the requisite medicines for the quelling of a wakeful anguish.

Prolonged night-writing had to be carried on by a light which we would think scanty and exhausting. The strain was more severe if the writer were also compelled to be a reader coping, for example, with a volume of Hall's close-printed chronicles without the benefit of a modern reading-lamp. There are several sad allusions to the dwindling oil and the guttering, inadequate candle. 'My oil-dried lamp and time-bewasted light' and 'my inch of taper' are mentioned by John of Gaunt (*Richard II*, Act II, Scene 1) as images of a sinking life, but such images can speak the author's

immediate mood of fatigue and distress. Similar exasperation may
have evoked Iachimo's

> *Base and unlustrous as the smoky light*
> *That's fed on stinking tallow.*
> (*Cymbeline*, Act I, Scene 6.)

The rich could cope with the dreariness of darkness. There was
a blaze of torches, lamps and candelabra in the halls of royalty and
of the festive noblemen when the revels were afoot. Bacon in his
essay *Of Masques and Triumphs* gives us a clear vision of the great
chamber well lit-up. 'These things are but toys,' he wrote of the
fashionable masques, 'but since princes will have such things, it is
better they should be graced with elegancy than daubed with cost.'
But cost there was and no economy on lighting in the provision of
illustrious entertainment. Bacon recommended as a source of
pleasure all manner of choir-singing 'taking the voices by catches
anthem-wise' and for great beauty as well as pleasure 'the alteration
of scenes, so it be quietly and without noise, to feed and relieve the
eye before it be full of the same object'. He added: 'Let the scenes
abound with light, specially coloured and varied.' The art of
elaborate stage-lighting was well-known to the designers and
stage-managers of the masquerades and when Shakespeare and his
colleagues could work in the covered Blackfriars Theatre they were
able to put on plays, as well as masques, with light abounding. But
as an author at the desk, particularly when young and poor, he had
no such help for the eye.

Amid this news of radiant revels we, in our age of electricity
which reaches even into remote Scottish glens, are apt to forget the
darkness of the streets and of the average Elizabethan home,
lodgings, or workshop during the murky winter days and always
in the winter evenings. The people then would have been struck
with Macbeth's special wonder by the flood-lit panorama of
London's riverside which we now enjoy. For use in the house good
candles were extremely expensive. A shilling bought only three
pounds of them and how could a Hired Man, with his actor's
weekly pay of eight shillings, afford to light properly what garret
he could rent out of that money? At the start of his Factotum career
Shakespeare, working on the early plays for a few pounds and acting
for a Hired Man's fee, must, like all the hard-driven quill-drivers of

the Henslowe management, have had his problem of domestic lighting and damned the 'unlustrous' product of the cheapest chandlery.

The countryman's wick of rush dipped in kitchen fats was a feeble defence against darkness. A Stratford boyhood gave full acquaintance with that in other people's homes, if not in his own when his father's business was flourishing and good candles could be bought. In considering the accuracy of printed texts we have to think of the printers setting the contents of long folio sheets, close-written in a possibly very difficult hand, behind small windows on a dark day or evening with only the oil-wasted lamp and stinking tallow for their assistance. That Shakespeare sometimes drove himself or was driven by his eager impetus of mind far into the night, cursing the 'inch of taper', is made the more probable by his daily occupation in the playhouse if he were caught up in morning rehearsals and afternoon performance and had to make writing his nocturnal homework.

Except when he was enjoying the comparative spaciousness of New Place at Stratford Shakespeare cannot have worked in much comfort, if in any. He was a lodger in the Bishopsgate district until 1596 or 1597, then spent some years, those of his greatest fertility of writing, on the Surrey Bankside, and then moved north to occupy a room or rooms with the tire-maker Mountjoy at the corner of Silver Street in the Cripplegate ward. The date of that move is uncertain: it may have been soon after the turn of the century. Wherever he was he could not rely upon a well-lit or a quiet life. We think of our towns of today as made intolerably noisy by the traffic. The Elizabethan and Jacobean pamphleteers had the same opinion of their own city.

In *The Seven Deadly Sins of London*, written soon after the accession of King James, Dekker gave this picture of the crowding and the din:

'In every street, carts and coaches make such a thundering as if the world ran upon wheels: at every corner, men, women and children meet in such shoals, that posts are set up of purpose to strengthen the houses, lest with jostling one another they should shoulder them down. Besides, hammers are beating in one place, tubs hooping in another, pots clinking in a third, water-tankards running at tilt in a fourth. Here are porters sweating under burdens, there merchants' men bearing bags of money. Chapman (as if they were at leap frog) skip out of one shop into another. Tradesmen (as if they were dancing galliards) are lusty at legs and never stand still. All are as busy as country attorneys at an assizes.'

Dekker may have been exaggerating, but obviously there was chaos and clatter in the streets. When Shakespeare was living in Southwark among the crowds flocking to the theatres, the Bear Garden and the grosser diversion of that fairground, there was even less peace than in the northern parts of the town.

Then there were the bells. The most popular poet of our day, John Betjeman, writes as one continually 'summoned by bells' and entranced by them. Shakespeare had other views. Dr. Caroline Spurgeon pointed out in *Shakespeare's Imagery* that 'the reverberation of chimes and ringing and tolling were continually in a Londoner's ear, for it was a city of a hundred and fourteen churches, full of towers and spires and belfries, some of which were probably always ringing.' Perhaps not 'always', but with dreadful frequency. The bells summoned people to work and their children to school. The watch rang their bells during their tramping at night. Worst of all, because of their melancholy message, were the 'passing bells', when somebody died, and the funeral bells, when they were buried. Dekker, describing the horrors of the plague epidemic of 1603 in *The Wonderful Year,* adds to 'the dismal concert' of the groans and ravings of the afflicted 'bells heavily tolling in one place and ringing out in another'.

We need not think only of the appalling and too often recurrent conditions of the plague years. The death-rate was normally high and the passing and the funeral bells were a macabre burden to Shakespeare's mind and nerves. Thrice he uses the adjective sullen of those ringings. In both his early poems he returns to this inescapable reminder of mourning which no ear could escape. In *Venus and Adonis* he wrote

> *And now his grief may be compared well*
> *To one sore sick that hears the passing bell.*

And in *Lucrece* bells sound with 'damnable iteration'.

> *For sorrow, like a heavy hanging bell,*
> *Once set on ringing, with its own weight goes.*

And constantly in the tragedies the bells are booming their intimations of morality. Even when the adjective sweet is applied by Ophelia to bells it is only to remind us of them in a jangled state, 'out of tune and harsh'. Shakespeare hated bells and one may fancy him writing Othello's

> *Silence that dreadful bell: it frights*
> *The isle from all propriety*

in a moment of exasperation endured by a lover of quiet striving to work amid the tintinnabulation of a hundred and fourteen churches. There were the time-telling bell and the midnight bell, mention of whose 'iron tongue and brazen mouth' does not suggest affection. The midnight chimes were gay in the memory of Mr. Justice Shallow with his recollecting of old frisks and capers and for Orlando parish bells which 'knoll'd to church' were part of a happy countryside. But the ubiquitous urban clang was no music to a poet devoted to the gentler harmonies. To him it was a constant nuisance, sullen as well as sepulchral, an echo of the lethal epidemics when as Ben Jonson said (*Volpone* Act III, Scene 2) the bells were in 'perpetual motion'.

The word study, meaning a reading-room and writing-room, is little used in the plays, but since the characters were so often unstudious people that is not surprising. Friar Laurence has a study attached to his cell in Verona and Prospero has a 'poor cell' with no study mentioned as a separate room. Shakespeare's Romans were better equipped in that matter. Brutus has a study in his house and so, somewhat surprisingly, has Titus Andronicus. We cannot say what sort of accommodation for writing Shakespeare was able to get in his London lodgings: he must have had some privacy assured, and Mountjoy's establishment may have been of a fair size since the demand for ladies' tires was a large one and much money was spent by the beauties and would-be beauties of the Court on these devices for elaborate dressing of the head. But, although Tennyson wrote of 'the spacious days of Queen Elizabeth' his adjective did not apply to the width of the Elizabethan streets or to the housing conditions of the ordinary citizen. Shakespeare in his various apartments would have 'room to turn round', but not much chance to accommodate what could be called a library.

A library makes only two appearances in the plays. Prospero, thanks to the charitable contrivance of Gonzalo, had been able to put on board, along with 'rich garments, linens, stuffs, and necessaries' books from his own library in Milan and on his island they proved to be 'a dukedom large enough'. For the other library we must turn again to the savage and blood-soaked Rome of Titus Andronicus who says to his son Licius

> *Come and take choice of all my library*
> *And so beguile thy sorrow.*

These early-written lines, with their characteristic cadence and melody of grief and consolation, are typical of Shakespeare at his ripest and should dispel the idea that he could not have been the architect of this juvenile Chamber of Horrors. Heminge and Condell passed the play as his and in far more passages than the one just quoted he signed it with his incomparable mark. Shakespeare took his essential books from one lodging to another as part of his 'necessaries', but a portable bookshelf could not make up a substantial library.

The books which he used have been the source of so much research and conjecture that they have created almost a library of their own. The editions of the separate plays always have a prefatory section on the old plays, chronicles, and story-books on which Shakespeare drew. When he first came to London, with the obligation to send back what money he could to his wife and three children in Stratford, he would have nothing to spend on books unless he prospered more rapidly than is known. The young author or part-author of the three *Henry VI* plays drew, we are generally told, on the *Chronicles* of Holinshed, Hall, Fabyan, Grafton, and Stow. It is surely a plausible idea that any company of actors demanding the history-plays, which were in popular demand, from their needy dramatists would have a small stock of books to make, if not a theatre-library, at least a theatre-shelf or chest. The university wits would have a book or two, unless they had pawned them, which was likely enough in the case of Robert Greene and others hard-pressed by their harassed landladies. Shakespeare, however, had a favoured position since he had a friend in the book trade and so could ignore the advice later voiced by his Polonius and 'a borrower be'. Dr. Johnson borrowed books from publishers. Why should not Shakespeare in his years of struggle?

His fellow Stratfordian Richard Field had come to London and apprenticed himself for a term of six years in 1579 to a Huguenot printer, Thomas Vautrollier. In 1587 Vautrollier died. Field married his widow Jacqueline and took over the business. We need not cynically suppose that this was no union of affection, but it was certainly also a prudent move, since only by inheritance or marriage could a newcomer enter the close corporation of master-printers. Six years later Field published the first of Shakespeare's long poems, *Venus and Adonis:* in the following year he issued *Lucrece.* By doing so he made immediate money, since both sold rapidly and had to be frequently reprinted. He also earned a posthumous place of honour in the reference-books. The friendship of the two men is attested by this collaboration. Since the printed texts are good ones it has been assumed that Shakespeare was able to revise the proofs himself. However that may be, he had a link with a man at the heart of the book trade working 'at the signe of the White Greyhound in Paule's Churchyard'. This was at the south end of an acre known as Little Britain which was the printers' quarter and the home of many hand-presses turning out prose and poetry for the increasing public of book-hungry Elizabethans. Conveniently for Shakespeare Little Britain was on the way from the northern theatres to the river and the Bankside. To have cordial acquaintance there was a great asset to a young playwright needing source-books for study in his lodgings.

Before the publication of his two long poems by Field Shakespeare had won the favour of the Earl of Southampton who accepted the dedication of both. Since an Earl would hardly prosecute a friendship by visiting the humble room of an actor-poet Shakespeare must have had the entry to Southampton House in Holborn, not far from Gray's Inn where the Earl was entered as a student of law in a community much addicted to watching the professionals act and acting for itself in amateur productions at the revels. Shakespeare and his fellows, now the Chamberlain's Men and on their way up in esteem and prosperity, played *The Comedy of Errors* at the Inn as part of the Christmas revels of 1594. In Holborn there was another valuable acquaintance for the dramatist who needed source-books for his plays. This was John Florio, who in 1591 had been appointed, or accepted, by the powerful Lord Burleigh as the tutor of his ward the Earl, then aged eighteen. Florio, then a man of thirty-seven, was the son of an Italian Protestant refugee: he had taken his degree at Magdalen College, Oxford, and had become a teacher of languages. He was later employed as tutor to the daughter of the French Ambassador. Strongly Protestant, Florio may in that quarter have been quietly useful to Burleigh's information service. His next appointment, at Southampton House, would be a shrewd move on Burleigh's part, since he would be there to watch any tendency on the part of the young Earl, a hereditary Catholic, to religious and political indiscretions and annoyance of the Queen.

Shakespeare was certain to meet Florio at Southampton House. Here was a man who, with the aid of his own personal library as well as the Earl's, could introduce him to the locality and themes of his plays set in Italy, especially the Novelle of Cinthio, Boccaccio and Bandello whence came a number of his plots. Florio could also translate what had not yet been translated into English and provide knowledge of the Italian cities and countries which was sometimes correctly used by the snapper-up of these useful trifles and sometimes not. We need not credit Shakespeare with a wide knowledge of Italian if he had Florio as a friend.

The deep reading and research which have sometimes been attributed to Shakespeare cannot have been practised when the theatres were open in London and the Factotum was busily engaged. There was, however, a good chance of leisure during the long plague epidemic which closed the theatres throughout 1593 and the early part of 1594. The Earl would take refuge in his country house at Titchfield in Hampshire with Florio attending, and it has been conjectured that Shakespeare did not go on tour as an actor all that time but was attached to this household for a period. In the dedication to *Venus and Adonis* the poet vowed to 'take advantage of all idle hours till I have honoured you with some graver labour'. This indicates a kind of leisure which he would not have in London. The promise was promptly kept with *Lucrece* whose dedication vows 'love without end', a phrase suggesting a growing and considerable familiarity. Whether the Earl and Florio brought books from London we cannot say: but Titchfield would have its own library in the manner of the time. Here were the 'idle hours' and the chance to get plays as well as poems under way. If he had Bandello as well as Brooke's English poem on *Romeus and Juliet*, Paynter's *Palace of Pleasure*, Bandello's other stories which had been translated by Sir Geoffrey Fenton, and Ovid's *Metamorphoses*, he had matter enough for poems and plays, and also a place in which to work in comfort.

The Comtesse de Chambrun, in her book *Shakespeare, a Portrait Restored,* gave special attention to the use of Florio and his books. In 1578 was printed 'Florio his firste fruites which yield familiar speech, merie proverbes, wittie sentences and golden sayings almost a perfect introduction, to the Italian and English Tongues'. This contained the observation 'We need not speak so much of love: all books are full of love, with so many authors, that it were labour lost to speak of love.' That Shakespeare drew his title for *Love's Labour's Lost* from this is probable. Florio would see to it that a man of ability read his book and also its successor: 'Second Fruits to be gathered of twelve trees of divers but delightsome tastes to the tongues of English and Italians.' In 1598 he published his English-Italian dictionary called *A World of Wordes* and subtitled as 'most copious and exact'. In 1603 came his best-known work, the translation of Montaigne's *Essays*.

That Shakespeare drew on Florio's Montaigne has long been accepted. Gonzalo's speech in *The Tempest* (Act II, Scene 1) about his ideal commonwealth is almost a transcription of a passage in Florio's version of the 'Essay on Cannibals'. The Comtesse shows at length the extent to which Shakespeare adapted Florio's own 'fruits' and his renderings of Montaigne. In the case of 'golden sentences' and 'merie proverbes' similarity does not prove copying, since the world's store of aphorisms about the truths and humours of life naturally contains repetitions, but there can be no doubt that Shakespeare had Florio often in or below the mind. Subconscious quotation is a common occurrence in the lives of writers.

A strong case is made out by the Comtesse for supposing that the pedantic schoolmaster Holofernes in *Love's Labour's Lost* was a joke at Florio's expense. The 'copious' tutor's love of alliteration and of flowers of speech can be regarded as part of the fashionable Euphuism which is mocked and renounced by Biron in the play:

Taffeta phrases, silken terms precise,
Three-piled hyperboles, spruce affectation,
Figures pedantical, these summer-flies
Have blown me full of maggot ostentation.
I do forswear them.

But the parallels between the spruce affectations and figures pedantical of Florio and Holofernes are so close that the satire seems to be aimed at a particular person and not a school of speech. Both, for example, use the adjective peregrinate for one who travels abroad. The first draft of this play, whose many cultural allusions and tricks of style distinguish it from the rest of the comedies, may have been written primarily to entertain the Southampton circle and the Gray's Inn wits. Here could be another product of the 'idle hours' of the plague years. With such an audience the skit on Florio's verbose ostentations would strike home the better. Whether the Italian had sufficient sense of humour to forgive the jest we cannot tell. Shakespeare long continued his familiarity with Florio's writings, if not with the tutor himself.

So here in Southampton's household was a man who could save Shakespeare much trouble in the choice of a suitable comic, romantic, or tragic theme with one of the Italian settings so much in vogue. If he did not visit Italy, he had Italy to talk to and consult. When a commentator announces that Shakespeare must have read this or that foreign and rare work we can reasonably have our doubts. He had the quick ear as well as the quick eye of a first-rate reporter and could pick up as much of what he wanted in a talk with the Italian tutor as he could get by laborious reading in the study.

I do not doubt that, like Hamlet, he had his 'tables' for recording the remarks of others and his own reflections.

My tables—meet it is I set it down
That one may smile and smile and be a villain.

It seems strange to us that a prince should walk about the castle with a notebook and pencil handy. Perhaps that was a habit surviving from the lecture-rooms of Wittenberg, though one cannot imagine Hamlet as a regular lecture-goer and sedulous recorder of academic instruction; perhaps, since there is generally supposed to be some self-portraiture in Hamlet's moods and thoughts, Shakespeare is reflecting a note-taking custom of his own, as he went about the town. Hamlet also talks of the 'tables of his memory' and Polonius speaks of a listener-in and recorder as one who 'played the desk and table-book'. Ulysses in *Troilus and Cressida* (Act IV, Scene 5) rails at the 'daughters of the game' who 'wide unclasp the tables of their thoughts' and so betray their wantonness to 'ticklish readers'. The shepherds and their girls in *The Winter's Tale* are purchasers of these notebooks, if only for the shopping list or for setting down the numbers of a flock, as well as buyers of printed ballads. Even the simple Mopsa is eager for printed sheets. (Here is an awkward fact for the anti-Stratfordians who tell us that Stratford and its countryside were populated by illiterate clots. Shakespeare plainly regarded a shepherd society as capable of reading and writing.) Autolycus, peddling his 'fairings' to the festive sheep-shearers, soon sold out his stock of 'trumpery' which included table-books along with ribbons, shoe-ties, and the rest. Tables were in demand as well as haberdashery.

There is no need to visualise Shakespeare, as Shaw did jestingly in *The Dark Lady of the Sonnets,* using his table-book assiduously and lifting his best lines from the conversation of others. But, since he says so much of tables in his plays, we may see him as a man with paper and pencil in his wallet and deciding, like Hamlet, when it was meet to set things down. Inside his desk at his lodgings there would be a convenient collection of these jottings.

The word desk he rarely used. Polonius, as was seen, linked it with the table-book. The only other mention of a desk in the plays is in *The Comedy of Errors* (Act IV, Scene 2). There it is not just a plain writing-table but a handsome piece of furniture which could be locked up:

> *In the desk*
> *That's covered o'er with Turkish tapestry*
> *There is a purse of ducats.*

If Shakespeare possessed an article of this substantial kind and took it with him from one lodging to another, it was useful not only to write upon but as a receptacle for his most needed and valued books as well as for his tables which, had they survived and been discovered, would now be sold in the auction-rooms for a thousand pounds an inch or line of scribble.

The playwright with a load of work on hand could save himself time and trouble by getting his plots out of other men's stories; he could also be thrifty of his toil by taking, adapting, and, in Shakespeare's case, vastly improving existing plays. Only two of his pieces, *Love's Labour's Lost* and *The Merry Wives of Windsor* were of his own invention and we are not absolutely certain about the former. The sense of property in land, material and money was strong in the Elizabethans and not least in Shakespeare himself. But in literature and drama there was a Communist attitude to available goods. A written play was there to be rewritten, as an anecdote or 'good story' is here today for anyone to retell. Now the play of the past is common property and is brought up to date with no shame at cribbing by such dramatists of high status as T. S. Eliot, Eugene O'Neill, and Jean Anouilh; to use the word cribbing is not to impugn the value of their re-interpretations of the old sagas.

We respect copyright for fifty years after an author's death. The Russian Communists have only a verbal respect for international copyright. The Elizabethans were with the Russians in their attitude to theatrical property and did not wait fifty years or even fifty months for their seizures. This was not regarded by them as a vicious practice. Printing-rights could be to some extent established by entering a book or a play at Stationer's Hall which in theory barred its theft by others. But anybody could rewrite an existing play-story himself if he got hold of it. This was a time-saver and Shakespeare, if he was to keep up with all the other claims on his attention, had to ration the hours of his writings and of his reading and research needed for historical plays. Short cuts were useful and the work of others provided them.

During the first half of the fifteen-nineties a play about Hamlet, possibly by Thomas Kyd, had proved popular. Its text has been lost and we do not know how far Shakespeare made use of it, if at all. Since here was a subject into which he flung himself with such energy and excitement that he wrote at far greater length than the playhouse usually required, we can assume that the previous piece was only used for the bare bones of the Danish Amleth story. For the boisterous comedy of *The Taming of the Shrew* he had a predecessor in *The Taming of a Shrew*. It has been suggested that 'A Shrew' was a faulty version of Shakespeare's play, but we need not here go into the problem of who used what: the essential point is that such usage was according to custom.

A clearer instance of the take-over occurred in the case of *King John*, usually assigned to 1596. An anonymous play called *The Troublesome Raigne of King John of England* had been published in two parts in 1592 and Shakespeare used it closely for the action, events, and some of the characters, including one that is almost as important as the King himself, the Bastard son of Richard Cœur de Lion, Faulconbridge. Sometimes the words were paraphrased, but Shakespeare naturally improved where he followed. Both plays contain contempt of Rome and patriotic as well as Protestant sentiments powerfully voiced. Shakespeare gave to King John the vehement defiance of the Pope in Act III, Scene 1, which is a fairly close translation of the other play's prose. 'Tell thy master', the latter makes John say to Pandulph, 'that John of England said it, that never an Italian priest of them all shall either have tythe, tole, or polling penny out of England, but as I am King, so will I reign next under God, supreme head both over spiritual and temporal; and he that contradicts me in this, I'll make him hop headless.'

Shakespeare drops the 'hop headless', but he gives us some of it nearly word for word, while lifting it with the dignity of fine rhetorical poetry:

> *Thou canst not, cardinal, devise a name*
> *So slight, unworthy, and ridiculous,*
> *To charge me to an answer, as the Pope.*

One can imagine cheers from the Protestant patriots in the audience and a muttering from the Catholics.

> *Tell him this tale, and from the mouth of England*
> *Add this much more, that no Italian priest*
> *Shall tithe or toll in our dominions:*
> *But as we, under heaven, are supreme head*
> *So under Him that great supremacy,*
> *Where we do reign, we will alone uphold*
> *Without the assistance of a mortal hand;*
> *So tell the Pope, all reverence set apart,*
> *To him and his usurped authority.*

The early play contains a passage of crude comedy in which the Bastard pillages a monastery to raise money for the King's wars. Written in rhyming doggerel, it is as rough as the comic scenes in Marlowe's *Faustus*. It is a long scene, covering four pages of text, and gave a chance to the company's comedian who could fool to the top of his bent as the Friar terrified by the Bastard's repeated threats to hang him with his own waist-cord. A nun is discovered hidden in a chest and the Bastard naturally has his fun with that piece of treasure-trove and delivers his mockery in rhyme:

What have we here, a holy nunne? so keepe me God in health,
A smooth faced nunne (for aught I know) is all the abbot's wealth.
Is this the nunries chastitie?
Beshrew me but I thinke
They go as oft to venery as niggards to their drinke.
Why paltry frier and pandar too, yee shamelesse shaven crowne,
Is this the chest that held a hoord,
*   at least a thousand pound?*
And is the hoord a holy whore?
*   Well, be the hangman nimble,*
Hee'l take the paine to pay you home,
*   and teach you to dissemble.*

The Bastard ordered both Friar and Nun to be hanged, but they apparently got off and escaped by handing over a hundred pounds sterling of church moneys. The scene is interrupted by the arrival of Peter the Prophet, selling his wisdom for cheese and bacon.

Shakespeare cut out these crudities altogether. That a man with strong Catholic opinions would have written the speech so fiercely defying the Pope and his titheing, tolling priests is unlikely. But a man of tolerance was not going to rustle up cheap and easy laughs with a caper of lecherous clergy and nuns in the sacerdotal cupboard. At a time of angry anti-Semitism in London, recently embittered by the trial and execution of the Portuguese-Jewish Doctor Lopez on a charge of trying to poison the Queen, he gave Shylock an opportunity to speak for Jews as human beings in a way that Marlowe did not in *The Jew of Malta*, written before the Lopez case. The anti-Romanism of *King John* was taken over where justifiable, and typically dropped when it became brutish and bawdy. What Shakespeare took he transmuted, touching nothing that he did not decorate.

This applies also to *The Famous Victories of Henry V Containing, the Honourable Battell of Agin-court*, an anonymous play written before 1588, since we know that Tarleton, who died in that year, appeared in it. It is a short, simple piece, all in prose. It curtails history so drastically that some of the matter of the *Henry IV* plays as well as *Henry V* is crammed into it. It has been argued by Professor Seymour Pitcher of Harpur College, State University of New York, that it was a very early piece by Shakespeare himself, written when he was twenty-two or thereabouts. If that is so—and I am not at all convinced—the young man had a lot to learn. It is worth notice that in *The Famous Victories* King Henry IV, at the point of death, says, 'I am very much given to sleep,' whereas Shakespeare gives to the King one of the most moving pictures of insomnia ever written. But the point need not be argued here. Whether Shakespeare used *The Famous Victories* or rewrote a juvenile effort he altered it out of all recognition, replacing very ordinary stuff with exceptional poetry, as was his way.

The books that he must have used for his historical plays were Edward Hall's Chronicle introduced as *The Union of the Noble and Illustrate Famelies of Lancastre and Yorke* and Ralph Holinshed's *The Chronicles of England, Scotland, and Ireland*. For the Roman plays he had North's translation of Plutarch's *Lives* which he followed very closely. Holinshed went back to very early and half-mythical events and helped Shakespeare with *Macbeth* and *King Lear*. The 1587 edition of Holinshed was at one time thought to be the principal source of the English historical plays, but Hall was much used too, despite the fact that he was a more prosy writer and more difficult to read easily and quickly. To look at one of his solid, under-paragraphed pages is no temptation to read on, and the text must have been still less tempting if it had to be scanned by 'smoky light of stinking tallow'. Hall's political preference was that of Shakespeare; he strongly championed the House of Lancaster and the Tudor succession which put an end to the anarchy and chaos of the baronial brawling of the fifteenth century and stopped the ruinous waste of massacre in civil war. Shakespeare, as a propagandist for a strong monarchy enforcing national union, was voicing the opinions of most men of his time who knew anything of the ugly, blood-soaked past from which the nation had been delivered by the victory at Bosworth Field; he was also echoing Hall.

A very interesting discovery was made by Mr. Alan Keen of a copy of the 1550 edition of Hall's *Chronicles* whose margins had been annotated in a hand of the time; the notes, which run to three thousand six hundred words, are often closely relevant to episodes which Shakespeare used in his plays on *Richard II*, *Henry IV*, and *Henry V*. The matter is fully discussed in a book called *The Annotator* by Alan Keen and Roger Lubbock. This copy of Hall was originally the property of Sir Richard Newport of Shropshire who put his name in it and the date 1565, five years before his death. It is argued, with a great deal of intricate research into the genealogies and movements of the great families of the time, that this book might have passed later into Shakespeare's hand; it is further suggested that Shakespeare himself might have been the Annotator. The handwriting has been very carefully examined and compared with the six Shakespeare signatures which are all we certainly possess of his handwriting. The ascription of 'Hand D' in the manuscript of the play on *Sir Thomas More* is not sufficiently proven to count in evidence. The specialist consulted, Mr. H. T. F. Rhodes, accepted the hand as of the right date and concluded that Shakespeare's and the annotator's lettering had significant similarities and 'indicate the probability that Shakespeare and the annotator were the same man, but do not by any means prove it'.

The pursuit of Sir Richard Newport and his kin, who included the Fittons and therefore the sisters who went to Court, Anne, known to Kempe and the Chamberlain's Men, and Mary, a strong candidate for Shakespeare's Dark Lady, makes a fascinating detective story. The securing of a final and decisive verdict is unlikely. What concerns the subject of Shakespeare at work as a writer is the great help which a well-read annotator could have given him, not only by marking and commenting on the salient passages in Hall but by delving about in other chronicles which some think Shakespeare himself consulted. There is report of such a man, a report which has been overlooked or pooh-poohed, but is of extreme interest to me because he exactly suits my idea of

Shakespeare as a hard-pressed writer who would welcome the service of one who could 'devil' for him and provide the succinct information that he needed. Reading Hall, as was said, is not an easy matter.

The title of the anonymous piece of writing in which this assistant appears, *An Essay Against Too Much Reading* is worth remarking. Writers who read too much may founder in the flood. It was published without signature in 1728. That admittedly was one hundred and twelve years after Shakespeare's death, but it was the time when the events of his life were beginning to excite the public. Rowe's edition of the plays, with his biography, had appeared in 1709 and introduced, rightly or wrongly, the deer-stealing from Sir Thomas Lucy's park at Charlecote. The curiosity was to be later met with further conjectures of a picturesque kind. Oldys added to them and in 1765 Dr. Johnson gave his authority to the story, handed on by way of Rowe and Pope, that Shakespeare had started and done well for himself by organising a service of horse-wardens for those who rode to the theatre. So the anonymous essayist comes fairly early into the supply of mingled fact and fable about what he calls Shakespeare's 'proceeding'. Of an annotator he wrote:

'I will give you a short Account of Mr. Shakespear's Proceeding; and that I had from one of his intimate Acquaintance. His being imperfect in some Things, was owing to his not being a Scholar, which obliged him to have one of those chuckle-pated Historians for his particular Associate, but could scarce speak a Word but upon that Subject; and he maintain'd him, or he might have starv'd upon his History. And when he wanted anything in his Way, as his plays were all Historical, he sent to him, and took down the Heads of what was for his Purpose in Characters, which were thirty times as quick as running to the Books to read for it: Then with his natural flowing Wit, he work'd it into all Shapes and Forms, as his beautiful Thoughts directed. The other put it into Grammar; and instead of Reading, he stuck close to Writing and Study without Book. How do you think, Reading could have assisted him in such great Thoughts? It would only have lost Time. When he found his Thoughts grow on him so fast, he could have writ for ever, had he liv'd so long.'

The essayist became tangled in his use of the word 'he', but the meaning is perfectly plain and it gives a plausible picture of the fluent Shakespeare for whom too much reading would mean too little writing.

The public has a ready appetite for stories of the bad boy, or of one reputed a bad boy, who 'makes good' and of the local lad who goes to town and conquers there. The shadow of Dick Whittington has worked its way into many a biography. Stories of this kind about Shakespeare multiplied during the eighteenth century. After the poaching and the whipping came such picturesque yarns as that of the drinking-bout at Bidford-upon-Avon which laid Shakespeare flat and gave legendary glory to the crab-tree under which he slept off the results of the carouse. (This was added to the legends in 1762.) We can easily understand why this kind of talk began and spread. But there was nothing exciting or picturesque about a writer's devil. Nobody could be less romantic to the ordinary Englishman than a book-worm. There was no saleable quality in a hungry historian who could speak of nothing else but the chronicles. Why should anybody bother to invent him?

On the other hand he would be a most serviceable fellow to have about the theatre and especially serviceable to Shakespeare who drew almost entirely on the past for his themes and, except in his Windsor comedy, left contemporary life alone. The studious one would know where to turn for the necessary facts; his needs were small and he would work for his modest keep and for the love of the job. I see the man as stage-struck as well as history-mad, delighted to be among the players and working for the up-and-coming dramatist of the day. The adjective chuckle-pated cannot have been used to suggest a stupid fellow since he was widely read and passionately a scholar. The word must be taken to mean eccentric. Here is a familiar type, unpractical, untidy, incapable of enduring and holding a workaday and routine job with regular hours, but devoted and most useful when working at his hobby. To Shakespeare, with no time for meanderings among historical authorities, he brought in summary what the Essayist called 'the heads of his purpose'. Then the 'natural flowing wit' could race on, which was 'thirty times as quick' as it would have been if he had to do his own slogging at research.

The chuckle-pate could possibly have been the annotator who made the marginal jottings in Mr. Alan Keen's copy of Hall. Whether he was that man or not, such a person would have been invaluable in and around Shakespeare's place of writing. His presence is, though anonymously, attested and his nature described with probability. If the essayist had not put the man on record, I should be glad to have invented him.

CHAPTER XI

Money Matters

During Shakespeare's lifetime, and especially during the last half of it, there was a considerable decrease in the value of money. This was a European as well as English occurrence which the economists attribute in part to the influx of gold and silver from the New World; of that and kindred treasures England's freebooting mariners had their share, to the great satisfaction of the Queen and of those who financed their voyages. The English explorers and merchant adventurers were also sailing east, to the Levant and far beyond, with frequently most rewarding results. Shakespeare's Antonio of Venice, with his trading argosies afloat, was a type whom the city and port of London were beginning to know well. But as a rule the English were more cautious than Shylock's potential victim and they split the risk by forming joint-stock companies to back their projects.

The sea-voyage projectors drew on the funds of speculators known as putters-out. They are given that name by Gonzalo in *The Tempest* a play based on an actual voyage to the Bermudas. These putters-out expected enormous profits if the luck was on their side. Gonzalo speaks of 'five for one', that is, in modern financial slang, 'a killing' of five per hundred per cent, and Ben Jonson mentions six hundred on a return 'from Venice, Paris, or some inland passage'. The danger came from the voracity of 'the sea-rats', the pirates who throve especially in the Mediterranean and Aegean Seas.

Thus Europe and its maritime nations in particular were rapidly adding to their monetary wealth with the familiar inflationary result of 'too much money chasing too few goods'. The vicious sale of monopolies by the Crown further stimulated the upward trend of prices, without an equivalent rise in wages. Sir Walter Raleigh, a successful competitor for the tin monopoly, argued that he could raise the earnings of the Cornish 'tinners' who worked in groups as 'tributers', often becoming small capitalists who took a share in the financial as well as the physical risks of shaft-sinking when the surface-tin was worked out. Whether or no Raleigh's claim of benefit to the workers was justified, the monopoly system was bound to afflict the consumer.

A monopoly in shipping sea-coal to London which had been obtained by some wealthy citizens of Newcastle produced a sharp rise in prices. During Shakespeare's lifetime the cost of fuel for the sea-coal fire in Mrs. Quickly's Dolphin-chamber, her 'snug' at the Boar's Head Tavern, had risen from four shillings a chaldron (thirty-six bushels) to nine. The price of bread varied according to the harvest and there were falls as well as rises, but the general trend was upwards. During the sixteenth century the charges for meat were more than trebled. In 1533 the prices of beef and mutton in London had been fixed by Act of Parliament at a halfpenny and three-farthings a pound. These had climbed to twopence and twopence three-farthings when Shakespeare's landladies were shopping in Bishopsgate and Southwark. It seems little enough to us, but the average London craftsman had to find a home and keep and clothe his wife and family on ten, twelve, or at the most fourteen shillings a week and keep a penny or two for a place among the groundlings if he took his pleasure at the play. The minor actors, whom he watched in lesser parts upon the stage, had even less to spend, unless they could pick up some extras by one means or another.

The social philosophy of the Middle Ages had withered away. The craft guilds were dwindling and the merchant companies were growing. The price which a man could get was supplanting the price that was fixed by authority as just and tolerable. Money was talking very loudly round the Palace of Whitehall and whispering in the suburbs where new small industries were springing up and the manufacturers were becoming their own salesmen to the great indignation of the old shopkeepers. To lend money at interest had once been called usury and had been forbidden by law. But as often happens, economic power gave its orders to political power. The law was altered. The new capitalism must have its capital; what had been stigmatised as usury was regarded as sensible and legitimate putting-out, and the ugly name of usury was reserved for extortionate rates of interest. In this connection Bacon's essay *Of Usury* throws a significant light on the change of opinion. There is the old repulsion mingled with the new acceptance.

'It appears, by the balance of commodities and discommodities of usury, two things are to be reconciled. The one, that the tooth of usury be grinded, that it bite not too much; the other, that there be left open a means to invite moneyed men to lend to the merchants, for the continuing and quickening of trade. This cannot be done, except you introduce two several sorts of usury, a less and a greater. For if you reduce usury to one low rate, it will ease the common borrower, but the merchant will be to seek for money. And it is to be noted, that the trade of merchandize, being the most lucrative, may bear usury at a good rate; other contracts not so.'

Bacon was, however, frightened of the recently arrived financiers.

'. . . Let it be no bank or common stock, but every man be master of his own money: not that I altogether mislike banks, but they will hardly be brooked, in regard of certain suspicions.'

Again he is treading cautiously. How could every man be master of his own money with the new projectors seeking loans and often profiting the lender? 'Common stock' was an essential means to the successful 'merchandising' of which Bacon approved.

It was in this atmosphere of freer trade, financial experiment, and a gradual inflation that Shakespeare and his colleagues were making their livings and driving upwards. They were not in the class of big investors; but they had to be borrowers, perhaps as individuals to buy themselves a Sharer's place in a Fellowship, certainly in common as lessees or purchasers of theatrical premises. Cuthbert Burbage has left us in no doubt about that. In his petition to the Lord Chamberlain in 1635 he mentioned 'the many hundred pounds taken up at interest' in order to build the house called The Theatre in Shoreditch in the years 1576–7 and the subsequent 'sums of money taken up at interest which lay heavy on us many years' necessary for building the Globe in 1599. The actors were used to dealing with the putters-out.

At Stratford Shakespeare had been brought up in an acquisitive and very litigious community whose investments were in land and whose frequent quarrels were over land-tenure and the recovery of loans. When he became a House-Sharer in the London theatres he was in the midst of playhouse borrowings and other mortgages; indeed no sooner had he bought the Blackfriars Gatehouse in 1613 for one hundred and forty pounds than he had to raise sixty pounds from the seller to buy a mortgage on it. He then leased it to a tenant. He was in a small way 'operating', as we say, in real estate. This does not mean that he thought excessively about his career as a man of property. He was an artist among artists, but those artists had to be projectors in their own modest way and closely watch the spendings and the earnings which their projects involved.

It is the experience of our own time that financial inflation, which is so cruel to those with fixed incomes, can be kindly to projectors and not least to the promoters of entertainment. The latter can thrive amid the partly fallacious prosperity of a seemingly affluent society. In the London of the early nineteen-sixties, a period of inflation which the Government tried in vain to check, theatre business prospered greatly while it was fighting for life in provincial towns and losing many of its battles. There were always incoming tenants for more than thirty playhouses within a square mile and the support for plays of all kinds was such that runs which used to be deemed satisfactory if they lasted for six or even four months were counted in years. This occurred despite the incessant rise in prices, with taxation more often added to than diminished, and with the cost of a stall in the West End priced at twenty, twenty-five shillings, or even more. The playgoers of the capital, largely made up of visitors to the capital, appeared to be inflation-proof.

So it was in Shakespeare's time. The Jacobean Court was even more play-loving than the Elizabethan. Command performances multiplied. The Crown set the tune of reckless spending. Any inflationary period will have its downs with its ups, its crashes of the too reckless putter-out, and its moods of despondency. But, on the whole, the arts, even those which do not cater for the widest and most shallow appetites, can flourish in a financial world of easy come and easy go. In our own years of inflation already mentioned the sale-rooms as well as the London theatres did enormous business and the prices of Old Masters of painting and of the work of some new men in fashion went soaring up to heights hitherto undreamed of.

When the King's Men, well established at the Globe, took over the Blackfriars with its comforting roof and its greater amenity and elegance, a putting-out only achieved, in the words of Cuthbert Burbage, 'with great charge and trouble', the experiment paid handsomely and there was a big advance, as much as a thousand pounds a year, on the money made on the Bankside. The audience was ready for it, with cash in hand. It was not so courageous an audience as those which had faced the great tragedies. It wanted bawdier comedies, which Fletcher was to provide, and romantic stories with more spectacle, to which Shakespeare contributed. But it was there and it paid well for what it got.

In his fascinating book called *The Great North Road*, which is not a guide-book to that great link with the north first forged by the Romans, but an imaginative excursion into English social history, Mr. Frank Morley describes 'the bad times' of James I with the dramatists despondent and box-office business falling off. In his words 'Ben Jonson, we may recall, died penniless. Shakespeare had retired from the arena very early. . . . At the age of forty-six he slipped away to Stratford. For three years or so he wrote, then wrote no more.' This can be disputed. There is no evidence of a decline in theatrical support. The fortunes of the Blackfriars indicate the reverse. Shakespeare between the years 1612 and 1616 was collaborating with Fletcher in *Henry VIII*, *The Two Noble Kinsmen* and possibly in the lost *Cardenio*. If theatrical business was in a bad way, why that urgency and success in immediately raising money to rebuild the burned-out Globe? Jonson died in poverty because he was a sturdy and quarrelsome individualist and never had the prudence to dig himself in as a Sharer in a well-established company. To be a good colleague was not his way. One can respect him for his independence, but it is misleading to generalise about the state of the theatre from his failure to see where the money lay. Shakespeare was able to slip away (incidentally he slipped back several times) because he could afford it; he was not leaving a sinking ship.

When Shakespeare came to London there must have been some years of extreme poverty unless he immediately found a patron such as the Earl of Southampton: but the winning of a wealthy friend would scarcely be immediate. We can believe, if we like, that tale of his horse-holding enterprise outside the theatres. A determined and stage-struck young man might do anything to keep alive while he forced his way in among the writers and rose in the ranks of the actors. The history of the stage is full of tough starts. If he got intermittent fees of a pound an act for contributing to the play-stock of a company and also drew the wage of a Hired Man as an actor he could hold on.

The cost of living in his youth was extremely low. We have the domestic budget of a master-baker in the year 1618 when prices had risen sharply above those current in the late fifteen-eighties. The weekly diet of the man and wife was put at five shillings each and of their children at seven shillings for three. Journeymen, apprentices, and maids each were fed at four shillings a week. Clothing of man, wife and apprentices was put at seven shillings and eightpence a week for all of them and the clothing and school-ing of three children at three shillings a week. 'Parson, Poor Rate, Scavenger, and Watch' collected a shilling a week between them. The weekly wages of a journeyman were two shillings and sixpence and of the two maids tenpence apiece, out of which, apparently, the journeymen and maids had to clothe themselves. (Their food has been allowed for.)

In Shakespeare's early working life such costs would be less by a considerable fraction than they were in 1618. So with less than ten shillings a week as a Hired Man and occasional writing fees he could find a room and victuals and pay his way. But it is hard to believe that during those years there could be anything at all sent back to Stratford for the maintenance of a wife and three children. We can make what conjectures we like about their way of life, supposing, for example, that John and Mary Shakespeare had enough confidence in their son's future as well as enough family pride to see that Mistress Anne and their grandchildren were reasonably well looked after. There is nothing unlikely in that.

As far as is known Shakespeare's first investment was to obtain his Actor's Share in the Chamberlain's Men at the end of 1593. These players were assembled from other groups about whose identity there has been much conjecture. The origins of this soon prosperous and eventually long-lived Fellowship need not concern us here. The important point is that a new company would have to acquire, either by buying from dissolving units or by fresh purchase, its stock of plays, costumes, and properties and have some working capital to meet production risks and pay the rentals of their early tenancies, since not till 1599 did the Chamberlain's

Men have a house of their own. They were briefly at Newington Butts in South London and then at the theatre and the Cross Keys Inn north of the river; later at the Swan in Southwark and the Curtain near Bishopsgate. With these charges to meet the amount of money needed was substantial. The public looked for the spectacle of rich costumes and the prices of these seem to us out of all proportion to the cost of other articles, especially housing. The twenty pounds for a cloth-of-gold cloak paid by Henslowe is a third of the price which Shakespeare paid some thirty years later for a house in the busy Blackfriars area. To become a Sharer in the new venture would need the putting-out of a fair sum.

We have no figures to indicate the value of an Actor's Share in the Chamberlain's Men at that time, but we know that a holding in the Admiral's Men changed hands for thirty-seven pounds ten shillings in 1589, for fifty pounds in 1602, and for seventy pounds in 1613. Here is further evidence of the alteration in money values during Shakespeare's lifetime and of the increased prosperity of theatrical ventures. The Chamberlain's Men were not yet established when Shakespeare joined them and he therefore may have got in, as the market says, 'on the ground floor'. But it is unlikely that he could be admitted without an investment of thirty or thirty-five pounds. It is difficult to see how he could have found that amount from his own purse at that period of his career, industrious Factotum though he had proved himself to be.

It is here that Rowe's story, 'handed down by Sir William D'Avenant', about the present of a thousand pounds by the Earl of Southampton becomes relevant. Rowe added that he would not have believed the 'singular magnificence' of this gift except for D'Avenant's report and called it 'a bounty very great and very rare at any time and almost equal to that profuse generosity the present age has shown to French Dancers and Indian Eunuchs'. Since then the size of the bounty has been generally disbelieved. Southampton was extravagant and on the edge of bankruptcy. Extravagant men are often recklessly generous to others and bankruptcy may come from bounty as well as from self-indulgence. But, even so, the sum is far beyond Shakespeare's needs, for there is no sign that he was ever prodigal. If we knock off one nought and suppose a gift of a hundred pounds that would provide Shakespeare with his Actor's Share and leave him with a useful sum in hand for his next known investment, the purchase of the big house, New Place, at Stratford in 1597.

New Place cost only sixty pounds, but it had to be furnished, perhaps sparsely at first, but not without further costs. It seems that some rebuilding or extra building had to be done since the Stratford Corporation bought some stone from the new owner for the sum of tenpence. This need not indicate only a few fragments. Stone was obviously cheap if a fine home was obtainable for sixty pounds. The transaction suggests a sale of surplus material left after the repairs had been made.

Shakespeare also made a small investment in the stocking of malt. There was then a rising market in grain of all kinds owing to a series of bad harvests. All over the country people were laying in stores and the Stratfordians were joining in this kind of speculation. Naturally this led to national discontent and the Privy Council in London ordered local justices to investigate the amounts held by the holders of stocks. This was several times done. After the wretched summer of 1595, probably described in *A Midsummer Night's Dream*,

> *The ploughman lost his sweat; and the green corn*
> *Hath rotted ere his youth attain'd a beard,*

there was a scrutiny at Stratford, but Shakespeare's name did not appear since he was not then a householder. But in 1598 he was found to have ten quarters of malt in hand. Since the total quantity of malt held in Stratford was then discovered to be six hundred and eighty-nine quarters, Shakespeare's share in this 'engrossing', as buying for a rise was called, was trifling. He had plenty to do elsewhere at the time, the beginning of his most copious spell of writing, and can have been rarely in Stratford during the first years of his possession of New Place. The purchase could have been made in his name by his wife or one of his brothers.

The investing and merchandising trend was to be seen at Stratford as elsewhere. Adrian Quiney, twice Town Bailiff, member of a family well known in the town and grandfather of Shakespeare's second and less reputable son-in-law, wrote to his son Richard, who was in London in November, 1598, suggesting that he raised money from Shakespeare to invest in the hosiery business at home. 'Knit stockings' were doing well in Evesham market. Richard

Quiney, who seems to have been a good spender, had also tried in that year to raise a loan of thirty pounds from 'his loving good friend' the poet. We do not know how these suggestions were met in either case. What is relevant is that Shakespeare, at work in London, was regarded as worth approaching in 1598 for a loan that was half the cost of New Place and also for a further amount for the Evesham speculation. So he was regarded as well set financially. It is likely that Shakespeare was reasonably shy of lending to young Quiney and had larger things in mind among the players than worrying about a share in the Avon Valley stocking-trade. But he would know about the valuable staple of the near-by Cotswolds. He had seen 'the spinsters and the knitters in the sun' who ply their crafts in his Illyria. They were visibly there in his neighbourhood to catch his eye, if not to attract his capital, on a summer day.

Demands for local taxes were not the kind of thing to which Shakespeare paid prompt and obedient attention. The collectors had to pursue and press him. But at a time when Richard Quiney thought that his fellow-townsman could be 'touched' for as much as thirty pounds he was a modestly housed lodger in London and not a substantial householder as he was at Stratford. He was assessed on goods, whatever the words may include, at five pounds in the parish of St. Helens. He did not, like Dogberry, have 'everything handsome about him'.

In 1599 came another important London investment when he took up one of ten House-keeper Shares in the new Globe Theatre. The Burbage brothers took five, Shakespeare, Heminge, Phillips, Pope, and Kempe one each. We do not know the amount of money needed for transferring the raw material of the theatre across the river from North to South London and then using it for the structure of the new playhouse, which had also to be well-equipped since this was to be an exemplary as well as a workshop of the Fellowship. After the fire which destroyed it in 1613 the second Globe was erected and furnished for about fourteen hundred pounds. The capital required for the earlier theatre was likely to be less since the players had the timber in hand and prices were lower than they were to be fifteen years later. If the putting-out was only eight hundred or a thousand pounds, Shakespeare had to find eighty or a hundred of them.

In Stratford his wife was evidently trusted in money matters, at least in small ones, since in 1601 she was acting as a warden of savings—banker would be too large a word. The will of the Shottery shepherd Thomas Whittington bequeathed 'unto the poore people of Stratford forty shillings that is in the hand of Anne Shaxspere, wyf unto Mr. Wyllyam Shaxpere'. In larger matters there was the poet's brother Gilbert to be his representative in business transactions. On May 1, 1602, there was 'sealed and delivered to Gilbert Shakespere, to the use of the within named William Shakespere' a document conveying to the latter one hundred and twenty acres of land in Old Stratford from William and John Combe. This was a large investment: the price was three hundred and twenty pounds. In September of the same year there was a small addition made to New Place by the acquisition of the copyhold of Chapel Lane Cottage with a quarter of an acre of land opposite the big house. In Shakespeare's will this was valued at fifty pounds: that was the amount left to his daughter Judith for surrendering it to her sister Susanna.

The largest of Shakespeare's local purchases was made on July 24, 1605, when he paid four hundred and forty pounds to Ralph Huband 'for his interest in a lease of tithes in Stratford, Old Stratford, Welcombe, and Bishopton'. After six years this investment was yielding him thirty-eight pounds a year, sixty pounds of gross income minus twenty pounds of rent. It proved to be a shrewd bargain since twenty years later, when the Corporation bought out Shakespeare's heirs, the valuation was ninety pounds a year. It is most unlikely that Shakespeare bothered to collect, with the aid of the law, the small debts of which two local creditors, Philip Rogers, a High Street apothecary, and Joseph Addenbroke, styled gentleman, were recalcitrant payers. If Gilbert acted for him in a large purchase, he could also look to the small defaulters. The total sum involved was only just over eight pounds.

In 1601 Shakespeare's father had died and so he inherited the family home in Henley Street, now known as the Birthplace. His mother continued to live there, presumably without rent, until her death in 1608. Then his married sister Mrs. Joan Hart was the occupant. The house was left to Mrs. Hart in his will at a nominal rent of a shilling a year. The successful poet was certainly not driving hard bargains with his family.

His two last investments were in London. On August 7, 1608, he took up one of the seven House-keeper shares in the Blackfriars Theatre. James Burbage, the father of Richard and Cuthbert, had bought this, in its early form, for six hundred pounds in 1596. When James died it was leased by Richard to Henry Evans and Nathaniel Giles who used it for the productions of the Children of the Chapel. In 1608 the King's Men took it over for their own use. In 1635 Cuthbert explained the financial history of the house, saying that it was first purchased by his father 'at extreme rates', and expensively adapted and improved. The remainder of the lease was bought back from Evans 'with our money' of which investment Shakespeare had a seventh share.

How much a Blackfriars House-keeper share originally cost is uncertain. We know that the later values fluctuated. In 1633 a Blackfriars share was worth sixty pounds and a share in both the Blackfriars and the Globe changed hands for a hundred and fifty-six pounds. But these give us no line on what happened in 1608. If Shakespeare became a House-keeper at the Globe for eighty or a hundred pounds, he might have to put out as much at the Blackfriars; possibly more, since at the opening of the Globe he was one of ten and when the later venture was founded he was one of seven.

The last of his investments has already been mentioned, the purchase of the Gatehouse in Blackfriars on March 10, 1613, for one hundred and forty pounds, with an immediate recovery of sixty pounds on a mortgage. This property he still held at his death: it was bequeathed with all his property in houses and land to his elder daughter, Susanna Hall. He had probably sold his theatre shares before he left London after his final visit, since there is no mention of them in the will. He may have transferred his Globe share when it involved further outlay for the building of the second Globe in 1614. He had put most of his money into land and tithes at Stratford. This involved him in local disputes, but it was not an investment likely to go wrong. He could spend his last years with the security of a moderately prosperous countryman.

He never put his money outside housing, land, tithe-rights, and theatre business. There were projects abounding in the London of King James, but he and his fellows stayed in the kind of finance which they understood and were not lured by the prospect of 'six for one' in a venturesome putting-out. They had the middle-class qualities of industry and common sense: there were avarice and recklessness among their wealthier patrons, but they preferred to buy a semi-rural house on the fringe of the expanding city, or a country home away from it all. In *An Historical Account of the English Stage* published in 1699, probably by the antiquary James Wright, it is said of the players of Shakespeare's time: 'All these companies got money and lived in reputation, especially those of the Blackfriars who were men of grave and sober behaviour.'

It is hard to assess Shakespeare's income during the twenty years of his growing success and of the likewise growing prosperity of the Fellowship. There are many elusive points to consider. The size of the Earl of Southampton's early gift is a difficulty. The receipts of an Actor-Sharer were bound to fluctuate: years of inhibition by the plague meant touring. This was generally ill rewarded, but it served to keep the company together and yielded fees enough for bed and board. Nor do we know how much the Globe was used in winter and the Blackfriars in the heat of summer. Further, there is no reliable information about the money which Shakespeare drew for his plays. It has been surmised that, when he did less acting or possibly none at all, he drew his Actor-Sharer's takings on the condition that he supplied a sufficient succession of plays, and supervised their production, but not at the early pace of two or even three a year. During the five years between 1607 and 1611 the whole output, according to the usual dating of the plays, was five or six. In the last five years of his life there was contributory work in assisting Fletcher and certainly a major, if not a sole, hand in *Henry VIII*.

The statement in the notebooks of the Rev. John Ward, Vicar of Stratford from 1662 to 1681, that Shakespeare 'supplied the stage with two plays every year after retiring to Stratford' is plainly wrong, but not so far wrong as the further announcement that 'he had an allowance so large that he spent at the rate of one thousand pounds a year, as I have heard'. The Vicar, who frankly confessed ignorance of the plays written by the great man buried in his church, had been listening to nonsense. A thousand pounds would be the equivalent of ten or even twenty thousand today. Sir Edmund Chambers, most careful and thorough of investigators, radically cut down the estimate of Sir Sidney Lee that Shakespeare drew one hundred and fifty pounds a year as a House-keeper from both the Globe and the Blackfriars and then had Actor-Sharer takings as well. The problem is so tangled by our ignorance as to Shakespeare's authorship fees and the possible sharing of the extra money paid for Command performances that we must abandon any attempt at accurate accounting.

My own guess, after reading most of the calculations, is that his London receipts over most of his life varied from two hundred to three hundred pounds a year according to the fortunes of the Fellowship, in addition to which there was the income from his Stratford investments as he enlarged them. That was plenty in those years for a man not socially ambitious.

In short, he was a citizen in good standing and 'comfortably off' as we say. With the exception of the Southampton gift he had worked for every penny of it and that gift may have been partly a payment for tutorship.

Shakespeare was one of the class about whom he preferred not to write. His rivals, with their eye on the town round about them, were eagerly concerned with the jollity of craftsmen's holidays and the acquisitive society of the putters-out. Ben Jonson in his later plays made the new projector one of his favourite targets. It is not difficult to satirise the ugliness and to ridicule the absurdities of greed and the writer who is himself poor, as Jonson was, takes most delight in this. Perhaps Shakespeare, though never in the big projector class, had enough sympathy with those who could look after themselves to leave them alone, preferring themes of far away and long ago. He limited his laughter at contemporary follies and types to the mockery of an occasional precious fop, such as Osric and Le Beau, and to deriding an affected way of speech and Frenchified vocabulary.

Yet he could, in the sweep of his imaginings which transcended thrifty habits, sympathise with the profligate extravagance which showed a reckless audacity. To Antony, whose careless bounty had no limits as he let kingdoms fall like plates from his pocket, he was generous in portraiture. There is nothing strange in being fascinated by qualities not one's own. The view that gambling is only contemptible when carried on within one's means is one that Shakespeare, an investor not a speculator, could have held. Means was a word unknown in the vocabulary of Antony as he pursued his personal passion and his gigantic political ends, a madness with no method in it, fantastic and picturesque in its bravado. The dramatist who made this dance to ruin immortal could be seized by the size and splendour of the Roman's temerity while he himself was adding acre to acre.

His imagination was not bounded by the nutshell of a small-town life as, with a squirrel's care, he provided for the winter of his life. He could take a just pride in the phrasing of his will:

'all that capital messuage or tenement with the appurtenances, in Stratford aforesaid, called the New Place, wherein I now dwell; and two messuages or tenements with the appurtenances, situate, lying, and being in Henley Street, within the borough of Stratford aforesaid; and all my barns, stables, orchards, gardens, lands, tenements, and hereditaments whatsoever, situate, lying, and being, or to be had, received, perceived, or taken, within the towns, hamlets, villages, fields, and grounds of Stratford-upon-Avon, Old Stratford, Bishopton, and Welcombe, or in any of them in the said county of Warwick. And also all the messuage or tenement, with the appurtenances, wherein one John Robinson dwelleth, situate, lying, and being in the Blackfriars, in London, near the Wardrobe; and all my other lands, tenements, and hereditaments whatsoever.'

The last sentence refers to nothing known but it is there for a fully inclusive legality. The man of property speaks to his own; yet we may note almost an echo of Antony's eloquence when he read Caesar's will in the Forum:

> He hath left you all his walks,
> His private arbours and new-planted orchards.

Here is the testament of the Stratford citizen, glowing with the modest splendour of a bourgeois pride.

To say that is to shock those who take a romantic view of poets and think that all of that profession must be Byronic or Shelleyan, rakish, spendthrift, or rebellious. When Bernard Shaw drew the unworldly poet Marchbanks in *Candida* he had, as he told me, Shelley in mind. Others may discover their favourite image of a poet in William Blake who saw angels in his London garden or in the company of alcoholics who have found solace and inspiration in a bottle. But many of the greatest in the arts have been none the worse in craft because they knew how to look after a contract and provide for the morrow. That the great writer can be a good business man has been abundantly proved, by Shaw not least. Not to be a fool in money matters does not prove a man to be a dull dog.

So this picture of a provident Shakespeare, which is attested by the known facts of his career, need not make him a drab figure. He retired to Stratford with his mind his kingdom as well as money in his purse. There are no better enemies of boredom than imagination and a sense of wonder and they were there to carry him far beyond the company of the shop-keepers and the cultivation of a garden. There is no need to think of him as smug because he was happy enough with his tithes and acres. He had worked hard and loyally with his fellows in the playhouse round, but he had had his random doubts about the actors' way of life. Members of a profession make high talk about the nobility of their callings at banquets and in public speeches. But they have their misgivings and Shakespeare had deplored the quality of the player in the privacy of sonnet-making. The occasional pangs of distaste, even shame, for the motley were felt when he was in lordly company. Few are wholly innocent of some snobbery, be it of rank or intellect. But obviously these moods passed. Back in the theatre there was work to be done, successes achieved, friendships to renew, and the 'shop' to talk; and few are happier talking 'shop' than theatre folk.

There was a background of the black despondencies as well as of the gleaming moment. It was impossible that he should forget the angers and despairs that had gone to the making of the dark comedies and to the savage pessimism of the tragedies. He had seen and known the failings of the spirit and the lusts of the flesh, especially amid the spreading corruption of the Jacobean Court where robes and furred gowns did not hide all. But the memories were mingled. He had walked amid happy hours. He had used in his Stratford youth and he could use again the sharpest of eyes for all the detail as well as the whole sweep of the world's beauty. Tiny things delighted him, the tender horns of a snail or the drops on the petal of a cowslip. Because he took a normal pleasure in his barns and fields he was conforming to the Stratford way of life, as he had conformed to the discipline and drudgery of a theatre Factotum. But for larger happiness he had his major wealth, his pen, his imagination, and his sense of wonder. Above all, he could still do what dull men cannot; he could laugh.

CHAPTER XII

Medical Report

THERE CAN be little doubt that Shakespeare began his life as a fairly strong and healthy boy. The world into which he was born was no place for weaklings. Parents of a large family did not expect to keep all its members. Before the birth of their first son, William, John and Mary Shakespeare had lost two girls in infancy. Though William died at fifty-two, only one of the young Shakespeares of Henley Street lived longer than he did; that was his sister Joan, later Mrs. Hart, who reached the age of seventy-seven. His brothers Gilbert and Richard, who probably stayed on in Stratford during most of their time, died at forty-seven and thirty-eight. The youngest, Edmund, who followed William's example and went to be a player in London, died there at the end of 1607, aged twenty-seven.

The idea that William was lame, either from childhood or because of some later accident, has been based on the lines in Sonnet 37:

> *As a decrepit father takes delight*
> *To see his active child do deeds of youth,*
> *So I, made lame by Fortune's dearest spite,*
> *Take all my comfort of thy worth and truth.*

But it is likely that the adjective lame is here used metaphorically, since the lameness mentioned is not contrasted with the faultless physique of the sonnet's recipient but with his beauty, birth, wealth, and wit. The poet is surely referring to his own lack of money and rank compared with the status and affluence of the man addressed. To complain about having to earn a living as a player instead of being able to lord it in one of the 'Lords' boxes' at the theatre may strike us as an unlikeable form of humility. But this kind of deprivation is the most plausible explanation of the lameness for which fortune's spite is blamed.

If Shakespeare had any serious deficiency of the leg or foot the actor's career would have been a most unsuitable one to choose. All that we know of the players' training demanded some ability to dance as well as endurance and agility in meeting the demands of stage-combat. In all that was related or handed down about Shakespeare's person there is no suggestion of a crippled or even of a limping man. The tradition that came to John Aubrey by way of the Beestons described 'a handsome, well-shapt man'. If he 'played kingly parts in sport', he would have to be of good carriage; the part of the limping Richard III was, we know, taken by Burbage. The old man Adam in *As You Like It* could have been played as lame, but not the Ghost in *Hamlet* assuming that Shakespeare did indeed take these assignments. It was a time of 'strutting' not of limping actors and the Ghost would be a strutter indeed, were it played in the way expected. If the poaching episode in Shakespeare's youth be credited, a lame man would be most unlikely to go out on risky ventures with a bolt for escape to be made in case of detection. The question put by Demetrius in *Titus Andronicus*

What, hast thou not full often struck a doe
And borne her cleanly by the keeper's nose?

suggests that a poacher was a reasonably nimble and athletic young man, fit for the sonnet's 'deeds of youth'. There is cause enough to discount a physical handicap in the use of the word lame.

Shakespeare survived epidemics of plague three times in his life. The first was in infancy. The pestilence fell upon Stratford-upon-Avon in July, 1564, three months after his birth. It was a dreadful visitation, worse for the poorer and more crowded families but falling severely also on those better off. It was a busy time in the graveyard beside the river. In the first half of the year there had been twenty-two burials in Stratford: in the second there were two hundred and thirty-seven. This was decimation in the full sense of that loosely used word, for the total population of the town at the time was about ten times that number.

Since Shakespeare's parents had already lost two daughters in infancy, anxiety for the male baby and only surviving child must have been acute. But a fortunate family could escape to the country near by. His mother's home was at Wilmcote, three miles to the north-west of Stratford, and this offered a likely retreat. There was plague again at Stratford early in 1597, but it was a much smaller epidemic and did not prevent the poet's purchase of New Place in May of the same year. The players in London suffered heavily in finance from the recurrent plague years, but their casualties were light compared with those of the general population. A William Kemp was buried at St. Saviour's in Southwark in the plague-stricken year of 1603 and he may have been the clown who had left the Chàmberlain's Men four years earlier, since there is no subsequent mention of his career. But otherwise the members of the Fellowship, by leaving London as soon as the theatres were closed, escaped. But they knew all about the peril and the danger of infection by breath as well as by contact. One treatment of the buboes was to place a live pigeon with its fundament naked to the sore and then replace it with another when the first died. This was supposed to extract the venom from the patient's blood: not surprisingly recovery was rare.

Modern destruction of vermin has been a serviceable factor in diminution of plague risk and now we have vaccines as prophylactics with streptomycin and the sulphonamides to provide remedial treatment of a power hitherto unknown. The Elizabethans were well aware of the deadly power of infection conveyed not only by personal contact but carried through the atmosphere. In *The Winter's Tale* Leontes prays to the blessed gods 'to purge all infection from the air' while Florizel is at his palace in Sicily. Caius Marcius in *Coriolanus* thus pours his curses on the retreating Roman troops:

> *Boils and plagues*
> *Plaster you o'er, that you may be abhorred*
> *Further than, seen and one infect another*
> *Against the wind a mile!*

Compulsory isolation of possibly infected persons was understood. The tragedy of Romeo's detention in Mantua was due to a prudent sanitary precaution. Friar John relates how

> *The searchers of the town,*
> *Suspecting that we both were in a house*
> *Where the infectious pestilence did reign*
> *Seal'd up the doors and would not let us forth.*

To the lovers the pestilence was indirectly fatal.

Furthermore Shakespeare knew that the infection was carried by mouth. Says Benedick of Beatrice in *Much Ado About Nothing:* 'She speaks poniards and every word stabs: if her breath were as terrible as her terminations, there were no living near her; she would infect the north star.' Accordingly it seems that the Elizabethans had an inkling of the germ theory of disease, but they did not use the word germ in that brief form. To Shakespeare the germin or germen—he used the term twice—was the source of growth, the seed, either vegetable or human. As a micro-organism or microbe the germ, as an agent of destruction, reached the vocabulary of medicine only in the nineteenth century. Bacilli and microbes achieved professional usage and dictionary status in the eighteen-eighties. Yet the plague-stricken world of Elizabeth and James had an instinctive feeling that, while contact was a dangerous carrier of the affliction, the mouth, even without kissing, could be a no less deadly agent. In *Timon of Athens* the raging misanthrope, calling 'plagues incident to men' to heap on his now hated city, cries 'Breath infect breath!' The word infection is common in Shakespeare's vocabulary and it is linked with breathing. The 'sowing' of infection in this way is regarded with fear and horror.

When Shakespeare used the word pox he may have been referring to smallpox as well as to venereal disease. The term 'small pokkes' first appeared in 1518 and there was a treatise on it published in 1593. Smallpox afflicted Elizabethan society from the highest to the lowest and its lurking presence must have been taken for granted, for there was evidently much less fear of it than of the plague.

Ill-health caused by decayed teeth and poisoning of the gums must have been general; the rank breath of the multitude was noted and loathed by Shakespeare. But halitosis and body odours were not restricted to the mob. Bacon recommended: 'sweet odours, suddenly coming forth, without any drops falling, are, in such a company as there is steam and heat, things of great pleasure and refreshment.' He was not writing of the populace but of the aristocratic revellers at a masque, who on a hot night 'steamed'.

Teeth were not wholly neglected. Andrew Boorde, who published a *Dyetary of Health* in 1542, recommended that teeth, as well as face and hands, should be washed daily in cold water, and the use of the tooth-pick was known and advised. Tooth-picking is three times mentioned in the plays: the Bastard in *King John* makes it part of the traveller's equipment. But with no regular dentistry the amount of pain and pyorrhoea must have been widespread and severe. When the victim was 'troubled with a raging tooth' there was nothing for it but extraction, for which a visit to the barber was the custom. The pain of an extraction could be modified. An 'outlandish physician' called Fenatus recommended a species of anodyne to Queen Elizabeth when she was terrified at the prospect of a tooth-pulling. The suggested method was to cover or fill the 'pugging tooth', as Autolycus described it in *The Winter's Tale*, by waxing fenugreek over it. This was a leguminous plant which was expected to have a loosening effect and so would enable the tooth to be removed later by a nip of the fingers, which would not hurt so much. But meanwhile the tooth pugged.

Shakespeare used the word tooth-ache five times in his plays and it is a curious fact that four of these mentions occur in one of them, *Much Ado About Nothing*. When Benedick complains of this affliction he is told to have the tooth drawn; there is no question of another remedy and no suggestion of alleviation by fenugreek. Towards the end of the piece Leonato says:

> For there was never yet philosopher
> That could endure the tooth-ache patiently,
> However they have writ the style of gods.

This return to the grievous subject (by one who himself could write 'the style of gods', at least in one sense) suggests that when this piece was being written the author was himself a sufferer. It is indicated by Jaques in his well-known address on the physical rise and fall in the stages of man's life that the very old could expect to be toothless as well as sightless.

Such larger nuisances as boils, carbuncles, and ulcers are frequently in mind. *Hamlet* is full of images drawn from disease. Was there some 'hectic in the blood' when he wrote it? Affections of the skin make frequent appearance. Shakespeare seems to have used tetter as a general term, like our dermatitis. He also twice expressly mentions serpigo, 'a medical term for creeping or spreading skin-diseases, especially ring-worm'. In *Timon of Athens* we find itches, blains, 'hoar leprosy' and ulcerous sores along with the 'potent and infectious fevers' which are 'plagues incident to men'. Scurvy is used frequently as an adjective of contempt and abuse, but not as a noun naming a particular tetter. But this was one of the greatest physical curses of the time.

It was caused by deficiency of vitamin C. The dietary of the age lacked the variety of fruit and vegetables that we possess to our great advantage. When the autumn fruit was finished there could be no opening of tins. What the sailors had long to endure at sea, until the value of limes was realised, even the inhabitants of the big house were suffering on land. It was of a much later period than Shakespeare's that G. M. Trevelyan wrote: 'Now for the first time since mankind took to farming the wholesale slaughter of stock at the end of Autumn ceased. Salted meat was replaced by fresh beef, mutton and other products. The immediate result was that scurvy and skin diseases which had afflicted the noblest families grew rare even among the poor.'

That Shakespeare, when in his later years he visited or settled at Stratford, discussed medical matters with his son-in-law, Dr. John Hall, is probable enough. The doctor was a graduate of Queens' College, Cambridge. He went to study in France, probably Montpellier, towards the end of the sixteenth century, returned to England in 1600 and settled at Stratford in the fine house which is now known (and open to the public) as Hall's Croft. There he built up a large and far-flung practice which included many titled folk. This we know from his clinical notes, which he wrote in Latin. Unfortunately only half of these were preserved. They were edited and put into English for common benefit by Dr. James Cooke of Warwick, who described himself as Practitioner in Physick and Chirurgery. They were published in 1657 under the title of *Select Observations on English Bodies or Cures both Empericall and Historicall, performed on very eminent Persons in desperate Diseases.* (Many of these exalted patients were scorbutic sufferers.) The book proved popular and was twice reprinted.

The ingredients of some of Doctor Hall's prescriptions are terrifying; not hesitating to be drastic, he applied what are called 'blunderbuss' cures. These were fired with some violence into the stomach and through the entrails. They caused purging and vomiting without stint. Thus he claimed to have cured the Countess of Northampton's dropsy in 1620 by ensuring forty-one 'stooles' in three days with a decoction containing twenty-eight herbs and drugs. He also cured with a prescription of seventeen herbs Mrs.

Wagstaff of Warwick. Aged forty-six, she was afflicted with 'hypochondriack melancholy, scurvy, beating of the heart, pain in the head and joints, opthalmia, vertigo, morphew and livid and purple spots'. (Morphew is 'a scurfy eruption'.) The body was 'righly purged', but the bombardment by blunderbuss was not so drastic as in the case of the Countess. But the effect was salutary. Presumably the pills were able to purge Mrs. Wagstaff's melancholy, for which her other ailments gave ample reason before the Doctor got to work.

Hall married Shakespeare's daughter, Susanna, in 1607, and was a close neighbour of his father-in-law when Shakespeare was at New Place. If we get a glimpse of the son-in-law in the physician Cerimon in *Pericles, Prince of Tyre,* a play written by, or adapted and added to, by Shakespeare about the time of Hall's marriage into the family, it is certainly a complimentary portrait of one who knew well

> *the blest infusions*
> *That dwell in vegetives, metals, stones.*

Cerimon describes himself as happy in his work and speaks of his skill in cures

> *which doth give me*
> *A more content in course of true delight*
> *Than to be thirsty after tottering honour,*
> *Or tie my treasure up in silken bags,*
> *To please the fool and death.*

These lines are signed with Shakespeare's style and they are both a memorable tribute to a devoted doctor in the play and a hint that the son-in-law was a happy, as well as a diligent, practitioner. It is made plain in the *Select Observations* that Dr. Hall was an expert in the uses of herbs, especially as remedies for skin troubles.

An exhausted brain-worker may be afflicted with these and Shakespeare had to nourish himself, in or out of Stratford, with the same diet that was having a general scorbutic effect. The many references to tetters of one kind or another suggest that he did have trouble of that kind. If so, he was, when at Stratford, in as good hands as the place and time possessed. Hall was on the watch for scurvy to such an extent that he was regarded as a skin-crank.

Dr. Cooke in his preface to the *Observations* remarked: 'It seems that the Author had the happiness (if I may so style it) to lead the way to that practice, almost generally used by the most knowing, of mixing Scorbuticks in most remedies. It was then, and I know for some time after, thought most strange, that it was cast as a reproach upon him by those most famous in his profession.'

It would not be surprising if, when he had completed his major tragedies, Shakespeare was a victim of exhaustion. A play which strongly indicates this is *Timon of Athens,* usually assigned to the year 1608. The patchy quality of its writing has led many to see the presence of 'another hand'. It has been supposed either that Shakespeare took up a minor colleague's feeble effort and poured his own genius into a weak vessel or that Shakespeare was too tired or too bored to finish effectively the work that he had begun and so let another take over and prepare it for stage-usage. (There is no evidence that it ever reached the stage.) Another view is that all the text is Shakespeare's, but that he lost heart and so only etched in a conclusion to which he never returned for the finishing touch.

It is essential, in my belief, for any consideration of Shakespeare's mental and physical condition that *Timon of Athens* should be carefully read. (The chances of seeing it in the theatre are small.) It tells the story of a rich Athenian who cossets his vanity by immense liberality. He gives away his great wealth with fantastic bounty, patronising the arts with a lavish hand as well as giving money to all who ask it and entertaining with the utmost extravagance. Inevitably he runs out of money and, when he looks round for help, his recent beneficiaries give him a very cold shoulder. Their meanness is in direct proportion to Timon's overflowing generosity.

The penniless Timon then retires to the woods and feeds on roots and berries while raging against mankind. The ferocity of his long-continued curses and condemnation is extreme. His real grievance is ingratitude, but he goes on to denounce all the sins of the flesh with a comprehensive fury. The play fails as a play, at least in the opinion of many of its students and critics, because it tends to become a Timonian soliloquy. Middleton Murry in his valuable book on *Shakespeare* called it 'almost incoherent in its savagery'.

It is true that Timon has visitors in his retreat to create a conflict;

but, apart from Apemantus, they are inconsiderable. The only spokesman for normal decency is the Steward and Shakespeare gave him a trivial part. Apemantus is a cynic philosopher of a churlish kind who is on Timon's side in detestation of mankind: they snarl at each other, but both snarl at the world and there is no real contrast of philosophies. Alcibiades, another man with a grievance against Athens and ready to destroy it in his anger, arrives accompanied by two of his mistresses: these wantons have nothing to do with Timon's story, but they give the misanthrope an opportunity to be misogynist also and to rail against the tyranny of the flesh. At last Timon dies off stage, presumably of mental and physical collapse combined. His last speech, announcing that he has arranged his sepulchre which is to be

> *An everlasting mansion*
> *Upon the beached verge of the salt flood*

has the true Shakespearian ring as well as the full Timonian pessimism in the conclusion:

> *Graves only be men's works and death their gain.*

Could despair of life go further than in a previous saying of Timon's as he resigns himself to death?

> *My long sickness*
> *Of health and living now begins to mend*
> *And nothing brings me all things.*

This is the quintessence of nihilism. To live is to be diseased: only by ceasing to live can we be cured. This statement of defeat and despair is the more impressive since it is so simply and concisely phrased.

There seems to be more than fatigue in the slack handling of a piece which, despite its display of tremendous and breath-taking power, has come to us in a careless, untidy form. I cannot avoid imagining a nervous and mental strain verging on psycho-physical collapse. How long and how grievous was this sense of life's futility it is impossible to say. There cannot have been a lengthy neurosis, because the poet had found the anodyne in renewed and happier work within a year or so. The theatre and the King's Men had to be served and the challenge was met.

To make this suggestion is to be in the company of the most respected authorities. Sir Edmund Chambers, not one to be accused of rash and airy suppositions, wrote: 'It is perhaps a subjective view that he dealt with it (*Timon of Athens*) under conditions of mental and perhaps bodily stress, which led to a breakdown.' Breakdown is not a clear-cut term; it can mean much or little, but it is a strong word for so cautious a writer as Chambers to use. Dover Wilson went further in the chapter called 'The Razor-Edge' in his *The Essential Shakespeare* a book which managed to say in small space far more than many have said in voluminous form. Just before and during the first decade of the seventeenth century came 'the bitter comedies' concerning which Dover Wilson wrote: 'the note of them all is disillusionment and cynicism, the air is cheerless and often unwholesome, the wit mirthless, the bad characters contemptible or detestable, the good ones unattractive.' There followed the tragedies of 1601 to 1608 and then 'the path he treads during those eight years may be likened to a mountain tract which, rising gently from the plain, grows ever narrower, until at the climax of the ascent it dwindles to the thinnest razor-edge, a glacial arête, with the abyss on either hand'. The abyss is what Chambers gently called the breakdown.

The picture accordingly is of the 'handsome, well-shap't' young man coming to London with enough energy, as well as brains, to work his way up in the strenuous conditions of a Factotum's life with the players. He had to work in a London where sanitation did not exist, where housekeepers got their scanty supplies of water from the local 'conduit' that drew on the Thames or a well which might be polluted. People either fetched it themselves or paid a Cob or carrier. Smallpox was endemic striking even at the highest in the land. Plague was epidemic and 'tetters' were all in the day's diet. Venereal disease was rampant. Shakespeare makes ugly play with this kind of pox in the brothel scenes of two plays and harps on it in *Timon of Athens* whose plot gives no excuse for dragging it in. There is precise reference there to the supposed remedies, especially the bath in which the patient was exposed to cinnabar fumes in a 'sweating-house', the treatment described by Pistol as the 'powdering tub of infamy'.

This provides no adequate reason to suppose, as some have done, that Shakespeare was himself a victim, infected by his Dark Lady.

The practices and sights of the town could evoke his violent fits of sex-loathing. He had to see every day the physical traces of one pox or another since the Bankside was the workshop of the prostitutes as well as of the players. To a man repelled by dirt and smells London must have seemed at times to be a lazar-house despite its vitality and the general relish of beauty in music, words and spectacle. Observant of everything Shakespeare was faced with continual examples of defacement and suffering among the passing crowds. In Timon's railings the symptoms of syphilis are mentioned in detail down to collapse of the nose and corruption of the bones.

Shakespeare had a comprehensive vocabulary of physical horrors:

'Now, the rotten diseases of the south, the guts-griping, ruptures, catarrhs, loads o' gravel i' the back, lethargies, cold palsies, raw eyes, dirt-rotten livers, wheezing lungs, bladders full of imposthume, sciatics, lime-kilns i' the palm, incurable bone-ache, and the rivelled fee-simple of the tetter, take and take again such preposterous discoveries!' (*Troilus and Cressida* Act V, Scene 1.)

According to a famous surgeon Mr. Alban Doran, who contributed the medical section to the composite volumes on *Shakespeare's England:* 'The names of the diseases in modern language would be syphillis, colic, hernias, catarrhs, pain in the loins ascribed rightly or wrongly to gravel or stone in the kidneys, apoplectic stroke with unconsciousness, permanent paralysis of the limbs, chronic inflammation of the lids with inverted lashes, obscure diseases ascribed to the liver, asthma, chronic cystitis, lumbago or sciatica (possibly a euphemism), psoriasis of the palm, bone-ache from any cause, and chronic ringworm'. It is a frightening catalogue compiled by a man who was appalled by the squalid side of illness.

I have suggested some nuisance from the common 'tetter' of a scurvy-ridden epoch and a serious degree of acute and even manic depression between the writing of the great tragedies and the romantic escape-plays of the final period. (In the case of *The Winter's Tale* there is a return to sex-loathing in the unsparing description by Leontes of our 'bawdy planet' savaged with lust, where 'physic for't, there's none'.) The inner conflict of a man both sensitive and sensual, to whom a Dark Lady could bring alternate ecstasy and torment, had been endured and was at last resolved. 'The labour we delight in physics pain.' His work was his refuge, whether in Stratford or London, and in his last years he was evidently no invalid until the lethal collapse in the spring of 1616.

CHAPTER XIII
The Last Years of Work

OF THE final phase of Shakespeare's life, that is to say the years from 1611 to 1616, we have enough information to form a plausible view of the ways in which his time was spent. He was by no means idle. He still had some writing to do as a collaborator and probably as a major hand in the play of *Henry VIII*. The return to Stratford was varied with regular visits to London. He was there on business of one kind or another in 1613, 1614, and 1615. Life at home was warmed by friendships and spiced by the contentions of a small-town community. There was usually a local lawsuit to cause discussion and create some enjoyable excitement among the shop-keepers and farmers in whom the sense of property and its defensible rights was strong. Duelling had declined as a manner of settling disputes; litigation was its popular successor and to be a lawyer in the countryside was to be kept in good practice. Shakespeare laughed at lawyers in his plays, but his writing is full of their language. He had his friends among them and not in his own town only: it was Francis Collins of Warwick who drew up and witnessed the will in which he was also a legatee.

A man with Shakespeare's vision could not be the yawning victim of a tedious retirement. Did Stratford seem petty and sluggish after the bustle of the Bankside, the splendours of Court patronage, and the challenge of pleasing royalty at a command performance and the public at the pay-boxes of the Globe and Blackfriars? If so, there were ample compensations in the local laughter which a man so observant of his fellows could share as a connoisseur of all absurdities to be seen among the humours of mankind. He was never to write comedy again with the abounding gusto of a dozen and fifteen years ago; but mirth made some return. New Place was not a 'Timoneum', as Cleopatra's Antony had actually called his place of embittered retreat.

Though he did not follow in his father's steps by taking a share in the official duties of local government, he knew all about the proceedings of the Borough Council. Two doors away from him at New Place lived Julyne Shaw, a general merchant. He was elected a Burgess in 1603 and later, like John Shakespeare, he became the Chamberlain and keeper of the 'Accompt', chosen for 'honesty, fidelity, and good opinion'. That Shaw was a companion as well as a neighbour is shown by his witnessing the poet's will. Another locally important neighbour, and a source of general laughter, was the self-important ex-schoolmaster, Alexander Aspinall who came to Stratford in 1582 and stayed for over forty years. He was forbidden to 'keep school' in the Chapel of the Guild and so may have found his way into *Twelfth Night* as 'a pedant that keeps a school in a church', a remark of Maria's which has no apparent relevance to life in Illyria. Aspinall had the pomposity of Malvolio and because of his pretentions and his Christian name of Alexander he was nicknamed 'Great Philip of Macedon'. He can also be considered a rival or joint claimant with Florio as a character on whom the pedant Holofernes in *Love's Labour's Lost* was based. (It is possible for an author to combine two types in one portrait.) After retirement from teaching Aspinall became Deputy Town Clerk and was renowned for his formalism and verbosity in the composition of a statement. Here was an abiding cause for amusement for the owner of New Place who, if he did not share in the labours of the Council, could say with his own Romeo:

'I'll be a candle-holder and look on.'

There were affairs, too, in which he could be active as well as observant.

In 1611 'Mr. William Shakespeare, gentleman' joined others in bringing a bill of complaint against William Combe of College House for failure to pay his share of the rent due on the Stratford tithes. In September of that year Shakespeare contributed 'towardes the charge of prosecutyng the bill in Parliament for the better Repayre of highe wayes'. As a traveller to and from London he had good reason to be anxious about this. Country lanes had been added to the ancient Roman roads and bridges had here and there replaced fords. Stratford, thanks to the road-crossing of the Avon handsomely rebuilt by Sir Hugh Clopton and still surviving, could have been renamed Stratbridge. But the roads themselves were untended and dangerously rough in winter. Milton wrote a generation later on that season:

Now that the fields are dank and ways be mire.

Even in London the main thoroughfare from the City to Whitehall, La Straunde, our Strand, was so full of holes that it was a continual scandal and caused those who could travel by river to do so and avoid a miry tumble. Naturally Shakespeare would be active in such a cause. For he had the long journey to the capital still several times to make.

In 1612 he had had another experience of the journey since he went to London to make and sign his deposition in the Belott-Mountjoy lawsuit. Shakespeare was described in the legal papers as living in Stratford, which is useful evidence of his retirement from London residence and playhouse routine. Eight years before, he had lodged in the Cripplegate Ward with Christopher Mountjoy, a Huguenot craftsman who specialised in ladies' 'tires', which were elaborate frames for dressing the head. There was trouble in the family. Stephen Belott, the tire-maker's apprentice, had married his master's daughter Mary in 1604. Eight years later he was accusing Mountjoy of failing to hand over the promised dowry of sixty pounds together with certain household stuff; there was a further charge of omitting to include a promised bequest of two hundred pounds in his will.

It was alleged that the 'Mr. Shakespeare that lay in the house' had persuaded Belott to make the match. Shakespeare was not a wholly effective witness, since he could not recollect the sums involved or the promise of a legacy. That is not surprising since he had much else to think about in and after 1604. His deposition testified to Belott's reputable character and admitted some part in persuading the young man to marry. His forgetfulness about the financial details of a bargain made in his landlord's house eight years earlier scarcely supports the view that his memory was already failing. He had played, as one might expect from the general approval of his friendly and 'gentle' character, a friendly and a co-operative part.

While in London, Shakespeare, with his interest as a Sharer and his readiness to be helpful as a writer, would naturally see to the business done at the Globe and Blackfriars Theatres and have talks with the company's new dramatist, on whom much call was to be made. John Fletcher, at first working with Francis Beaumont and, after the latter's early death in 1616, independently, was to be a main prop of the King's Men. During discussions about their future work he probably agreed to help Fletcher by taking a main part in *Henry VIII* and by working also on *The Two Noble Kinsmen*. The fact that the great man was ready to be a collaborator with a younger and lesser writer argues his modesty and generosity. There is no evidence that the egotisms and the claims to priority in status and billing, so prominent in the theatre of today, existed in the team.

We do not know when *The Two Noble Kinsmen* was first played. There is a Revels Office mention of a production in 1619; but that was probably a revival. The text was registered and published by John Waterson, printed by Thomas Cotes, and sold at the sign of the Crown in St. Paul's Churchyard in 1634. It was described as 'written by the Memorable Worthies of their time; Mr. John Fletcher and Mr. William Shakespeare, Gent.' It was included in the second Folio of Beaumont and Fletcher's plays in 1679, but was omitted, like *Pericles,* by Heminge and Condell from the Shakespeare First Folio of 1623, in which they had included *Henry VIII*. But modern authorities are agreed in the main that there is a great deal of authentic Shakespeare in the last of these three as well as in *Pericles.*

This opinion is reached partly by statistical calculation of the lines with light or weak endings and by relating these figures to the usage of the poets. More important is the consideration of the imagery and of the parallels with Shakespeare's image-clusters elsewhere. To my mind the shape, rhythm, and vocabulary of the lines are valuable evidence; to anyone with an eye and an ear for Shakespeare's touch there is intermittent but striking evidence of his contributing hand. For those interested in the play there is full survey of the evidence by Professor Kenneth Muir in volume eleven of the annual *Shakespeare Survey* (1958), edited by Allardyce Nicoll for the Cambridge University Press. Muir decides that *The Two Noble Kinsmen* has as much right to be included in editions of Shakespeare as *Sir Thomas More, Titus Andronicus, Henry VI, Part I,* and *Pericles.* While agreeing with him about this I would point out a small piece of evidence which he has overlooked. In Act V, Scene 4, of the play, a section generally claimed as Shakespearian,

Palamon, doomed to death, says:

> *We expire*
> *And not without men's pity. To live still,*
> *Have their good wishes, we prevent*
> *The loathsome misery of age, beguile*
> *The gout and rheum that in lag hours*
> *For grey approaches.*

'Prevent' here, of course, does not mean escape, but anticipate. What Palamon means is that to go on living is for grey-haired men, slowly nearing their end, to suffer the maladies of age. Then the speaker adds:

> *We come to the gods,*
> *Young and unwappered, not halting under crimes*
> *Many and stale.*

Wappered is a very rare word for jaded or exhausted. But it does occur once in Shakespeare's work (*Timon of Athens,* Act IV, Scene 3), when Timon, in an undoubtedly Shakespearian passage, curses the power of gold and says:

> *This is it*
> *That makes the wappen'd widow wed again.*

We have only the Folio text and that prints 'n' instead of 'r', but obviously the same word is being used, whether it be wappened or wappered. More significant, the *Oxford English Dictionary* describes wappered as a Cotswold word and gives a quotation referring to a journey with a wappered horse to Stratford itself.

There can surely be no doubt that Shakespeare wrote his share of *The Two Noble Kinsmen.* It has the flower-painting that is typical of Shakespeare's vision and recording. Consider this passage in Act II, Scene 3:

> *O Queen Emilia,*
> *Fresher than May, sweeter*
> *Than her gold buttons on the boughs, or all*
> *The enamelled knacks o' the meads or gardens, yea,*
> *We challenge too the banks of any nymph*
> *That makes the stream seem flowers: thou, a jewel*
> *O' the wood, o' the world, hast likewise blest a place*
> *With thy sole presence.*

That is Shakespeare, Shakespeare using his latest, loosest rhythm and versification, but Shakespeare still unwappered.

Spending his last years mainly at home in Stratford Shakespeare was involved, during 1614 and 1615, in a confusing and tiresome dispute about the enclosure of common land at Welcombe, a mile to the north-east of the town. He was concerned as a leaseholder of the Welcombe tithes. The Stratford Corporation strongly opposed the enclosure which was being attempted by William Combe with two men called Mainwaring and Replingham as his agents. Shakespeare was offered compensation. The enclosure was, in the end, prevented by a verdict of Lord Justice Coke given at Warwick. Shakespeare seems to have been on the side of the Corporation.

As the faithful son of a litigious community he may have been interested by this long and angry tussle which had led to the verge of local rioting. But he was more probably wearied by it, especially when the quarrel followed him to London which he was certainly visiting in the November of 1614. Thomas Greene, who was Clerk to the Stratford Corporation, was then also in London and wrote on November 17 that he had called on 'my cousin Shakespeare' and discussed the matter. (Greene's claim to this relationship with Shakespeare is a mystery.) Shakespeare, with his interest in landed property, would be concerned; but he was in larger company and confronted with an urgent problem of the King's Men, the conduct of the newly opened second Globe Theatre in addition to the maintenance of an attractive programme at Blackfriars. Here was work in which he had a professional interest and work after his own heart.

During much of the previous year, when he was in London for his investment in the purchase of the Blackfriars Gatehouse, he may have developed a pastime as a painter. At that time Francis Manners, the sixth Earl of Rutland, wished to take part in a tournament of tilting arranged to honour the tenth anniversary of the succession of King James. For an exercise of this kind it was the custom of the competitors to carry a decorated shield which displayed their family emblem and motto. This was called an impresa or impreso. The Earl's steward recorded in his accounts a payment of forty-four shillings in gold to 'Mr. Shakespeare about my Lord's impreso'. The same amount was paid to Richard

Burbage for his share in the work. This sum indicates two of the gold coins called a 'jacobus', worth twenty-two shillings each.

But there was another 'Mr. Shakespeare' then at work in the same field and so doubt has been thrown on the idea of our Shakespeare as a part-time graphic artist. But he was on the spot at the time and it is odd that the partner in the job should be his actor-colleague, Burbage. So it may be true that the poet Shakespeare was trying his hand at least as a colourist and emblem-designer. Burbage was known to use what leisure he had, which cannot have been much, in painting portraits and he may have suggested to the dramatist that here was a pleasant and even profitable hobby. Forty-four shillings would be a useful help in paying for the trip to town. Sir Winston Churchill has memorably advocated painting as the happy solace of old age and has practised according to his theory. Shakespeare, still under fifty, was certainly not old by our standards, but he was a man of advancing years according to his own and those of his period. Even if he had not begun to feel what Sir Winston has called with typical eloquence 'the surly advance of decrepitude' he may well have taken up as a pastime the Churchillian cure for that depressing condition.

Fripp suggests that Shakespeare went to London in November 1613 to assist the King's Men in the presentations at Court during that winter. The company was busily engaged. In that month it gave performances three times for the King and twice for Prince Charles, then aged only thirteen but an early devotee of playgoing; his later taste for reading Shakespeare in the First Folio is well known. There were eleven more command appearances before Lent. If Shakespeare stayed in London, or moved to and from Stratford, he had a busy winter. It is also surmised by Fripp that during this season he was acting his old parts, but this is a conjecture. If he was so occupied, decrepitude was making no surly advance on him.

Meanwhile, as was said, the new Globe, described as 'the fairest theatre that ever was in England' was going up, with tiles for roofing to replace the previous, inflammable thatch. This building was to have thirty years of life, more than twice as long as the life of its short-lived predecessor. It was pulled down in 1644 'to make tenements in the room of it'. The Blackfriars Theatre suffered the same fate in 1655. Pulling down theatres in order to put up offices or flats yielding greater returns for the space occupied became a practice constantly proposed, keenly challenged, and only sometimes prevented three hundred years later. But during the Cromwellian regime there had been a closure of the theatres and there was the constant hatred of the play-actors to support the financial policies of the up-rooters of these 'work-shops of the Devil'. If Shakespeare was back in Stratford after the opening of the new Globe in June, 1614, an occasion which he would not like to miss, he had another spectacle of conflagration. There was then a disastrous outbreak of fire round his home, which was fortunately spared while fifty-four dwelling houses were destroyed.

As far as we can tell, Shakespeare's last visit to London was made during April and May of 1615 when the Gatehouse property involved him in more business. He and others had to issue 'A Bill of Complaint' against one Matthew Bacon in order to get, through the Court of Chancery, the title-deeds of the Lodging of the Prior of Blackfriars in which stood the recently purchased Gatehouse. The surrender of the deeds by Bacon, from whom Henry Walker had bought the Gatehouse in 1604, was apparently not disputed. But the issuing of 'the Bill' and formal surrender may have necessitated Shakespeare's presence in order to avoid the delay caused by transferring the papers to and from Stratford.

The last years had their disappointments. There is no sign of any response to the two late Roman tragedies, *Coriolanus* and *Antony and Cleopatra*. No mention remains of any contemporary performance of either and there were no Quarto editions. The known triumphs of Burbage include no reference to his having conquered again by embodying the pride of Caius Marcius in the former play or by displaying the squandered powers and passions of Marcus Antonius in the latter. Yet to us it seems that these were vast opportunities for the leader of the King's Men, then at the height of his capacities and public estimation. Had it not been for their inclusion in the First Folio we should have no knowledge that these plays ever existed. To us who are increasingly accepting and admiring the incisive ironies and fine sweep of portraiture in the Rome and Antium of *Coriolanus* and are amazed at the irresistible surge of poetry on which Antony and Cleopatra faced and finally rose above disaster in their deaths, the silence of Shakespeare's time is a mystery.

Three of the four great tragedies written between 1600 and 1606 held their place in popular and royal favour and were not dropped from the company's repertory. That *Hamlet* remained in strong demand is shown by the recorded training of Joseph Taylor in the title-role after the death of Burbage in 1619. (We may wonder whether Burbage was still playing Hamlet at the age of fifty-one.) *Othello* was seen at the Globe by Prince Frederick of Württemburg in 1610 and was in the list of plays selected for the revels before the marriage of Princess Elizabeth in the winter of 1612. *Macbeth* was seen by Dr. Simon Forman at the Globe in April 1611. So these pieces certainly did not drop out. Concerning immediate performances of *King Lear* we know only that it was given at Whitehall before the King on St. Stephen's Night, December 26, 1606. We hear of no other revival until D'Avenant staged it soon after the Restoration and Nahum Tate 'rectified' it with a happy ending. But that *King Lear* did not disappear hurriedly is suggested by the appearance of a Quarto, issued by Nathaniel Butler, in 1608 and by the fact that the printer Jaggard deemed it profitable to print it, without the permission of the King's Men, in 1619. This annexation would scarcely have been risked in the case of a play that had failed and been forgotten.

Neither Jaggard nor anybody else thought it worth while to borrow or steal the texts of *Antony and Cleopatra* and *Coriolanus*. Both were considered only fit for 'rectification' during the theatrical revival in the reign of Charles II. Dryden turned the former into his *All for Love* in 1678 and that was constantly brought to the stage: *Coriolanus* was twice 'rectified' by Nahum Tate in 1682 and John Dennis (with the title *The Invader of his Country or the Fatal Resentment*) in 1719. This version was so fatally resented by the playgoers that it had to be abandoned after three nights.

Conjecture can range at will among the possible explanations of the failure, in Shakespeare's time, of plays wherein we in our time discover the poet's genius at full stretch. In neither case was he taking over and gloriously reshaping another man's second-rate script. In both cases he was working on lives related in North's rendering of Plutarch and chosen because of their rich dramatic possibility. Into *Coriolanus* he poured wry and acute reflection on matters of government as well as on human self-destruction by a demon of pride. In *Antony and Cleopatra* there was more pulse of feeling in the writing as well as more sympathy for the failings of the principal characters: Shakespeare, himself thrifty, had responded with a fascinated wonder to grand extravagance and a surrender to a consuming sensual passion. It cannot possibly be said that those pieces disappointed because they were the hack-work of a tired man. They are essential Shakespeare, brimming with energy and revealing his penetration of mind in the one case and his wealth of sympathetic comprehension in the other.

J. B. Priestley has convincingly argued that in the person of Falstaff we see the struggle between the surface and rational side of Shakespeare, which constantly approved of law upheld by a strong ruler, and the subconscious side in which there was an abounding relish for the boisterous and unruly element in man. The subconscious won and Falstaff came towering in spirit, as well as in bulk, out of that deep well within the author. This he did with such overwhelming vitality and power that he bestrode both the plays in which Prince Hal was to become the rake nobly reformed into a model king. One might similarly urge that in the case of *Antony and Cleopatra* the intellectual respect for order has been completely submerged by the subconscious addiction to the splendours of a majestic misrule: Shakespeare, the defender of discipline in national life and the cautious investor in his own, had been swept aside altogether by Shakespeare the man of feeling for whom waste became pardonable and even glorious when perpetrated on a cosmic scale and with an all-devouring recklessness.

The two failures were not the product of carelessness or potboiling. Nobody can think of *Antony and Cleopatra* as written to order or for lack of a better theme. Here was the man himself, the established favourite of the public. Was he ceasing to be wanted? We can make our guesses, that Burbage was ill and did not play the leading and very important roles, or that he was tired and played them well below his best. We can readily imagine that the boy-player confronted with the colossal challenge of playing Cleopatra in a way to match the richness of the part was so inadequate as to fail the author and the company, and that to a ruinous degree. We may also suppose that the public was tired of ancient Rome or that it was turning away from high tragedy to lighter and easier themes. Certainly the mood of the audience was changing and Shakespeare was soon to take the hint and turn from tragical-historical to fantastical-romantical.

But the failures must have been a grievous disappointment. A man who has unbosomed such stuff as went into *Antony and Cleopatra* may console himself, if he is a detached intellectual, by reflecting on the shallowness and folly of an 'incapable' audience. (That adjective was applied by John Webster to his public after the failure of *The White Devil*.) But Shakespeare was no isolated artist. He was Shakespeare the Sharer as well as Shakespeare the playwright: thus failures hit both the company's purse and his personal pride, and he may have felt the former blow quite as strongly as the latter. Whatever his loyalty to the company it cannot have been pleasant to realise that he was doing far better financially for himself and his colleagues by patching up another man's *Pericles* than by asserting his matured powers independently and to the height of his capacity.

A chilly reception for *Timon of Athens,* a play of the same period, he could have taken without much surprise or distress. He had used it, in the words of Macbeth, to

Raze out the written troubles of the brain

and

Cleanse the stuffed bosom of that perilous stuff
Which weighs upon the heart.

He could not expect success and did not get it. There was no publication of *Timon of Athens* in Quarto and the pagination of the First Folio has suggested that it was only put in to fill a gap. If that is so, it is by accident that we have it at all. There was no recorded performance in Shakespeare's time or before the Restoration, when it was rehashed by Shadwell and later given a score by Purcell. *Timon* was blown away on the winds of its own rancour. Shakespeare may not have regretted its disappearance. But the public refusal to accept the two Roman tragedies of his own devoted workmanship was a set-back, even a calamity, which was bound to hurt.

But a partnership play, following the Roman tragedies, had an immediate and continuing success. *Pericles, Prince of Tyre* was a piece of collaboration in which Shakespeare, intervening at the close of Act II, took a third-rate romance as it were by the scruff of the neck and forced it to have at least some look of strength and beauty. The feeble start had obviously been made by another hand, probably that of George Wilkins who had published a novel in prose on *The Painful Adventures of Prince Pericles,* as 'lately presented by the ancient and worthy Poet John Gower'. The presence of Gower as chorus in the play indicates that Wilkins had tried to dramatise his novel and done it so poorly that somebody had to come to the rescue if the King's Men were to make use of it. In this Shakespeare, ready as ever to play for his team, courteously obliged, but the editors of the First Folio evidently decided that there was so much work by the other hand that it could not, despite its popularity, be properly included in the Shakespearian canon.

The play is a curious mixture of near-Eastern travel, 'when knights were bold' romance, incestuous lust, comprehensive villainy, far-fetched fairy-tale with miraculous revivals of the seemingly dead, and squalid brothel-humour. After his participation had begun Shakespeare displayed his ability to create a storm at sea with a typhoon of words, which he was to do twice again in *The Winter's Tale* and *The Tempest.* He showed his skill, also to be repeated, in the picturing of girlish innocence without a touch of mawkishness or sugar in his writing. There was the flower-painting too.

> No, I *will rob Tellus of her weed,*
> *To strew thy green with flowers; the yellows, blues,*
> *The purple violets, and marigolds,*
> *Shall, as a carpet, hang upon thy grave,*
> *While summer-days do last.*

One cannot see Wilkins, or indeed anybody but Shakespeare, writing that. But it may not have taken him long to do his share. In this case, with the experience so ripe and the facility so assured, the exquisite could also be the easy. Without the character of Marina, obviously of Shakespeare's fathering, *Pericles* would be mainly a tiresome and occasionally a dirty piece of work. Perhaps one should not use piece of work dismissively, for piece was a word very precious to Shakespeare in his appraisal of womanhood. Now piece is a playful slang-word for an attractive girl, but Marina was 'a piece of your dead queen', Imogen 'a piece of tender air', Perdita 'the most peerless piece of earth that ere the sun shone bright on', and the salute to Queen Elizabeth that is spoken by Cranmer in *Henry VIII* calls her 'a mighty piece'. In the playhouse sense *Pericles* is far from being a mighty piece, but Marina deserves as much as Imogen the charming tribute of 'a tender piece of air'. She disinfects even the repulsive scenes in the stews of Mytelene.

But the piece had results which could be called mighty in terms of public favour. The First Quarto, published in 1609, advertised it as 'the late and much admired play'. It was certainly not late then in the sense of dead for it continued to be the darling of the Court as well as of the playgoing commons. The authorship was attributed in the Quarto to William Shakespeare only, but that was salesmanship. His name was an attraction. The Folio Editors did not agree. The Quarto title adds 'as it hath been divers and sundry times acted by his Majestie's Servants at the Globe on the Banckside'. So it was well in demand and continued so. There had to be another Quarto issued the same year and between 1609 and 1635 there were four more printings. There was a midnight performance in the King's Great Chamber in May 1619 and it was chosen in June 1631 to be part of a thanksgiving performance for the cessation of the plague.

The continuing success of *Pericles* infuriated Ben Jonson, who chose for it, as we shall see, the adjective 'mouldy'. But it must have been a triumph with a sting in it for Shakespeare who had recently seen *Coriolanus* and *Antony and Cleopatra* staged with no demand for immediate printing or renewed performance. (We have, as a matter of fact, no evidence that they were ever staged at all.) He did not live to discover that there would be more Quartos of *Pericles* than of any other play in which he had a hand, either single or sharing. Would he have smiled or groaned had he lived to learn that, with perhaps a few day's work, he had turned the feeble piece by Wilkins into such a solid asset for his successors in the King's Men?

Shakespeare, though modestly helpful to the newcomers, must also have known that their work was considerably inferior to his own. Fletcher's type of play substituted fancy for imagination and his verse ran loosely without the power to strike out a mighty or a memorable line. That is the judgment of our time. It is significant that *The Oxford Dictionary of Quotations* includes sixty-seven double-column pages of citation from Shakespeare and less than two from Beaumont and Fletcher together. In these Beaumont's share, extracts from poems not plays, provide the only well remembered elements: Fletcher alone, though he could occasionally be effective in a lyric, is represented only by the commonplace. Shakespeare, if, as is most likely, he worked with Fletcher in *Henry VIII* and *The Two Noble Kinsmen,* was giving a hand to a comparative weakling. How many other writers have ended their working lives by assisting an inferior rival in their own field? Magnanimity could not go further.

It would be foolish to say about any character, unless we know him intimately, which is out of the question in the case of those long dead, that he had no taint of egotism or conceit. If such a fault is sought in Shakespeare's character, it is possible to pull out of the *Sonnets* a boastful couplet concerning the endurance of his work.

> *Not marble, nor the gilded monuments*
> *Of princes, shall outlive this powerful rhyme.*

Quoting this, Bernard Shaw observed that 'the timid cough of the minor poet' was never heard from Shakespeare. But the real test of a man's modesty is that he is not so convinced of his own importance as to be continually thrusting forward his personality and his opinions. Shakespeare was one who could have justified self-assertion by pre-eminent ability. We could have been spared a mass of conjecture, to which it may be complained that I am adding, if Shakespeare had exposed and exhibited himself the more. What a flood of controversy and speculation was to emerge from his silences!

Ben Jonson behaved far otherwise. Being full of himself, he declared himself, especially on the nature of audiences, in a way that Shakespeare did not. Through the mouth of Hamlet, it is true, the latter had taken a side-shot at the 'barren spectators', as well as at the faults of the actor, but in his own epilogues he was tact itself. We have only to reread the ingenious pleasantries with which Rosalind sends home the audience at the close of *As You Like It* to realise how courteously and adroitly Shakespeare could do this kind of thing. Others could not take defeat as he did. Let his continuance after the failure of response to *Antony and Cleopatra* and *Coriolanus* be compared with Ben Jonson's surly outburst of self-pity and abuse after the failure of his late comedy *The New Inn*:

> Come leave the loathed stage,
>   And the more loathsome age;
> Where pride and impudence, in faction knit,
>   Usurp the chair of wit!
> Indicting and arraigning every day,
>   Something they call a play.
> Let their fastidious, vain
> Commission of the brain
> Run on and rage, sweat, consure and condemn;
> They were not made for thee, less thou for them.
>   Say that thou pour'st them wheat,
>   And they will acorns eat;
> T'were simple fury still thyself to waste
>   On such as have no taste!
> To offer them a surfeit of pure bread,
>   Whose appetites are dead!
>   No, give them grains their fill,
>   Husks, draff to drink and swill:
> If they love lees, and leave the lusty wine,
> Envy them not, their palate's with the swine.
>   No doubt some mouldy tale,
>   Like Pericles, and stale
> As the shrieve's crusts, and nasty as his fish—
>   Scraps, out of every dish
> Thrown forth, and raked into the common tub,
>   May keep up the Play-club:
> There, sweepings do as well
> As the best-order'd meal;
> For who the relish of these guests will fit,
> Needs set them but the alms-basket of wit.

The retort made to Jonson by a writer called Owen Feltham was crushing with its reference to those 'who pay dear for your declining wit' and its chiding remark

> *Let's suffice*
> *Had you been modest, you'd been granted wise.*

As we can tell from his writing and from his reputation for civility, Shakespeare, though he had strained himself to the uttermost and suffered some failure in his time, never sulked in public, never earned a rebuke for an unwise immodesty, and never evoked a reprimand for the 'self-conceit and choler of the blood' which Feltham scolded in Jonson.

He had won a social position in the country; but on this dignity he did not stand. An epithet then applied to an established man of property was the Latin *generosus*. When Shakespeare bought his Stratford home, New Place, from William Underhill in 1597, he was named in the deed simply as William Shakespeare while Underhill was styled *generosus*. Shakespeare, by his rise in the world, soon won the formal epithet for himself. He was *generosus* in a document of 1602. The word indicated rank and did not mean generous in our sense; but generosity, as we understand it, was a large and most likeable part of his professional quality.

The Elizabethan dramatists were lusty quarrellers and had their 'war of the theatres' among themselves as well as their conflicts with the Puritan City and the censorious officers of the Crown. They hit out at each other freely in some of their plays. If the character of Ajax in *Troilus and Cressida* was aimed at Jonson, there was some mockery there. But allusions to other authors are sparse and, to us, sometimes cryptic; in the case of Marlowe the reference by quotation, not by name, was a gracious tribute. He may not have been speaking directly for himself in the words of the poet who is one of the characters in *Timon of Athens*. But, if a poet-dramatist brings a poet on the stage, one may expect some personal note. Says Timon's bard,

> *No levell'd malice*
> *Infects one comma in the cause I hold.*

Whether or not Shakespeare was there speaking of himself, it was a statement applicable to the conduct of his life and work.

It has been suggested that during his last years at Stratford Shakespeare was putting his play-scripts together and revising them for publication. He probably had heard that Ben Jonson was thus engaged. But there is no evidence that Shakespeare was doing anything of the kind.

It seems almost incredible to us, in our age of profuse editing of old texts and new printing of all kinds, that so great a writer should have been so little tenacious of his work as Shakespeare apparently was. He had poured not only magnificence of writing but also the essence of his feeling into many of his plays; had his intention been only to serve the players' need and do a financially rewarding job, he had no need to write at greater length than the traffic of the stage required. So regarded, the vast length of *Hamlet* was simply a waste of time and effort. His thoughts did run beyond the reaches of the stage. Yet for the preservation of those thoughts no care was taken.

Shakespeare had published his early narrative poems with approved results. That he disliked the printing of the *Sonnets* is probable: they were composed, as Meres said, for his friends and there were good personal reasons for maintaining their privacy. When plays were pirated and printed in the truncated or vitiated texts of the Bad Quartos steps were taken by himself or his colleagues to present the authentic version. But the plays not thus issued were left to linger and possibly moulder in the Book-keeper's hands with the risk of vanishing altogether by accidental loss. *Hamlet* had been printed in its fullest form and so saved from oblivion, but much of the finest was never guaranteed against disappearance. There was no Quarto printing of *Othello* in the author's lifetime and none at all of *Macbeth* or *Twelfth Night* or *Antony and Cleopatra* to mention only three of the eighteen un-published plays, all of which might have been lost to us if Heminge and Condell had died early or been too busy to edit the First Folio.

If Shakespeare had believed that he had any kind of ethical doctrine to expound, as many commentators think that he had, it is inconceivable that he would have been so careless about his texts. The doctrinaire dramatist is naturally most eager to see that the message is preserved: Shaw not only printed his plays but empha-sised their instruction and implications with prefaces sometimes longer than the plays themselves. Shakespeare knew that his audiences were there to be amused and excited and not lectured, and, if he had wished to be a preacher, he would have written tracts and pamphlets, as was frequently done by others at that time. He did not do so. Nor had he Jonson's feeling of self-importance. The stuff could remain with the players, for use if revival was demanded, for neglect if there were no demand.

A possible explanation is that a play is different from a book and a dramatist may be different from an author of books. The maker of a play has written primarily for actors acting and for people listening, and this was certainly the case amid the quick turnover of the Elizabethan and Jacobean theatres. The playwright's mind is on the moment: the product meets the occasion and passes, perhaps with failure, perhaps with success. It is there; it has gone; there is more to be done. The modern dramatist has property in his work and wants it printed, not only to gratify his professional pride, but as a source of future income from the touring, repertory, and amateur rights. But in Shakespeare's time there was no author's property: the play went to the company. Whether the author received any payment for subsequent performances we do not know; probably he did not. The players were using what they had bought. So Shakespeare could have murmured, 'Good-bye to all that', when he had passed a play to his colleagues. A dramatist, not a book-man, he went on to the next job, turning out the perishable goods with the unconcern of his profession in that period. No playwright of the age, except Jonson, had his collected plays printed in Folio during his lifetime.

Finally, it is quite likely that Shakespeare, when he was back in Stratford, had not got copies of all the plays with him. To take home books of the plays printed in Quarto was easy enough. But the eighteen not so printed were held by the King's Men, whether as the writer's own Foul Papers, Fair Copy, or in scriveners' reproductions. The number of these, as was earlier noted, was few. To have them copied in plenty took time and money: manuscripts were scanty and had to be guarded against piracy. It is quite possible that Shakespeare did not have the whole of his work with him at New Place and that collecting, revising, and editing would have meant working in London and not in Stratford. A man who was certainly modest and possibly tired could shrug the task aside. So he was ready to let it go, with perhaps a word to the Fellowship that somebody might care to do something about it sometime. By the most blessed of all accidents in the history of writing Heminge and

Condell were not struck down, and yet another fire, which might have reduced all their play stock to ashes, did not visit the second Globe. That the world's Shakespeare-worship could have soared and swollen to its present enormous extent with our possession of half the plays, those preserved in Quarto, is most unlikely. Our gratitude goes to Heminge, Condell, their Book-keeper, and a run of luck.

CHAPTER XIV

Work Ended

❦

BERNARD SHAW, as reported by Hesketh Pearson, observing that
Shakespeare's life had no Third Period, quoted some examples of
what grandeur this late maturity had achieved. He argued that the
finest work of an artist had often been done after the flush of youth
and the hard climb of middle age. Beethoven composed the Ninth
Symphony and the Mass in D at the age at which Shakespeare died.
Handel was fifty-eight when he produced his *Messiah*. Ibsen wrote
The Master Builder at sixty-eight. Shaw himself wrote his Meta-
biological Pentateuch, the five-plays-in-one called *Back to Methuselah*, which is the fullest expression of his opinions on First and
Last Things, when he was sixty-five, and *Saint Joan* when he was
sixty-eight. The fact is that Shakespeare did have his Third Period;
but he had it early and then had a Fourth too.

His career can be divided into four stages of some six years each,
ranging up from the early and fairly crude to the mature histories
and comedies, then on to the great tragedies, and so to this Fourth
Period of partial retirement with continued but less frequent service
of the King's Men. Shakespeare had done the best of his work by
the time he reached his middle forties and in the second sonnet he
had expressed his opinion of that brow-furrowing age when
'youth's proud livery' becomes 'a tattered weed'. We now have
happier ideas of the fourth and subsequent decades, but time
galloped for the Elizabethans who could hold high commands on
land and sea before they were twenty and were ready to shine as
brief candles in the theatres and had no hope of being enduring
lamps with a blaze to come in the fifties.

The theatre-men, coping with their business affairs as well as
with the swift repletion of their play-list, were especially liable to
burn themselves out and to be as much exhausted at fifty or even at
forty as Shaw was at ninety. They did not shape their way of life

with longevity in view. Shakespeare's Fourth Period was not as strenuous as his early ones, but we cannot regard his energies as steadily dwindling. His writing was still unique and to bring zest to the later years he had his interests and obligations in London as well as in Stratford until the beginning of 1616, when his fifty-third birthday was also the day of his death.

The belief that Shakespeare's end was caused by 'a merry meeting' with his old friends and rivals Ben Jonson and Michael Drayton is based on evidence so flimsy that it leaves the cause of death an open matter. The Vicar of Stratford from 1662 to 1681 was the Rev. John Ward. He had begun life as a medical student and later preferred a 'cure of souls' to the healing of bodies. He kept notebooks which were acquired by the Medical Society of London. In the section of those notes which covered the period between February 14, 1661 and April 25, 1663, he made some jottings about Shakespeare. These can be taken to echo the current local hearsay about one who had died nearly fifty years before. The subject was apparently not of a kind in which the Vicar was naturally or deeply interested. His remarks simply indicate a feeling that he owed a duty to one who had been a distinguished parishioner of Stratford.

Addressing himself, the Vicar uttered a cautionary statement to the effect that he must remember to peruse and become versed in Shakespeare's plays that he 'be not thought ignorant in the matter'. This makes it certain that he knew little or nothing of the local hero until he came to Stratford. He had plainly been no student of poets and poetry. There he heard that Shakespeare 'was a natural wit without any art at all'. This valuation was not quite so foolish then as it seems to us, since the word art is now given a much wider meaning: to Ward it signified what we should call artifice or technique. The Vicar was repeating the fairly common opinion generated by Ben Jonson that Shakespeare was a natural dramatist and had not plodded up the 'steps to Parnassus' with a text-book on classical methods as a playwright's manual.

Ward added that Shakespeare spent his 'elder days' at Stratford and 'supplied the stage with two plays every year'. He added the random statement, already discussed and dismissed, that Shakespeare had an allowance so large that 'he spent at the rate of £1000 a year'. His final remark is the often-quoted assertion that 'Shakespeare, Drayton and Ben Jonson had a merry meeting and it seems drank too hard, for Shakespeare died of a fever there contracted'. We cannot prove that this over-indulgence in 'the social glass' did not happen, but the anecdote is the kind of thing that gossip likes to repeat and to enlarge. So here is a tatler's notion of the picturesque finale to what cannot in fact have been a sottish and was certainly a hardworking life. Such tales may cling.

Gossip likes to enlarge drinking stories instead of playing them down. John Aubrey was not one to diminish a tale of human frailty; but he reported the tradition that Shakespeare declined risky invitations with suitable excuses because he 'would not be debauched'. It is likely enough that after a bout of concentrated work at the writing table or a new production in the theatre Shakespeare was ready for an escape into celebration: he praised the creative quality of drinking as forcibly as he deplored the sad effects of wine within upon brains above. Frank Harris thought that Shakespeare became an alcoholic and anything can be proved by poring over the shaky signatures of a dying man. Naturally Shakespeare's life had had a number of merry meetings, but these did not make him a sot: he was too busy to be that.

So there may have been that gathering. The arrangements for his second daughter's wedding early in the February of 1616 had been suggested as a banqueting occasion. Shakespeare was a probable host to Drayton who was a regular visitor in the Stratford district. That poet's flame or, as he more coolly expressed it, his Idea, Anne Goodere of Polesworth, had married above the rank of the writers. Her husband was Sir Harry Rainford of Clifford Chambers, a village two miles south of Stratford and today worth a visit for its looks apart from any literary associations.

Though a rejected suitor, Drayton was welcome there and ready to be a visitor. His Stratford connections are shown by his becoming a patient of Shakespeare's son-in-law, who cured him of a fever by an infusion of violets. Among the tributes to Shakespeare was Drayton's salute, made eleven years later, to the smoothness of his 'comic vein', the strength of his conceptions, and clearness of his 'rage', which must refer to the great speeches of anger and despair in his tragedies. So it was likely enough that Drayton was an admiring neighbour from time to time and visits may have occurred in the early spring of 1616. But we have no other mention of Jonson as a visitor to the district; his reference to the 'Swan of Avon' need not imply that he had actually watched the swans upon that river. But he could possibly have been there in 1616. His visit to Scotland proved him a ready traveller.

But hard drinking does not usually produce a fever. A severe headache, for which, in the absence of our cures for a 'hang-over' the accepted alleviation of the time lay in small ale, was more likely than a fatal collapse. Another suggestion is that Stratford was visited by an epidemic in 1616, since Shakespeare's brother-in-law William Hart, the hatter who had married Joan Shakespeare, died on April 16. But this nearness of one death to another is no evidence of the same cause. The early spring is always a likely season for epidemics since winter has reduced human powers of resistance to infection. This was especially the case then when people had been compelled to feed unhealthily through the long winter, were suffering, as was earlier stated, from lack of vitamin C, and were so run down as to be easy victims of a visiting malady.

Of John and Mary Shakespeare's family of seven, five died between February and the end of April in one year or another. These were the poet's sisters Margaret and Anne, his brothers Richard and Gilbert, and William himself. His daughter Judith and her husband, Thomas Quiney, both died in February and their three sons died in January and May. The poets of the time were often and naturally vocal about vernal joys, but a cold spring could, like the green Christmas of the proverb, make a full churchyard.

Dr. Simpson in *Shakespeare and Medicine* agrees 'though it can only be conjecture', with the notion of an epidemic; his surmise is typhoid. He believes that Stratford was in those days subject to this killing fever when the Avon had been in flood. He finds in the records that 'the year 1616 was the most unhealthy from this cause in the early part of the century'. So, like Falstaff, Shakespeare (and William Hart as well) may have died 'of intolerable entrails'. Typhoid is also Fripp's surmise. The progress of the fever could be discerned, according to this opinion, in the growing feebleness of the handwriting in Shakespeare's various signatures of his will. Dr. Mitchell, author of *The Shakespeare Circle* offers a different view and diagnosis, suggesting a 'a cerebral haemorrhage or apoplexy that quickly deepened and soon became fatal'. For this he gives three reasons.

'Firstly, the hurried reconstruction and inter-lineated clauses of the Will not allowing time for it to be copied afresh before signature; secondly, the earliest and clearest impressions of the Droeshout frontispiece of the First Folio show outstanding shadings, suggesting marked thickening of the left temporal artery—a sign of atheroma and arterio-sclerosis; and thirdly, such a termination is quite common in men who have undergone such continuous mental and physical strain over a prolonged period as our actor-manager-dramatist must have been subjected to throughout his, undoubtedly, strenuous career. Richard Burbage, who daily shared the same theatrical life, himself died of such a seizure after twenty-four hours' illness, and within a year or two of Shakespeare's death.' That is plausible, but we cannot take the Droeshout portrait as serious medical evidence; the artist was only fifteen when Shakespeare died and must have been copying another likeness. Dr. John Hall, close neighbour as well as close relation by marriage, must have known the cause of death and recorded his 'observation' on this most precious of his 'English bodies'. But chance has kept it from us. We have only his clinical notes of later years.

Whether the death was caused by too much wine at table or by too much water on the flooded Stratford fields is a question we must shelve. The death occurred and the funeral in the parish church was two days later. Those who wish to discredit Shakespeare as a mere actor and to allot the writings to another and socially exalted figure like to point out the lack of immediate comment on the death of so famous a man. And why, they ask, was he not laid in Westminster Abbey if a far less distinguished servant of the theatre, Francis Beaumont, could be given that honour? One answer is obvious. In 1616 news did not travel apace; it moved no faster than the speed of a horse. London would not immediately or even quickly know of the light that had gone out a hundred miles away. The transport of a body by cart or carriage to London was a slow business, essential, no doubt, in the case of a king, but not easily considered in the case of a poet. There was no time for dilatory messages and consultations. If we allow three days for the arranging and conveyance of a message to London, none of his fellows knew of the death until after the funeral.

There may have been some social consideration in that award of Abbey funerals. Beaumont was the son of a knight and an

Oxford and Inns of Court man. His more famous and much more productive partner, John Fletcher, did not receive the Abbey honour. Being the son of a clergyman he was buried with other poets and actors in what is now Southwark Cathedral but was then the parish church of the players. Ben Jonson is his introductory verses to the First Folio appears to be apologising for Shakespeare's absence from the Abbey where he was later to go himself, which was natural since he was a Westminster man by education as well as residence and had long remained a prominent and laureate figure in London. He politely claimed that Shakespeare's greatness rose high above such minor issues as the placing of a tomb:

> *My Shakespeare rise! I will not lodge thee by*
> *Chaucer or Spencer or bid Beaumont lie*
> *A little further, to make thee a room:*
> *Thou art a Monument without a tomb,*
> *And art alive still, while thy Book doth live*
> *And We have wits to read and praise to give.*

Jonson was more prophetic than he knew.

How much attention was devoted by Shakespeare to theological considerations or the routine of religious observances is a question which has naturally aroused the excitement of zealots and considerable conflict of opinion. The Comtesse de Chambrun, a strong Roman Catholic who gave much of her life to Shakespearian research, claimed with a passionate intensity that his heart and that of both his parents remained with the Old Religion. There must have been some local hearsay that he died in that faith, since it was repeated in notes made by the Rev. Richard Davies who was Vicar of Sapperton, a Cotswold village, from 1695 to 1703 and then became Archdeacon of Coventry. Like Ward, he did not worry to be precise. For example, he jotted down that William Shakespeare was born at Stratford-upon-Avon 'about 1563-4'. He could easily have confirmed the exact date if he had taken the trouble to consult the church records at Stratford, but he was more of a gossip than a historian. He related the deer-stealing anecdote about Shakespeare and stated that 'Sir Lucy had him oft whipped and sometimes imprisoned and made him fly his native country to his great advancement'. Davies next said that when the refugee had become a dramatist he got his revenge by creating the character of 'Justice

Clodpate'. His last assertion about Shakespeare is that 'he died a papist'.

Davies cannot be cited as an exact recorder. He wrote Clodpate where he should have put Shallow. The former word was never used by Shakespeare either as a descriptive noun or personal name. What way the opinions and feelings of a sinking man may tend, we cannot tell. The Arden in Shakespeare's blood may have been at work, as he, with his own work ended, let his mind range back to the Stratford boyhood and the outings to his grandparents at Wilmcote, a Catholic household. But that he was a Roman Catholic in his active lifetime is most unlikely. It is true that he and his fellows had every reason to dislike the fanatical Puritans who would gladly have prevented the practice of his profession. But the Reformed and National Church had more quarrel with the Puritans than with the players and churchmen did not regard the latter as public nuisances and corrupters of public morals for the good reason that some of them were well known to be men of faith and works. It must not be forgotten that we owe the First Folio to a couple of Anglican churchwardens.

Orthodoxy was Shakespeare's political attitude. The player and playwright of a company closely attached to the service of the Throne could hold no other views in public. But it is noticeable that the devotion of the King's Men was to the Crown and not to the Court. Monarchs had no particular objection to writers laughing at and even passing scathing comments on the courtier-class, about whose fawnings, intrigues, and hypocrisy of the bended knee and cunning mind Shakespeare was quite as outspoken as ever he was about the gullible and slippery mob. He saw the monarchy as a strong foundation of national unity. But, while the mind was the advocate of order, impulse could work the other way. Instinctively he had a plain man's sympathy with the gaily rebellious and riotous side of human nature.

There is nothing strange in such dualism: we know, as Shakespeare did, that some officialism is necessary to the maintenance of order and that without some order there can be no equitable spread of liberty. None the less we love to see officialdom mocked and the Clown make game of the Policeman. The pantomimic side of drama has always exploited this kind of irreverence. So we can think of Shakespeare as a loyal supporter of established things but as one who could quietly smile as he observed Jack Pudding getting the better of Jack-in-Office.

In a portion of his latest work he definitely supported the new establishment in religion as in secular affairs of State. In Cranmer's speech in Act V, Scene 4 of the play *Henry VIII* there is a blessing of the child who is to be the great Protestant Queen. Shakespeare proclaimed that in the reign of the babe, now being christened Elizabeth, 'God shall be truly known'. Here is complete approval of the Reformation. If Shakespeare had been secretly a convinced Roman Catholic, he could scarcely have attached his name to a play carrying this strong endorsement of the break with Rome, and this assertion of a consequent enlightment. The christening scene had proudly to remind the public of the splendour of Queen Elizabeth's reign and tactfully, even fulsomely, to approve her successor, who was the patron of the author and the players presenting the play, but there was no need to include a statement of confident belief in Protestant truth. A Catholic sympathiser could have evaded the issue by confining his praise to the secular prowess of England during the past century and remaining silent about the correct knowledge of God.

The life-long theatre worker was to receive a snub in his own town shortly before his death. There had been a strengthening of the Puritan element in Stratford and a majority in the Corporation decided to keep players from visiting the guildhall, citing the example of 'other well-governed cities'. However much Shakespeare may have resented this intolerance and the insult to himself as a player and play-maker he did not break with the parochial life of his Protestant church; it is on record that he entertained a visiting 'preacher' at the house during the Christmas of 1614. This was an arranged hospitality on 'expense account', as we say nowadays, since the Corporation paid for the wine (one quart of sack and one of claret) which cost twenty pence. The members of the Corporation would not have found the money if the 'preacher' accepted at New Place had not been one acceptable to local Protestant opinion.

That Shakespeare accepted the beliefs and practices of his parish church is apparent. But, if we look to his plays, we find few traces of strong religious enthusiasm. We can sense sympathy with the sympathetic attitude of Friar Laurence to the lovers in *Romeo and*

Juliet. We find no admiration for a sanctified and dedicated life of the spirit. For a young woman to be 'in shady cloister mew'd' and to be 'a barren sister' all her life, 'chanting faint hymns to the cold, fruitless moon', is an existence that could be respected for its mastery of the blood, but is by no means recommended.

> *But earthlier happy is the rose distill'd*
> *Than that which withering on the virgin thorn*
> *Grows, lives, and dies in single blessedness.*

It is risky, of course, to make excision of passages in a play and attribute their opinions to the author, but the sentiment of Duke Theseus in the first act of *A Midsummer Night's Dream* does seem to have a personal urgency behind it. The Duke with his reference to cloisters is obviously thinking of Christian practices and not of devotion to the gods of ancient Athens or his Amazon Queen.

The declaration of faith in a life everlasting made in Shakespeare's will has hardly an echo in the plays, where death seems continually to be viewed as a sleep and a forgetting and not as a summons to a fuller, purer, and more glorious life. Here again one must be careful in the matter of extracting quotations. Duke Theseus of ancient Athens did discuss Christian views of the good life for young women, but on the whole we should not expect to find Christian views of heaven in the plays of the pre-Christian centuries. Why should a Roman general or an Egyptian queen utter the confident opinions about a future life that are expressed in a Christian liturgy? But in the plays of subsequent centuries we can fairly look for some orthodoxy if that orthodoxy had been powerfully lodged in Shakespeare's mind and temperament. It is true that in *The Merchant of Venice* Lorenzo speaks of immortal souls escaping from the muddy vesture of the body, but in the later plays set in the Christian epoch death is constantly envisaged not as the gateway to a glorious life but as an escape from a dim and melancholy existence. Death is sleep, and this sleep is the great refuge, bringing the boon of tranquillity after life's strains and fevers.

The Christian Duke's great speech in the third act of *Measure for Measure* beginning 'be absolute for death' is one of the most moving salutations to non-existence that has ever been written. To die is to escape the curse of consciousness, not to gain a new and rich awareness.

The best of rest is sleep,
And that thou oft provokest; yet grossly fear'st
Thy death, which is no more.

So the life everlasting is reduced to the comfort of a coma. What is that creed but an enforcement of pagan Timon's assertion that health and living are a sickness and that 'nothing brings me all things'? Death, thus viewed, is a discharge from that ward for incurables, which is our world.

There is a striking contradiction between the Shakespearian and the Wordsworthian outlook. To Wordsworth birth is 'but a sleep and a forgetting'; as infants we come with intimations of immortality, trailing clouds of a past existence in glory to which, after a sojourn in this world, we may have a glorious return. We have lived before in a 'vision splendid'; to the 'imperial palace' we may be restored. To Shakespeare it is death that is the salve of care, the medicine which promises the sweet serenity of an unbroken sleep. To Wordsworth 'Heaven lies about us in our infancy'. He could not possibly think of a babe as one 'that smells the air and needs must bawl and cry since he has come to the great stage of fools'. That sad view of the human arrival cannot be taken as authentically Shakespearian: some of the outcries in *King Lear* are a document in madness, proper to the play, but Shakespeare in his later years did seem to take a frequent relish in giving to life-hatred the utmost vehemence of his expression. He could have appreciated Swinburne's thanksgiving for annihilation:

From too much love of living,
From hope and fear set free,
We thank with brief thanksgiving
Whatever gods there be
That no life lives for ever
That dead men rise up never,
That even the weariest river
Winds somewhere safe to sea.

Shakespeare's mind seems, at least after the year 1600, to have run much closer to Swinburne's than to Wordsworth's.

Shakespeare did, it is true, preface his will with the orthodox phrases of Christian hope. This was a routine affirmation which did not necessarily convey any fervency of belief behind it. That throughout his life he was a convinced Christian worshipper, outside the church-going compulsions of the law, is difficult to believe. The conformist element in his attitude to society would make him accept the prescribed offices without rebellion. But that may well have been the limit of his observance.

The tolerant and kindly way of life, call it Christian or humanist as you will, he obviously admired. He hated persecution. In the play on *Sir Thomas More*, in a passage which is now widely accepted as a piece of Shakespearian collaboration, there is a striking utterance of compassion for the foreign craftsmen whom the London workers wished to drive out as rival claimants for work and wages. Shakespeare's pitying mind imagines

> *those wretched strangers*
> *Their babies at their backs, with their poor luggage,*
> *Plodding to th' ports and coasts for transportation.*

Those who would abuse the rights of asylum to persecuted people are sternly warned of the precedent which they are setting:

> *Other ruffians, as their fancies wrought,*
> *Would shark on you and men like ravenous fishes*
> *Would feed on one another.*

Again and again the cause of mercy evokes his most persuasive poetry. But there could be crimes beyond pardon. Shakespeare was a humanist, living in a society where savagery to man and beast was accepted as normal and aroused little protest. But for him too there were inhumanities not to be excused or spared. Murder was one and

> *Mercy but murders, pardoning those that kill.*

It is the verdict of the Duke Escalus in *Romeo and Juliet* and the Duke speaks in that play with the authority of the Greek Chorus in a tragedy.

But, for the rest, the nobler action did not lie in vengeance or vendetta. By the hypocrisy of a so-called justice whose lance broke 'hurtless' on the rich while it was driven against the poor, Shakespeare was shocked into violent protest. These, lines, if they were spoken in Court performances, were as dangerous as gallant.

Bigotry he loathed as much as he hated the abuse of the power whose robes and furred gowns concealed iniquity. Referring to the remark of Davies that Shakespeare 'died a papist' Fripp adds at the end of his second volume: '. . . Neither his father nor his son-in-law would have judged him sound in the Protestant faith. He was no zealot, and he has drawn none, Jesuit or Puritan. Shylock and Isabella are his nearest approaches to fanaticism; and the one he would have abjure his Judaism, the other leave the convent door and be a wife. He cared for man more than doctrine, and for God more than creed. The Bible was a book of men and women rather than of saving truth. Worship was dearer to him than sermons, and worship was not always at Church.'

This is a reasonable judgment. It was part of Shakespeare's genius to give to every opinion its best possible utterance. His profession of playwright and painter of character gave him full opportunity to do that. When he spoke for any humour or passion of human nature, he did so with such comprehension and such a gift of phrase that he made whatever he touched unforgettable.

Fripp says confidently that Shakespeare loved 'the noble parish church' in which he was buried. To Sunday service he had to go; it was the law of the land. But my final fancy is of occasional annoyance at an intolerant or lengthy sermon vexing the ear of a drowsy pew-holder. If his way of mind was not to be contained in any formal creed his thoughts would wander out of church, back to another and a larger river than the Avon, and to that sometimes enchanting and sometimes exhausting and harassing workshop of the one-time Factotum and the later Sharer.

In this book there has been no intention to write of Shakespeare's personal experience outside that work-shop, inevitably a theme of multifarious and conflicting conjecture. That other world from which the Sonnets came, a world of intense devotions and passions, deep pleasures and bitter disenchantments, came back to mind inevitably along with the memories of the day's labour and the chances and changes of the play-house; the old ardours and angers, the humours and satisfactions of a working theatre-man could be affectionately recollected in the evening light. Prematurely, as we see it now with our different notions of life's expected span, night fell in the April of 1616. It fell upon a failing hand that was shaky in its penmanship. But what a hand it had been! The supreme master of words and word-music, went, in the haunting phrase of his fellow-dramatist, John Webster 'to study a long silence'.

Note on Books
and Index

Note on Books

Of the enormous Shakespearian library, in which I have been delving for many years, I have been especially indebted to the following works of assembled fact and, in some cases, of well-argued fancy.

W. Bridges-Adams, *The Irresistible Theatre*

H. Granville-Barker, *Prefaces to Shakespeare*

M. C. Bradbrook, *The Rise of the Common Player.*

Sir Edmund Chambers, *The Elizabethan Stage* (two vols), *William Shakespeare* (two vols)

Comtesse de Chambrun, *Shakespeare—A Portrait Restored*

Margaret Chute, *Shakespeare of London*

Edgar Fripp, *Shakespeare. Man and Artist* (two vols)

Sir Walter Greg, *Henslowe's Diary and Papers, Editorial Problems in Shakespeare*

F. E. Halliday, *A Shakespeare Companion, The Life of William Shakespeare, Shakespeare in His Age*

Alfred Harbage, *Shakespeare's Audience*

G. B. Harrison, *Shakespeare at Work*

Martin Holmes, *Shakespeare's Public*

Leslie Hotson, *I, William Shakespeare, Shakespeare's Motley, The First Night of Twelfth Night, Shakespeare's Wooden 'O'*

Allardyce Nicoll, *British Drama, The Elizabethans,* Editor of the *Shakespeare Survey* (annually)

A. W. Pollard, *Shakespeare's Fight with the Pirates, The Foundations of Shakespeare's Text*

M. M. Reese, *Shakespeare*

Dr. R. B. Simpson, *Shakespeare and Medicine*

A. C. Sprague, *Shakespeare and the Actors*

J. Dover Wilson, *The Essential Shakespeare* and introductions to the Cambridge University Press Editions of the Plays.

Index

Academy of Love, The (John Johnson), 21
Admiral's Men, 28, 114, 177
Alchemist, The (Ben Jonson), 42, 74
Alleyn, Edward, 27, 49, 62, 64–6, 74, 114–17, 129, 140, 142
All's Well that Ends Well, 17, 146
Antony and Cleopatra, 70, 205–8, 210, 212, 214
Armin, Robert, 38, 39, 45, 46, 59, 72, 142
Aspinall, Alexander, 199
As You Like It, 12, 70, 72, 110, 111, 125, 135, 187, 211, 228
Aubrey, John, 68, 69, 97, 109, 110, 117, 187, 219
Avenant, Sir William D', 45, 101, 137, 177, 206

Bacon, Francis, 20, 102, 153, 172, 173, 189
Bacon, Mathias, 205
Baker, Sir Richard, 22
Bandello, 159, 160
Baring, Maurice, 99, 104, 133
Bartholomew Fair (Ben Jonson), 80, 81
Beaumont, Francis, 139, 201, 211, 221
Beeston, Christopher, 69, 97, 107, 187
Beeston, William, 69, 97, 109, 187
Belott, Stephen, 200
Betterton, 45, 101
Blackfriars Gatehouse, 68, 174, 181, 203, 205
Blackfriars Theatre, 9, 38, 39, 42, 46, 56, 61, 75, 82, 102, 109, 153, 174, 175, 181–3, 200, 203, 204
Bonduca (Beaumont and Fletcher), 139
Bridges-Adams, W., 33, 88
Brome, Richard, 120, 123
Brooke, 160

Burbage, Cuthbert, 38, 39, 41, 47, 50, 51, 53, 56, 109, 173, 174, 179, 181
Burbage, James, 37, 181
Burbage, Richard, 9, 35, 37, 41–6, 48–49, 53, 59–62, 65, 72, 73, 95, 99, 101, 102, 107–10, 113, 116–18, 121, 123, 129, 131, 139, 179, 181, 187, 204–7, 221
Burleigh, Lord, 159

Cardenio (suspected Shakespeare), 8, 175
Catiline (Ben Jonson), 41, 144
Chamberlain's Men, 8, 11, 26–8, 37, 38, 44, 47, 53, 57, 58, 60, 67, 74, 94, 97, 106, 107, 112, 114, 116, 121, 131, 133, 158, 167, 176, 177, 188
Chambers, Sir Edmund, 110, 136, 142, 182, 195
Chambrun, Comtesse de, 160, 222
Chapel Children's Company, 45, 68, 80, 120
Charles I, King, 43, 82, 204
Charles II, King, 111, 206
Chettle, Henry, 60, 64, 106–8
Chronicles of England, Scotland and Ireland, The (Ralph Holinshed), 157, 166
Chute, Margaret, 9
Collins, Francis, 198
Comedy of Errors, The, 104, 158, 162
Command performances, 11, 12, 31–4, 67, 68, 104, 124–6, 135, 174, 183, 204, 206, 210
Condell, Henry, actor, 38, 39, 41, 46, 48, 63, 65, 107, 109, 139
   editor of First Folio, 61, 62, 69, 85, 100, 106, 136, 138, 142, 143, 157, 201, 216
Cooke, Alexander, 49, 62, 107
Cooke, Dr. James, 191, 193

Copia Rerum et Verborum (Erasmus), 20
Coriolanus, 70, 83, 100, 148, 188, 205, 206, 210, 212
Cory, William, 124, 125
Cowley, Richard, 37, 45, 46, 65, 94
Crane, 136, 141, 143
Curtain Theatre, 37, 177
Cymbeline, 52, 70, 102, 132, 153
Cynthia's Revels (Ben Jonson), 80, 82, 97

Daborne, Robert, 140, 141
Davies, John, 108, 110, 118
Davies, Sir John, 29, 31
Davies, the Rev. Richard, 222, 223, 228
Dekker, Thomas, 35, 54, 55, 59, 60, 89–91, 154, 155
Derby's Men, Lord, 37
Digges, Leonard, 144, 148
Donne, John, 66, 70
Downes, John, 45, 101
Drayton, 60, 218, 219
Droeshout, 18, 221
Dryden, John, 117, 137, 206, 218
Duchess of Malfi, The (John Webster), 41, 48, 77
Duke, John, 94, 107

Eliot, T. S., 11, 163
Elizabeth, Queen, 32, 67, 68, 93, 159, 165, 171, 189, 190, 224
Elizabeth's Men, Lady, 64
English Traveller, The (Thomas Heywood), 14
Erasmus, Desiderius, 20, 21
Essex, Earl of, 11, 67, 68
Every Man in his Humour (Ben Jonson), 42, 69, 77, 94, 107, 108
Every Man out of his Humour (Ben Jonson), 42

Fabian, 157
Faustus, Dr. (Marlowe), 115, 165
Feltham, Owen, 212, 213
Field, Nathan, 39, 68, 142
Field, Richard, 158
First Folio, 18, 27, 41, 45, 61, 70, 85, 94, 100, 101, 106, 108, 125, 136, 137,
139, 141, 142, 144, 145, 148, 149, 201, 204, 205, 208–10, 214, 221–3
Fitton, Anne, 167
Fitton, Mary, 167
Fletcher, John, 8, 9, 60, 100, 139, 140, 175, 182, 200, 210, 211, 222
Fletcher, Laurence, 46, 130
Florio, John, 11, 159–61, 199
Fortune Theatre, 55, 65, 114
Fripp, Edgar, 10, 204, 220, 228
Fry, Christopher, 11, 16

Gardiner, William, 19, 68
Garrick, David, 137
Gilburne, 45, 50
Globe Theatre, 9, 31, 34, 36–40, 42 (burning of), 44, 46, 56, 61, 67, 71, 76, 77, 85 (burning), 104, 145, 173, 174, 175 (burnt-out), 179 (new theatre), 181–3, 200, 203–6, 210, 216
Grafton, 157
Granville-Barker, H., 100
Greene, Robert, 8, 28, 64, 88, 106, 107, 157
Greenwich Palace, 32, 67
Greg, Sir Walter, 136, 141–3
Gull's Hornbook, The (Thomas Dekker), 54, 89

Hall, Edward, 72, 157, 166–8, 170
Hall, Susanna (Shakespeare's daughter), 181, 192
Hall, Dr. John (Shakespeare's son-in-law), 191, 192, 221
Halliday, F. E., 47
Hamlet, 13, 15, 19, 20, 51, 58, 72, 85, 101, 110, 135, 137, 151, 187, 190, 206, 214
Harbage, Professor Alfred, 47, 55
Hart, Joan (Shakespeare's sister), 180, 186, 220
Hart, William (Shakespeare's brother-in-law), 220
Hathaway, Anne (Shakespeare's wife), 44
Haymarket Theatre, 55

Heminge, John, 44, 49, 65, 67, 71, 72, 92
  actor, 44, 45, 57, 107, 109, 131
  Treasurer and business manager, 41, 42, 44, 73, 81, 125
  Sharer, 38, 39, 53, 57, 61, 65, 179
  editor of First Folio, 46, 61, 62, 69, 85, 100, 106, 136, 138, 142, 143, 157, 201, 214–16
  as churchwarden, 62, 63
Heminge, William (John's son), 39
Henry IV, 166, 167
  Part I, 131, 135
  Part II, 11, 113, 135
Henry V, 47, 78, 104, 121 (film of), 121, 135, 137, 166, 167
Henry VI, 77, 106, 157
  Part I, 27, 201
  Part III, 106
Henry VIII, 100, 101, 175, 182, 198, 201, 210, 211, 224
Henslowe, Philip, 26–8, 33, 34, 38, 40, 42, 43, 46, 51, 59, 60, 64–6, 74, 76, 84, 103, 104, 114, 129, 140, 141, 154, 177
Herbert, Sir Henry, 140
Hesketh, Sir William, 44
Heywood, Thomas, 14, 15, 32, 34, 140
Holinshed, Ralph, 72, 157, 166
Hope Theatre, 75
Hotson, Dr. Leslie, 55, 75, 76, 145, 146
Hunsdon, Lord, 37

Irving, Sir Henry, 33, 117
Isle of Dogs, The (partly Ben Jonson), 66
Isaacs, Professor J., 89, 90, 96

James I, King, 11, 32, 38, 40, 46, 66, 69, 71, 102, 108, 117, 124, 125, 130, 154, 175, 181, 189, 203
Jew of Malta, The (Marlowe), 28, 115, 165
Johnson, Dr., 22, 136, 137, 158, 168
Johnson, John, 21
Jones, Inigo, 74, 102
Jonson, Ben, 9, 18, 21, 22, 41, 42, 47, 50, 60, 66, 69, 73, 74, 77, 78, 80, 86, 94, 97, 98, 107, 109, 117, 118, 120, 142, 144, 148–50, 156, 171, 175, 183, 210, 211, 212, 215, 218, 220, 222

Julius Caesar, 59, 72, 76, 77, 135

Keen, Alan, 44, 167, 170
Kempe, Will, 38, 39, 44, 45, 58, 59, 72, 95, 107, 113, 123, 131, 142, 167, 179, 188
King Lear, 21, 104, 132–4, 166, 206, 226
King John, 164, 165, 189
King's Men, 8, 12, 29, 38–41, 43, 45, 47–9, 51, 53, 60, 61, 65, 77, 101, 106, 108, 109, 124–6, 129–32, 136, 139, 141, 142, 174, 181, 194, 201, 203–6, 209, 210, 215, 217, 223
Knight, 136, 139–41
Kyd, Thomas, 88, 116, 163

Lodge, Thomas, 72
Love's Labour's Lost, 31, 59, 91, 104, 135, 160, 163, 199
Lowin, John, 41, 46, 48, 65, 101, 107, 139
Lubbock, Roger, 44, 167
Lucy, Sir Thomas, 168, 222

Macbeth, 70, 99, 144–7, 152, 166, 206, 214
Marlowe, 18, 27, 28, 37, 59, 115, 165, 213
Masefield, John, 144, 146, 150
Measure for Measure, 104, 225
Merchant of Venice, The, 104, 135, 225
Meres, 60, 214
Mermaid Inn, 68, 118
Merry Wives of Windsor, The, 12, 104, 135, 137, 141, 144, 146, 151, 163
Midsummer Night's Dream, A, 33, 77, 82, 91, 113, 150, 178, 225
Milton, 21, 124, 144, 200
Montaigne, 11, 160
Montgomery, Earl of, 142
Mountjoy, Christopher, 10, 37, 154, 156, 200
Much Ado About Nothing, 58, 72, 135, 138, 189, 190
Munday, 60
Murry, Middleton, 193

Nashe, Thomas, 27, 29, 30, 32, 63
New Place, Stratford, 36, 178–80, 184, 188, 192, 198, 199, 213, 215, 224

Newport, Sir Richard, 167
Nicoll, Allardyce, 87, 88, 201
North, 166, 206

Oldys, John, 110, 111, 168
Ostler, 39, 45
Othello, 13, 206, 214
Ovid, 160
Oyly Carte, Richard D', 86

Pallant, R., 94
Pallant, R., 94
Pembroke, Earl of, 12, 39, 56, 112, 116, 124, 125, 142
Pembroke's Men, 129
Pericles, Prince of Tyre, 20, 34, 71, 100, 192, 201, 208–10
Phillips, 38, 39, 45, 46, 50, 65, 67, 107, 179
Platter, Thomas, 30, 54, 59, 71, 73, 77, 80
Plutarch, 166, 206
Poetaster, The (Ben Jonson), 120
Pollar, A. W., 136
Pope, Alexander, 168
Pope, Thomas, 38, 39, 65, 95, 107, 179
Priestley, J. B., 17, 151, 207
Purcell, 137, 208

Quartos, 58, 71, 85, 136, 138, 139, 141, 145, 205, 206, 208, 210, 214–16
Queen's Men, 93, 124
Quiney, Adrian, 178
Quiney, Judith (Shakespeare's daughter), 220
Quiney, Richard, 178, 179
Quiney, Thomas (Shakespeare's son-in-law), 220

Raleigh, Sir Walter, 171, 172
Rape of Lucrece, The, 8, 10, 20, 57, 155, 158, 159
Ratsey, Gamaliel, 126–9, 133
Reese, M. M., 36, 37, 121
Rice, 47, 50
Richard II, 67, 68, 71, 129, 152, 167

Richard III, 114
Rich Cabinet ('T.G.'), 119, 121, 123
Robinson, Richard (Dicky), 43, 45, 139
Romeo and Juliet, 11, 20, 29, 57, 71, 83, 137, 224, 227
Rose Theatre, 27, 55
Rowe, Nicholas, 63, 110, 111, 168, 177

Second Part of the Seven Deadly Sins, The (Richard Tarleton), 93, 96, 102
Sejanus (Ben Jonson), 9, 42, 46, 73, 107, 109, 144
Shakespeare, Anne (sister), 220
Shakespeare, Edmund (brother), 186
Shakespeare, Gilbert (brother), 180, 186, 220
Shakespeare, John (father), 112, 154, 176, 186, 187, 199, 220
Shakespeare, Margaret (sister), 220
Shakespeare, Mary (mother), 176, 186, 187, 220
Shakespeare, Richard (brother), 186, 220
Shakespeare, William, joint authorship with others, 8, 9, 60, 143, 167, 175, 201–3, 208–11, 227
speed of writing, 9, 11, 12, 17, 99, 135, 143–52
actor, 7, 9, 10, 22, 42, 44, 57, 99 10 106–12, 115–20
Sharer, 9, 24, 38–42, 44, 47, 56, 57, 106, 107, 109, 129, 139, 173, 176, 177, 179, 181, 183, 200
on tour, 12, 123–6, 129–34
demands of his audiences, 12–17
legal disputes, 19, 68, 199, 200, 203, 205
Hired Man, 44, 119, 153, 176
his family, 36, 44, 63, 157, 176, 178, 180, 186, 187, 220
his Fellowship, 53–70, 85, 90, 99, 100, 129, 142, 176, 179, 182, 183, 188, 215
his mild nature, 67–9, 98, 107
creation of a new play, 25–8, 72, 73, 77, 141
possible direction of own plays, 96, 99–101, 104, 106, 110, 111

accuracy of Shakespeare texts, 136–9, 141–3, 145

sources of inspiration, 72, 157, 159–61, 163–8

investor and property owner, 173, 174, 176–84, 203

his Will, 144, 180, 184, 198, 199, 221, 225, 226

his health, 186, 187, 192–5, 197

retirement to Stratford, 198, 199, 203, 215

possible cause of death, 218–20

his religion, 222–8

Sharpe, Richard, 48, 49

Shaw, George Bernard, 23, 72, 87, 162, 184, 185, 211, 214, 217

Simpson, Dr. R. B., 220

Sir Thomas More (Shakespeare perhaps part-author), 143, 167, 201, 227

Sly, Will, 30, 46, 107

Sonnets, 8, 11, 69, 73, 111, 112, 130, 131, 186, 211, 214, 217

Southampton, Earl of, 10, 11, 31, 40, 57, 107, 112, 158, 161, 175, 177, 182, 183

Spanish Tragedy, The (Thomas Kyd), 88, 116

Spenser, Edmund, 130

Staple of News, The (Ben Jonson), 82, 98

Stow, 157

Strange's Men, Lord, 27, 28, 37, 93, 114, 131

Stratford-upon-Avon, 10, 20, 42, 44, 63, 65, 100, 124, 130, 135, 154, 157, 162, 173, 175, 176, 178–81, 183–5, 187, 188, 191, 192, 198, 199, 203, 205, 215, 218, 224

Swan Theatre, 19, 54

Tamburlaine the Great (Marlowe), 59, 115

Taming of the Shrew, The, 35, 137, 151, 163

Tarleton, Richard, 65, 93, 117, 123, 166

Taylor, Joseph, 45, 101, 206

Tempest, The, 22, 102, 137, 141, 160, 171, 209

Theatre in Shakespeare's day, hours of performances and rehearsals, 25–8, 29, 32, 35, 79, 103

provincial tours, 25, 32, 123–9, 132, 133

front of house arrangements, 79–81

backstage workers, 81–4

piracy of plays, 84–6

possible stage directors, 87–93, 95–102

styles of acting, 109–16, 121, 122

training of actors, 119–21

copying of play manuscripts, 139–43

Tilney, Sir Edmund, 32, 103, 104

Timon of Athens, 21, 150, 189, 190, 193, 195, 202, 208, 213

Titus Andronicus, 71, 187, 201

Tooley (or Towley), 49, 77

Trevelyan, G. M., 191

Troilus and Cressida, 121, 135, 162, 196, 213

Twelfth Night, 70, 135, 145, 146, 199, 214

Two Gentlemen of Verona, 17, 141

Two Noble Kinsmen, The (John Fletcher and perhaps Shakespeare), 8, 175, 201, 202, 211

Underwood, John, 39, 45, 62, 77

Union of the Noble and Illustrate Famelies of Lancastre and Yorke (Edward Hall), 166, 167

Venus and Adonis, 8, 20, 21, 155, 158, 159

Volpone (Ben Jonson), 74, 156

Waite, 19, 68

Ward, the Rev. John, 218, 222

Webster, John, 8, 30, 41, 48, 77, 144, 208, 228

White Devil, The (John Webster), 30, 208

Whitehall Palace, 31, 104, 172, 206

Wilkins, George, 209, 210

Wilson, J. Dover, 136, 148–50, 195

Wilson, Robert, 60

Winter's Tale, The, 70, 141, 148, 162, 188, 196, 209

Worcester's Men, 59